Understanding and Recognizing Dysfunctional Leadership

Since the early twentieth century, scholars have researched leadership and it is one of the most researched topics of our time. Understanding how to be a strong leader and what makes a good leader is something that we continue to strive to understand. Research ponders various positive leadership models such as transformational, servant, authentic, charismatic, situational and ethical leadership to name but a few. Yet, we find that a small number of our leaders are truly transformational. While scholars continue to provide examples of positive and influential leaders, we still struggle to understand what a dysfunctional leader is. Practitioners and followers are quick to identify a leader that is a nightmare, yet they can't name what type of dysfunction that leader possesses. Day in and day out, we struggle with these leaders and how to intervene when dysfunctional behavior arises. This is most evident with recent scandals that have plagued the media involving characters such as Bernie Madoff, Dennis Kozlowski, Tyco, Enron's Kenneth Lay and Jeff Skilling.

It is vital to understand the importance of dysfunctional leadership and its impact on organizations, followers and society. The recent literature focuses on the psychology of dysfunctional leadership and the destruction of organizations. Little has been written in relation to the characteristics, traits and behaviors of dysfunctional leaders. In addition, little has been included on how to deal with this type of behavior within organizations. Individual books have been written on each of these types of characteristics, but no one book has been written that focuses on all of these characteristics and studies the subtle differences of these behaviors, interventions that can be employed to address this type of behavior and how to recognize the impact on our organizations.

Understanding and Recognizing Dysfunctional Leadership will be of interest to professionals and researchers in this field.

Dr Annette B. Roter is Assistant Professor of Leadership, Change Management and Healthcare Management at Viterbo University. She has written several articles on the topic of dysfunctional leadership related to healthcare and provides consulting on the topic along with executive coaching. She is associated with the Midwest Academy of Management and the International Leadership Association.

Understanding and Recognizing Dysfunctional Leadership

The Impact of Dysfunctional Leadership on Organizations and Followers

Annette B. Roter

First published 2017
by Routledge
2 Park Square, Milton Park, Abingdon, Oxon OX14 4RN

and by Routledge
711 Third Avenue, New York, NY 10017

Routledge is an imprint of the Taylor & Francis Group, an informa business

© 2017 Annette B. Roter

The right of Annette B. Roter to be identified as author of this work
has been asserted by her in accordance with sections 77 and 78 of the
Copyright, Designs and Patents Act 1988.

All rights reserved. No part of this book may be reprinted or reproduced
or utilised in any form or by any electronic, mechanical, or other means,
now known or hereafter invented, including photocopying and recording,
or in any information storage or retrieval system, without permission in
writing from the publishers.

Trademark notice: Product or corporate names may be trademarks
or registered trademarks, and are used only for identification and
explanation without intent to infringe.

British Library Cataloguing in Publication Data
A catalogue record for this book is available from the British Library

Library of Congress Cataloging in Publication Data
A catalog record for this book is available from the Library of Congress

ISBN: 978-1-4724-8565-6 (hbk)
ISBN: 978-1-315-54928-6 (ebk)

Typeset in Bembo
by Swales & Willis Ltd, Exeter, Devon, UK

To Clemens and Rosemarie Roter

Contents

List of illustrations	xiii
Preface	xiv
Acknowledgments	xvi

PART I
Introduction to dysfunctional leadership — 1

1 Introduction to dysfunctional leadership — 3

Leadership 3
Dysfunctional leadership 4
A history of dysfunctional leadership 4
Defining dysfunctional leadership 5
Is a dysfunctional leader truly a leader? 6
Dysfunction in today's work environment 7
Different terms used for "dysfunctional leadership" 7
    Toxic leadership 8
    Destructive leadership 10
    Abusive leadership 10
    The Dark Side of Leadership 11
    Passive-aggressive leadership 12
The costs of dysfunctional leadership 13
The role of power in dysfunctional leadership 13
The role of charisma in dysfunction 15
Negative charisma 15
The structure of this book 16

2 Bullying — 19

Introduction 19
Bullying defined 20
The characteristics of bullying 21
The bully 21

viii   Contents

Types of bullies 22
 The public bully or direct bully 22
 The silent or indirect bully 24
 The critical bully 25
 The friendly bully 26
 The hoarder bully 28
 The opportunistic bully 29
Mobbing 30
Gender and bullying 31
Bullying tactics 32
Summary of the classification of bullying 35
Incivility versus bullying 36
The impact of bullying 36
 The individual impact 36
 The organizational impact 37
The organizational role in bullying 37
How to recognize bullying 38
Why targets are bullied 39
Dealing with a bully 40
Conclusion 42

3   Tyrant leadership   **45**

Introduction 45
Tyranny 45
Petty tyranny 46
Tyrannical leadership 46
The historical tyrant 47
 Joseph Stalin 48
Modern-day tyrants 50
 Robert Mugabe 50
 Bashar al-Assad 51
 Saddam Hussein 52
 Vladmir Putin 54
 Kim Jong-un 56
Summary of political tyrants 57
Organizational tyrants 57
 Leona Helmsley 57
 Albert J. Dunlap 59
 Mark Pincus 59
 Larry Ellison 60
Other organizational tyrants 60
What leads to the ultimate downfall of the tyrant? 61

Contents ix

4 Unethical leadership 62

Introduction 62
Understanding ethical leadership 62
Ethical principles 63
Unethical leadership 63
Unethical leadership crossover 65
Characteristics and traits of an unethical leader 65
Temptation and greed 65
Unethical leadership behavior/tipping points 66
Examples of how unethical leadership impacts organizations 67
Why people follow the unethical leader: What is in it for
  the follower? 69
Conclusion 69

PART II
The Dark Triad 71

5 The Dark Triad 73

Introduction 73

6 Narcissism 75

Introduction 75
  Narcissism defined 75
Overview of corporate narcissism 76
The two faces of narcissism 77
  Proactive/constructive/productive narcissism 77
  Reactive/destructive/unproductive narcissism 77
  How a narcissist becomes a reactive
    narcissist 79
  Summing up the two faces of narcissism 80
Understanding the characteristics and traits of a
  reactive narcissist 80
Narcissism and leadership 86
Narcissism and gender 87
The impact of narcissism 87
  Organizational impact 87
  Followership impact 88
Why people follow narcissists 89
Addressing the narcissist 91
Survival guide: Dealing with the narcissistic leader 92
Conclusion 93

x   Contents

7   Psychopaths running our organizations   95

Introduction to corporate psychopaths 95
Definition of "psychopath" 96
The difference between "psychopath" and "sociopath" 97
The evolution of the corporate psychopath 98
Corporate psychopaths in leadership 100
The narcissist versus the psychopath 101
The characteristics and traits of a corporate psychopath 102
Hiring a corporate psychopath leader 106
Why people follow the psychopath leader 107
Addressing the psychopathic leader 108
Building the skills to recognize the behavior of the corporate psychopath 109
Conclusion 109

8   Machiavellian leadership: The story of a prince   111

Introduction 111
Niccolò Machiavelli 112
Machiavelli on leadership 113
Machiavellianism defined 115
Machiavellian research 115
Ethics and Machiavellianism 116
The principles of Machiavellianism 117
The positive lens of Machiavellian leadership 118
The characteristics and traits of a Machiavellian leader 118
Machiavellian leadership in modern times 119
Conclusion 119

PART III
Addressing dysfunctional leadership from an
organizational and individual standpoint   121

9   The role played by organizations and followers in
dysfunctional leadership   123

Introduction 123
Impact on the organization 123
Organizational culture and dysfunction 126
    Organizational values 127
    Organizational norms 127
    Behaviors 128
Organizational influence on dysfunction and impact 128
    Organizational commitment 129
    Social justice 129

Contents xi

Organizational stress 131
Organizational structure 131
Results and dysfunction 132
    Followership and enabling 133
Organizational conflict and dysfunction 133
How dysfunctional leadership impacts followers 134
Dysfunctional leadership behavior and job satisfaction 134
Emotional impact 135
    Work and family conflict 135
    Depression 135
    Anxiety 135
    Humiliation 136
    Isolation 136
    Lack of personal control 136
    Post-traumatic stress disorder 137
    Self-harming behavior 137
Physical impact 138
Financial/economic impact 138
Bystanders 139
Stages of understanding 139
Conclusion 140

10 Addressing dysfunctional leadership　　　　　　　　　　**142**

Introduction 142
    Fear of retaliation 142
    Lack of training (individuals) 143
    Making sense of the situation 143
    Suffering in silence 143
    Speaking up 144
Coping mechanisms 144
Negative coping mechanisms 144
    Trying to appease the dysfunctional leader 145
    Denial and avoidance 145
    Self-medicating 146
    Example of negative coping 146
Positive coping mechanisms 147
    Problem solving 147
    Addressing the situation 147
    Checking emotions 147
    Timing is everything 148
    Document, document, document 149
    Getting out of the situation 149
    Other ways to address the behavior 149

xii Contents

Organizational mechanisms for individual coping 150
    Human Resources 150
    Employee Assistance Programs 151
    Going higher up 152
    Seeking legal advice 152
Organizational coping 153
    Understanding organizational processes 153
Helping the target 154
Healing from dysfunction 154
Legal rights 155
The organizational role in dysfunction 155
Addressing the work environment 165
Internal organizational interventions 165
Conclusion 169

Index   171

List of illustrations

Figures

2.1	Spectrum of workplace violence	36
7.1	Perceptions of the corporate psychopath leadership candidate	107

Tables

1.1	Researchers and dysfunctional leadership types	8
1.2	Comparison of charismatic leaders	16
2.1	Bullying factors from the Negative Acts Questionnaire-Revised (NAQ-R)	35
2.2	The individual and organizational impact of bullying	37
3.1	Characteristics of organizational tyrants	57
5.1	Dark Triad traits	73
6.1	Comparison of constructive and reactive narcissism	79
6.2	Gender traits of narcissists	87
7.1	Comparison of the narcissist leader and the psychopath leader	101
9.1	The impact of dysfunctional behavior	124
9.2	Psychological symptoms	138
9.3	Physical symptoms	138
10.1	Laws related to harassment by country/state	156

Preface

This book brings together various insights and experiences that I have collected over the years related to research and experiences of endless hours of interviews and studies. Through the years I have experienced bad leadership, but never before had I experienced dysfunctional leadership until I met my match in 2009. The following shares my personal experience and the jumpstart that would one day become my research platform.

Personal experience

I remember my first encounter with a dysfunctional leader. We had spent several hours going over the project that she had assigned to me two weeks prior. This was the tenth iteration of the document. She had made so many changes to the document and here we sat in the room looking at the original document that was submitted two weeks ago, and she decided that this document was actually good enough to move forward with. We were back to the original format and content, essentially back to square one. I was confused. This was the original document – why did we go through all the changes, edits and frustration only to come back to the original document? I questioned her and she became furious. Her eyes bulged from her head as she screamed at me, calling me incompetent, an idiot and a waste of oxygen. Then she took the folder with all the changes, bound it with a rubber band and threw it at my head, screaming "Get out of my office and never, ever question me again." I remember leaving her office, my head swirling in confusion and disbelief. My co-workers in the office heard the insults and I was mortified as well as embarrassed. During the course of the day, several co-workers came to me and tried to comfort me. Several said to me "You get used to it" and "That wasn't that bad, I have experienced worse from her." During the next few days, I heard horror stories about this leader and that they had secretly nicknamed her "Satan's Mistress." I was left wondering what was happening and how a leader could get away with this type of behavior. I started asking myself questions. What type of leadership is this? Can this even be called leadership? I didn't respect her as a leader and I certainly found myself questioning the institution that allowed a leader to act in this way. It was then that I started to explore the topic.

As I started my research, a plethora of research unfolded focusing on positive leadership. I moved on and found the words "bad leadership." While I was getting close to the topic, I felt that this experience was very different from the overbearing, hands-off, or micro-managing leader that these sources were describing. This leader was different. She was a leader who was destructive, abusive and harmful to followers and to the organization. I stumbled upon information that described toxic leaders (dysfunctional leaders) as individuals who by their destructive behavior and dysfunctional personal qualities generate serious and poisonous effects on their followers. This is what I was looking for. This definition matched the leader that my co-workers and I were experiencing. As I spoke to my co-workers, I realized that this type of leadership was destroying the lives of this leader's followers and that the organizational unit was slowly eroding away.

In the case of my dysfunctional leader, I left the organization only after three months. She was the type of person that when I saw her, I would duck into the nearest office, meeting room or washroom just to avoid her. I became physically ill thinking of seeing or having to interact with her. Friday afternoons were slow to approach and I spent the weekend feeling relieved from her craziness. Sundays came, causing me to feel depressed, ill and anxiety-ridden thinking about what the following week would entail. I was stuck and humiliated, and I felt my self-confidence slowly diminishing. I left the organization having no place to go and for the first time in my career, I didn't care. For my sanity and my self-preservation, I needed to be out of the organization and away from this person. During this time I felt hopeless and lost. I was thinking that I was the only one who had ever dealt with this type of negative experience. In the end, I did land another job. It was a positive environment where I felt valued and appreciated by the leadership. However, I never got this leader out of my mind. During my exit interview, I shared my experience with legal and human resources, but nothing was done. After I left, she directed her attention toward another target and slowly others started to leave the organization. Eventually, more people started to speak out and she was let go. She went on to another organization and landed on her feet, and my understanding is that she is wreaking havoc within that organization.

It was because of this experience that I started to research the topic and to seek understanding. During my years of research, I started to learn more about the topic and heard examples and stories of leaders that made my dysfunctional leader seem as though she was actually normal. It was because of this experience that I wanted to help others, including organizations, to recognize the different types of dysfunction in leadership and what could be done to address the situation.

Acknowledgments

The author would like to take this opportunity to acknowledge the following people for their support and assistance during this project: Mr Paul Capparelli for endless hours of research and finding sources related to topics; Ms Jami S. Kohl for hours of editing and last-minute changes – thank you for coming through for me; Ms Tiffany Smith and Ms Nicole Van Ert for reviews of outlines and listening to the stories and supporting this effort; and Dr Sara Cook, Dr Tom Knothe and Viterbo University for allowing me to work on this project along with supporting my research.

A special acknowledgment to my family for their continued love and support, especially to my mother Rosemarie Roter for her strength and ear when I needed it; to Petra Roter for helping out when I needed a break and needed time to complete this project; and to Greg Roter for pointing out articles for me to read. Thank you to Ron for your support, friendship and encouragement years ago that got me to where I am today. It was one conversation that changed the direction of my life and I will be forever grateful. Thank you Eric for encouraging me to write this book and to shop the idea around – your encouragement and direction helped to bring it to life. Thank you to all who have supported this work and the efforts put forth, including my students, who have taken my Dark Side of Leadership course and have encouraged me to move forward. This was a labor of love and a topic that has become my being.

I would like to take this opportunity to acknowledge the many participants who have come forward over the years to support this research with stories and experiences related to their dysfunctional leaders. Research participants willing to share and discuss their understanding of this topic. It is through these stories and experiences that I am able to help others and to support them. Thank you for your courage and strength.

Part I

Introduction to dysfunctional leadership

Chapter 1

Introduction to dysfunctional leadership

At some point in our careers, we will experience a leader who is less than stellar. For many of us, we are no strangers to the concept of a dysfunctional leader and will either experience this phenomenon directly or indirectly throughout our careers. However, many who have witnessed or experienced dysfunctional leadership are left wondering what is happening in relation to this type of behavior, as it is not normal and is something that they have not experienced before. People question the leader and then in turn question themselves; after all, aren't leaders supposed to act in the best interests of the organization? Don't we expect our leaders to treat followers with respect and dignity? After experiencing a dysfunctional leader, it makes a person wonder "what is this insane behavior?"

Dysfunctional leadership behaviors are beginning to gain attention from scholars and the media. These behaviors include physical and psychological abuse. In recent years, this type of behavior has received more and more attention as the topic continues to be researched. However, despite being researched on a more frequent basis, this type of leadership is not studied in schools or organizations. Many people do not know how to address the problem or situation when confronted with this behavior.

Leadership

Leadership functions as the visionary, the guiding force and, most importantly, the role model for followers within the organization. The leaders of an organization are faced with many different opportunities and challenges. Today's world demands leaders who provide a foundation for the organization to move forward. Leadership needs to be free of egos and the promotion of personal agendas. The behaviors and characteristics of a leader influence the actions of employees within the organization. Positive follower experiences correlate with higher job satisfaction, commitment and willingness to stay with the organization, and increased productivity. Negative experiences with a leader will drive a decrease in employee commitment to the organization, higher turnover rates, lower job satisfaction and a reduction in productivity. Because of these aspects, one can easily assert that the behavior of the leader impacts both the follower and the organization.

The construct of leadership can be difficult to understand. While there are a number of leadership models and theories, the concepts of leadership still remain a confusing topic. Different models ranging from autocratic to democratic, transactional to transformational and numerous others exist. During the history of leadership studies, thousands of books and articles pertaining to the topic have been written. Critics argue that most of the results

4   Introduction to dysfunctional leadership

are insignificant and fail to address the true concepts of leadership. Without an understanding of leadership, individuals and organizations are at a disadvantage in their ability to truly identify and develop effective leaders. In addition, organizations struggle with identifying and addressing the constructs of negative leadership. If it is difficult to understand the positive models of leadership, it is equally difficult to decipher the dysfunctional side of leadership. Modern leadership studies continue to explore what makes a great leader, but without a clear understanding of the different constructs of leadership, organizations will continue to struggle with identifying the good, the bad and the destructive behaviors of leadership.

The focus on the constructive aspects of leadership provides insights into leaders who support their followers, provide a clear and defining vision, and provide a work environment that is satisfying and engaging. However, that is not always the case with leadership. In many cases, employees will stumble upon a leader who does not support their followers. Instead, the leader undermines, belittles, and does not provide a clear and articulate leadership approach. Yet, research on the topic of dysfunctional leadership is limited. The topic is still new and the approaches are fragmented. With recent revelations of wrongdoing in leadership, focusing on the abuse of power and leadership in areas such as politics, religion and business, one could argue that there is a need for further exploration into the negative sides of leadership. In order to understand the negative sides of leadership, it is important to identify and to decipher the theories related to the topic of dysfunctional leadership.

Dysfunctional leadership

Dysfunctional leadership negatively impacts followers and the organization. Researchers have said that it takes only one bad leader to take down a whole organization. This has been demonstrated through the course of the last several years with the downfall of organizations such as Arthur Andersen, Enron, Tyco, and WorldCom. While these examples are large in scale, organizations all over the world are faced with varying levels of dysfunction within their leadership ranks and continue to struggle with identifying and defining dysfunctional leadership behaviors. In addition, these organizations wrestle with what to do with these types of behaviors and it becomes the proverbial elephant in the room. Organizations adopt the philosophy of "if we don't talk about it or address it, then maybe it does not exist." The problem with this mindset is that the negative leadership behavior continues to occur and will only continue to fester the longer it is ignored. In the meantime, morale erodes, productivity declines and turnover increases, while employees suffer with the actions of the dysfunctional leader.

A history of dysfunctional leadership

Through the years, there have been several different titles or names associated with dysfunctional leadership, including petty tyranny, toxic leadership, destructive leadership, bad leadership, leadership derailment, evil leadership, narcissism, and Machiavellian leadership. The evolution of dysfunctional and destructive types of leadership can be traced back hundreds and thousands of years. The following provides insights into several leaders throughout history who can be classified as dysfunctional leaders:

- *Caligula, Roman Emperor* (37–41 AD): Caligula led through the use of fear, cruelty and extravagances, and was known for his insatiable lusts. During his rule, he was known for having affairs with his sisters and with his opponents' wives. He declared himself to be a living god and his horse was treated better than his followers; living in a marble stable, it was named a senator and had 18 servants tending to it. After four years of destructive leadership, Caligula was eventually assassinated.
- *Genghis Khan* (founder and ruler of the Mongol Empire, 1206–1227): In his early years, Genghis Khan led a difficult life. He experienced poverty, imprisonment and persecution, but was known as a military genius. By 1206, he was the ruler of most of Mongolia and was given the title Genghis Khan, "Ruler of the Universe." As his military forces moved through the country, they slaughtered or imprisoned those they conquered. He was responsible for killing over 40 million people during his rule. He utilized tyranny, genocide and carnage as part of his military strategy and leadership tactics.
- *Ivan IV "The Terrible"* (Tsar of Russia, 1533–1584): Ivan showed his cruelty and vengeance early in his childhood. He handed down his first death sentence at the age of 13. During his early reign, he was influenced by his wife, who was considered to be extremely kind and compassionate. It is believed that she was poisoned and murdered. It was after this point that Ivan's leadership changed. He believed in killing people and that proving their guilt was pointless. Some believed that Ivan took great pleasure in killing others and coming up with new methods of torture, and would use techniques such as burning people at the stake, boiling people and impaling them on sticks. It was during his leadership that Russia doubled in size and he was believed to be quite strategic, intelligent and talented at conquering other territories.

While history provides many different examples of dysfunctional leaders, it was not until recently that scholarly research surfaced relating to the topic. The works of Freud have been linked to narcissism from a psychoanalytical approach and, in the 1980s, research emerged on dysfunctional leadership traits from this viewpoint. Dysfunctional leadership at this time was termed as paranoid, compulsive, dramatic, depressive and schizoid. Researchers Kets de Vries and Miller (1985) found that negative leadership behaviors have a significant impact on followers and organizations. Their research indicates that these behaviors can cause organizational environments and cultures to transform in order to accommodate the dysfunction of the leader. These changes result in the culture becoming dysfunctional. Other researchers described ineffective leaders as suffering from a dysfunctional point of view. Later, Bing (1992) used the terms "problem boss" and "crazy boss," and then went on to label them as the bully, the narcissist, the paranoid and the disaster hunter. He found that these leaders were extremely successful and motivated depending on their dysfunction. Also noted was that it was their followers who suffered the impact of these leaders for months and even years following the event.

Defining dysfunctional leadership

There is an over-abundance of definitions and nomenclatures related to dysfunctional leadership. There is no single agreement on one name or one clear definition. Dysfunctional leadership has many different names, including toxic leadership, the Dark

Side of Leadership and the Dark Triad. Researchers have primarily focused on leadership that has gone bad. For example, Kets de Vries (2001) explained that some leaders go far beyond the normal ways of functioning – they go off the deep end. Later in his research, he expanded upon this by explaining that all leaders, whether in organizations, communities or other countries, are susceptible to the darker side of power. Tepper and Duffy (2002) went on to describe dysfunctional behavior or abusive leadership as behavior that negatively impacts an individual's ability to create and maintain relationships with others, to be successful in the organization or to form a favorable reputation in the workplace. These behaviors are alleged to be thoughtless and result in frequent harm to the follower. Finally, Kellerman (2004) simply reiterates that there are two types of leaders: good leaders and bad leaders.

Researchers found that the definition of dysfunctional leadership depends upon the interpretation of each individual and can have many different meanings. In order to provide some construct upon this type of leadership, different definitions emerged to address the phenomenon. One definition suggested that dysfunctional leaders are characterized by destructive behaviors, such as leaving their followers worse off than they found them. Traits associated with dysfunctional leadership include lack of integrity, insatiable ambition, arrogance and reckless regard for one's actions. As we can see, dysfunctional leadership remains a topic that has not been systematically researched and leaves much room for interpretation in relation to the definition or meaning.

Is a dysfunctional leader truly a leader?

We understand that the themes of positive leadership include the ability to inspire, motivate, provide a guiding vision and lead followers toward the successful completion of a goal or strategy. In contrast, the definition of dysfunctional leadership is an individual who leads with power, causing harm either psychologically, physically or both. There are many people who believe that a leader is someone positive and therefore if we look at someone as a dysfunctional leader, they cannot be classified as such. However, they still hold the title of leader. We see many examples of dysfunctional leaders who meet the definition of positive leadership based on their ability to inspire, motivate and provide a vision, guidance and strategy to lead people. An extreme example of a dysfunctional leader who would characterize this definition of leadership would be Adolf Hitler. As we know, his negative influence has had a major impact on the twentieth century. Yet, he was able to inspire, mobilize and direct his followers. He was viewed as someone who would take Germany forward to address the problems that the country was facing. During the early stages of his period of leadership, he was extremely charismatic; he was able to inspire millions to follow him through his mesmerizing speeches (Kellerman, 2004). He possessed qualities of positive leadership and was a strong visionary for Germany. However, the darker side of his leadership caused the death and destruction of millions of people, and the devastation he imposed is something that humankind hopes never to experience again. So the question still remains: was Hitler a leader or something other than what we would consider to be a leader? Through what we understand of leadership, he is one who can be classified as a dysfunctional leader.

Burns (1978) was unwilling to label individuals who obliterate and attack their followers as leaders. Instead, he labeled these individuals as power wielders. He believed that what sets these individuals apart from leaders was the treatment of their followers. Power wielders do not treat followers as people but as objects, and whose goal is the meeting of personal gains and the achievement of their own agendas. Once the follower was of no use to the power wielder, they were simply tossed aside.

The debate on whether or not these individuals are truly leaders is far from settled. For the sake of this book, we will use the term "dysfunctional leader" or "dysfunctional leadership." This term is used in order to provide context to the topic and to focus specifically on dysfunction at a leadership level.

Dysfunction in today's work environment

The world in which we work today has changed dramatically. Organizational leaders are asked to become leaner while working with fewer resources in a complex, volatile and ambiguous environment. We are asking leaders to adapt quickly to these changes. In addition, organizations have become highly competitive, causing the workplace to become a predatory environment full of leaders who are bullies, narcissists, psychopaths and tyrants. Dysfunctional leadership is not isolated to just one industry; we find dysfunction in all industries, as well as at all levels of leadership.

Researchers Erickson and Freud (1962) explained that during times of complexity and multifaceted relationship, it is important to focus on civility and treating others with respect. In today's work environment, we find complexity relating to global interactions, rapid changes in technology and competing resources. These complex interactions have placed an increasing amount of stress on leaders, causing them to step outside of their normal boundaries. Often, these stressors, coupled with low levels of emotional intelligence, force leaders to take on dysfunctional leadership behaviors in order to achieve results and to survive the complexity of the work demands placed upon them.

The reality of a dysfunctional leader is that they will eventually self-destruct. Before they actually self-destruct, they will inflict as much damage and harm on individuals, teams and the organization. In the meantime, we watch good people leave organizations and become demotivated, and watch as organizations also start to unravel. When the dysfunctional leader starts to realize they are losing control of the situation, they will move on to another organization and will begin to wreak havoc in this new environment.

Different terms used for "dysfunctional leadership"

This book will examine several different types of dysfunctional leadership including bullying, tyrants, unethical leaders, and the three components of what is referred to as the Dark Triad. The Dark Triad includes Narcissism, Psychopathy and Machiavellian Leadership. There are a number of different terms related to dysfunctional leadership. As you read further, you will notice that in many cases there are subtle differences as well as similarities between the different terms or constructs that are used. As was discussed earlier, the field of research on this topic is still new. It is important to understand the work being done around the topic and how these foundational works inform the direction of research. The following table provides insights of researchers associated with different types of dysfunctional leadership.

8 Introduction to dysfunctional leadership

Table 1.1 Researchers and dysfunctional leadership types

Researchers	Dysfunction
Kets de Vries	Narcissistic leadership
Ashforth	Petty tranny
Keashly	Emotional abuse
Baron and Neuman	Workplace aggression
Hoel, Rayner and Cooper	Workplace/leadership bullying
Namie and Namie, Ferris, Zinko, Brouer, Buckley and Harvey	
Duffy, Ganster and Pagon	Undermining supervision
Kellerman	Bad leadership
Lipman Blumen	Toxic leadership
Kusy and Holloway	
Einarsen, Schanke and Skogstad	Destructive leadership
Padilla, Hogan, and Kaiser	
Paulhus and Williams	Dark Triad

Toxic leadership

Lipman–Blumen (2005a: 18) defined toxic leaders as those who "inflict serious and endur-
ing harm" on their followers by their "destructive and dysfunctional characteristics."
Research shows that toxic leadership is multidimensional. In the case of a toxic leader,
they are aware of their behavior and will consciously feed their followers with illusions
that help to enhance their own power while damaging the ability of their followers to
act independently. The toxic leader creates the illusion that they are the only person who
can save the organization. These same leaders will work proactively to create dissension
amongst followers and to persuade them that there is conflict, even if no conflict exists.
While followers are focused on the conflict that is created, the leader will implement their
personal agendas and plans to fulfill their own goals. The leader will look to promote
incompetence and corruption within the organization and will thrive and flourish in the
chaos within the organizational system.

The impact of a toxic leader on the organization can be devastating. Kusy and
Holloway (2009) focused their research on toxic leadership in relation to its impact on
the organization. They provided the following definition related to toxic leaders: "The
insidious effect on organization life and the welfare of both the organization and those
who work diligently in pursuit of the organization's success" (Kusy & Holloway, 2009). A
toxic leader's motivation is inwardly focused, destructive and violates the best interests of
the organization. To support their assumptions related to toxic leadership and the impact
on organizations as well as employees, Kusy and Holloway conducted empirical research
with more than 1,000 participants and the results demonstrated alarming evidence in relation to toxic leadership:

- 94 percent of victims stated that they work or have worked with a toxic person;
- 50 percent say they are not skilled in addressing verbal abuse from a toxic individual;
- 68 percent reported a decline in personal productivity;

Introduction to dysfunctional leadership 9

- 78 percent stated they were less committed to the organization;
- 92 percent rated their emotional pain between 7 and 10 on a 10-point Likert scale (with 10 being the highest);
- 12 percent of victims quit their jobs;
- The fully loaded costs of staff turnover is 1.5–2.5 times the exited person's salary (including lost productivity, lost opportunity costs, recruitment and overtime).

As their research demonstrates, toxic leadership correlates to higher rates of turnover, emotional distress, a decline in productivity and reduced organizational loyalty. Even with this evidence, we find that toxic leaders continue to remain with an organization for many years.

Toxic leaders may not always be seen in a negative light. Lipman-Blumen (2005a) stated that one person's toxic leader is another person's hero. Toxic leaders can be very charming and will align themselves with people who can help them to promote their personal agendas. Since they are very conscious of their behavior, they will reward followers who are supportive of their toxicity while on the other hand destroying those who do not. During investigations of toxic leaders, some employees will share that the leader in question is charming, talented and one of the best leaders they have ever experienced or worked with. Others will share that the leader is abusive, detrimental, destructive and toxic. This contradictory information can be confusing for organizations and does not help to address what the problem actually is. On many occasions, the tables are turned and the person making the complaint is viewed as the toxic individual instead of the leader. Toxic leadership results from the leader's charm, intelligence, admiration expressed by the follower and an environment that supports these forms of behavior. All of these elements help fuel the power of the toxic leader (Klein & House, 1995; Popper, 2000).

There are many different behaviors associated with toxic leadership. Lipman-Blumen (2005a) suggested that the toxic leader will use charismatic tendencies to manipulate, isolate and ostracize their followers. Other behaviors include:

- a violation of human rights;
- feeding illusions creating dependence instead of independence;
- playing to the fears of the follower;
- encouraging compliance and stifling critical thinking;
- misleading followers;
- ignoring ethical processes and organizational structure;
- encouraging followers to hate and to destroy others;
- failing to mentor or nurture others;
- constantly identifying scapegoats;
- making themselves indispensable to the organization;
- ignoring or promoting incompetence and corruption.

As we continue through this book, we will see that many of the dysfunctions discussed will encompass some of the components of toxic leadership. It is important to recognize that the toxic leader is aware of their behavior. They know that their behavior is destructive toward others and is aimed at obtaining personal rather than organizational goals.

Destructive leadership

The behaviors of destructive leaders are considered to be similar to those of toxic leaders. The characteristics of destructive leadership are referred to as inward and outward behaviors. Inward destructiveness involves actions that leaders do to themselves and may reflect moodiness, lack of integrity, irritability and arrogance (Hogan & Hogan, 2001; Hogan & Kaiser, 2005). Outward destructive behaviors purposely target the leader's followers or peers. Neuman and Baron (2005) stated that outward destructive leadership can involve acts of physical abuse, including shoving, throwing things and inappropriate physical conduct, which is not limited to sexual contact.

Destructive leadership plays a major role in the destruction of the organization and the followers (Pellitier, 2009). Einarsen, Aasland and Skogstad (2007: 208) defined destructive leadership as "systematic and repeated behavior by a leader, supervisor, or manager that violates the legitimate interest of the organization by undermining or sabotaging an organization's goals, tasks, resources, effectiveness and/or motivation, well-being, or job satisfaction of subordinates." It also embraces behaviors directed toward employees, organizational goals and strategies, such as imposing goals on followers without their agreement or regard for their long-term welfare. The destructive leader is characterized by their charisma, personalized need for power, negative life history and ideology of hate. However, in order for this leader to achieve the power to lead, they need followers who will implement their agenda. The Bond Institute identified the construct of destructive leadership and created clusters that apply to this type of leadership:

- Cluster 1: Makes bad decisions based on bad information, lies, engages in unethical behaviors and is unable to prioritize or delegate.
- Cluster 2: Lacks critical skills. Unable to persuade, negotiate, motivate or inspire others.
- Cluster 3: Is unable to make good decisions, but tends to micro-manage and apply overly controlling behaviors toward direct reports.
- Cluster 4: Is unable to effectively handle conflict. Plays favorites and is often inconsistent with their behavior.
- Cluster 5: Does not seek the input of others. Won't change their minds and is unable to coordinate others or the work of others.
- Cluster 6: Isolates the team or group from the organization.
- Cluster 7: Creates situations of despair, misery, bullying, lying and engaging in unethical acts.

We find that this type of destructive leadership is both anti-organization and anti-follower. Abuse inflicted by the leader includes passive acts, such as not providing subordinates with feedback or failing to protect a subordinate (Neuman & Baron, 2005). Destructive leadership styles can be blatant, illegal and easy to identify. Leaders who act in a destructive way that is not blatant or illegal may have a hard time admitting that they have behaved in a negative manner and may believe that their behavior is appropriate (Illies & Reiter-Palmon, 2008).

Abusive leadership

Abusive leadership has been defined as the follower's perception of the extent to which leadership engages in the unrelenting display of hostile, verbal and non-verbal abuse;

however, this behavior excludes physical abuse. Actions of an abusive leader include: public criticism, use of derogatory names or comments, condescending tones, intimidation, tantrums, rudeness, coercion, public ridicule and blaming followers for mistakes that they did not make (Hornstein, 1996). Other definitions of "abusive leadership" include volatile behavior by a leader who harms or intends to cause harm to an organization and/or followers. The abusive leader will encourage followers to pursue goals that contradict the legitimate interests of the organization. These types of dysfunctional leaders utilize a leadership practice that involves the use of harmful methods of influence directed toward followers regardless of justification for the negative behavior. They follow a set of leadership procedures that are used to satisfy their own self-interest. Abusive leaders have the skill to create the impression that what they are doing is actually in line with the right thing to do, as well as for the good of the organization. They encourage or ignore the use or sale of dangerous and unsafe products even when the company supports safety. These shortcuts in safety are used to increase profits and to focus on gaining recognition regardless of the safety of employees. In order to motivate employees, the abusive leader uses a combination of negative and verbal actions to influence others. This behavior may include rude comments, bullying, public criticism and coercion (Bies, 2001). These forms of behavior may appear when the leader's goals are thwarted or when they experience obstacles in trying to reach their goals and agenda. These personal goals may include economic gains, increased social status, self-image and assumed professional competence. When these goals are threatened or questioned, they will lash out negatively.

Followers exposed to a dysfunctional leader's actions often demonstrate lower self-esteem, higher psychological distress, increased job tension and emotional exhaustion. Employees will experience reduced organizational commitment, an increase in organizational deviance, organizational injustice, and an aggressive rejection of organizational norms and environmental factors. Followers who had experienced abusive leadership stated that they believed the leadership of the whole organization was unjust, which led to a negative influence on their attitude to work, the organization and the environment. Starratt and Grandy (2010) found that employees identify abusive leadership with the following characteristics: playing favorites, assigning dirty work as punishment, threatening employees, blurring the lines between personal and professional conduct, talking behind employees' backs, putting employees down, public criticism, unrealistic expectations, telling lies and illegal practices.

The Dark Side of Leadership

Another term used for dysfunctional leadership is "The Dark Side of Leadership," which is defined as the systematic and repeated behavior by a leader, supervisor or manager that violates the legitimate interests of the organization by undermining or sabotaging the organization's goals, tasks, resources and effectiveness. In addition, it is focused on negatively impacting the motivation, well-being and/or job satisfaction of followers. Traits related to the Dark Side of Leadership include argumentativeness, interpersonal insensitivity, narcissism, impulsive behavior, perfectionism and a fear of failure. The continued pattern of these traits reflects negatively on the follower, the results of strategic outcomes and the organizational culture. There are four dimensions related to the Dark Side of Leadership: (1) abuse of power; (2) inflicting damage on others; (3) the over-exercise of control; and (4) rule-breaking to satisfy personal needs. Followers believe these leaders to

12 Introduction to dysfunctional leadership

be untrustworthy, overly ambitious and disingenuous. These characteristics are designed to alienate followers and interfere with team formation.

The Dark Side of Leadership reflects on the impression made on others when the leader lets their guard down or when they are at their worst (for example, during periods of stress or illness). These leaders come across as arrogant, compulsive, over-controlling, insensitive, aloof, overly ambitious and unable to delegate or make decisions. These behaviors typically co-exist with well-developed social skills that mask or compensate for their actions. However, this is only in the short term. Over time, the dark personality traits will emerge and begin to erode trust and undermine any relationships that may exist.

Passive-aggressive leadership

The passive-aggressive leader is a challenge in the workplace. They will often speak over or dominate discussions, ignore ideas presented and pass over people for promotion for no reason. When the person is confronted, they will act as if nothing is wrong and as if there is no issue. In many cases the leader may say that the follower is being too sensitive and is over-reacting to situations that never happened. Typically this type of leader does not know how to deal with or address conflict. The passive-aggressive leader typically feels that their feelings are more important than those of others and that they should be the center of attention. They will express their feelings in a negative way, but will avoid any form of confrontation. Typically, these behaviors are learned at a young age and are used as a coping mechanism to repress their feelings, and often they may not be aware of the negative impact of this type of behavior.

The passive-aggressive leader will come across as agreeable and will agree to certain projects or requests. Later, they will resent these requests, the person making the request and in turn will act out by missing deadlines, undermining others and ignoring input or meetings. In many cases they will use the excuse of forgetfulness or will blame others for not informing them. For example, they will often say "I sent that report to you last week. I can't believe that you forgot." When the person points out that they did not receive the report, the passive-aggressive leader will say "Check your emails, you must have deleted it." The blame will be placed on the recipient. When asked to resend the report, the passive-aggressive leader will then act as though they are looking for it and then may say that they thought they sent the report, but had so much to do that they must have forgotten to hit the send button. They will come across as cold, aloof and passive, and will appear to be depressed or withdrawn. Direct reports, peers and/or upper leadership will always be seen as unreasonable or demanding and at fault.

Unlike other leadership positions that recognize the importance of aligning themselves with leadership, the passive-aggressive leader will resent people in positions of authority. Their resentment may appear subtle, but under the surface it is often boiling over. When they don't feel pressured, they will produce high-quality work and these behaviors will appear minimal. When put under pressure by the upper leadership, their work quality will decline and their passive-aggressive behaviors will escalate. Their work or directions to direct reports will be inconsistent and when those inconsistencies are pointed out to them, they will become hostile toward others and will deny it, make excuses, blame others or just cite being forgetful. During times of constructive feedback to the passive-aggressive leader, they will move toward a victim position, feeling as though they are being wrongfully attacked by others, and will blame either leadership or direct reports (or both). Their behavior frustrates upper leadership and direct reports. For the passive-aggressive leader, this frustration is a feeling of accomplishment, since that is their ultimately their goal.

The costs of dysfunctional leadership

The cost of dysfunctional leadership is multifaceted and impacts the target, bystanders and the organization as a whole. The psychological and physical toll it takes on followers includes feelings of desperation, incompetence, embarrassment, guilt and shame. This state of mind will often manifest itself in low self-esteem, poor performance, work alienation, poor team performance and feelings of helplessness. In order to cope with these feelings, employees may become vengeful, separating themselves emotionally from the job or organization and in some cases leaving the organization in order to cope. Other means of coping include causing personal harm to themselves, including the use of recreational drugs, increased alcohol use, over-eating or under-eating, along with other unhealthy and destructive forms of behavior. In extreme cases, targets have been known to contemplate or even commit suicide as a way to permanently escape from the situation. As these feelings continue to develop, they may manifest themselves in physical reactions impacting the employee's health and well-being. Physical symptoms may include headaches, cardiac issues, hypertension, skin irritation and myriad of other ailments. Individuals often suffer for months and even years with these physical and psychological issues. In some cases, they may seek professional help, but most often they choose to suffer in silence. These health issues also impact organizations by increasing absenteeism, loss of productivity, decrease in morale and a multitude of other organizational concerns. These costs from a monetary standpoint can be quite significant, impacting the bottom line.

The role of power in dysfunctional leadership

Power has many different definitions. Generally it relates to the ability or potential to influence others. The first definition of power focused on the works of Max Weber as he defined the link between class, status and power. In 1925, Weber defined power as "the ability of an individual or group to achieve their own goals or aims when others are trying to prevent them from realizing these them" (www.biography.com). He identified power as having two components: authoritarian or coercive. Authoritarian power is exercising power that is considered to be legitimate. The other side of power focuses on coercive, which is the use of force where a person is forced into doing something that is against their will. According to Somech and Drach-Zahavy (2002), power is defined as the potential for one person (leader/agent) to cause another person (follower/target) to act according to the leader's wishes.

Influence relates to the leader's actions that cause either behavioral or attitudinal change in their followers. One cannot ignore the role that power plays in dysfunctional leadership. Power is the ultimate foundation in influencing others, whether positively or negatively. The more power a leader possesses, the higher the likelihood that an individual will comply and follow these actions. Just like followers, leaders can be enticed and motivated by power. For some, the power of individual leaders is an intoxicating drug that can never satisfy them. However, it is important to recognize that power and influence do not make a good leader. Leaders throughout history have

14 Introduction to dysfunctional leadership

utilized power in a negative way to promote their own personal agendas and goals. The misuse of power and influence has caused disastrous results for many leaders, followers and organizations.

Power and influence utilizes a leader's indirect or direct messages and behaviors to leverage a response from others (Barbuto & Gifford, 2009). Depending on the leader, power can be viewed as a way to make someone feel superior and unique in the eyes of their followers. Dysfunctional leaders justify their power through their positions in order to achieve either the goal of the organization or their own personal goals and agendas – most of the time, it is used for personal gain. When the leader's personal agenda comes into the mix, it supersedes the goals of others or the organization. Jacques (1995) believed that leaders can lead using manipulative abuse of personal power due to a mismatch between organizational roles and their capabilities. Wyatt and Hare (1997) stress that leaders or managers who lack personal power will abuse their role in order to gain power, status and prestige. They are often provoked by their own lack of self-confidence and fear. It is when their power or status is threatened that a dysfunctional leader will turn to negative leadership approaches in order to regain or maintain power. They will attack others who they perceive as a threat, whether that perception is real or not. Their beliefs are biased. They will spend little time building relationships and will rely on their perceived understanding of a person, whether this is right or wrong. They create stereotypes of others, resisting feedback, especially if it is delivered by someone who is at a perceived higher level of status or influence. Followers who have little power will become over-cautious, defensive and critical of others. With the combination of their high power status, their reluctance to receive feedback and the low power status of their followers, who are now critical and cautious, little can be done to move the department or organization forward.

There are several different levels of power that can be utilized by a leader. The first focuses on hard power, which is linked to rewards and punishments. Rewards come in the form of raises, promotion and bonuses. Punishments are delivered through the use of threats, termination of employment and intimidation. In contrast, soft power is used to get followers to follow. Leaders typically use soft power by delivering a clear and compelling vision and building positive relationships with followers.

Other forms of power include coercive, reward, legitimate, expert and referent power. Coercive power is utilized through the methods of punishment and penalties. The leader has the ability and power to punish the target and to prevent them from achieving rewards. Methods of coercive power can be displayed through physical force or reduction of salaries and hours. Reward power is focused on just that – rewarding behavior through extrinsic or intrinsic rewards. The leader rewards behavior and efforts accordingly. Legitimate power is related to power in a position, for example, the position of a judge, doctor or CEO. These types of positions imply power linked to a particular position or by a system of responsibilities and obligations. Expert power is based on what the person knows and their knowledge to drive their power base. This may include experience, schooling, knowledge and skills. This type of power is connected to the individual's expertise. Referent power is based on the admiration others have toward another person. Followers may be drawn to a person based on the level of admiration one has for that leader and they derive power from that admiration. Referent power is the ability to elicit feelings of personal acceptance or approval from others (Barbuto & Gifford, 2009: 274). At any given time, a leader will draw on any one of these power levels, depending of course upon the situation.

In dysfunctional leadership, power is utilized by the leader as a means for counter-productive activities. Rewards are used as a way to recognize negative behavior; for example, a bonus that is tied to financial earnings can be used as a method to reward an unethical leader. Punishment is delivered as a way to stifle an individual who is viewed as a threat to the leader's personal power, status and influence. Followers who are connected to leaders who rely on coercive, reward and legitimate power are less satisfied in work environments (Hackman & Johnson, 2013; Johnson, 2015). Not only are they less satisfied, but they are also typically less engaged or committed to their organizations.

The role of charisma in dysfunction

In the late 1990s, researchers explored the negative impact of charismatic leadership and the negative influence these leaders had on followers. It was discovered that these behaviors may not be intentional. Researchers then explored the dark side of charismatic leadership. In order to understand this phenomenon, it is first necessary to understand what charismatic leadership is.

Charismatic leaders exude a magnetic and motivating presence that followers find both attractive and compelling. According to Lovelace and Hunter (2013), a charismatic leader is always thinking about the future. This is a technique that they use to inspire their followers. They lay out a futuristic path and orientate their personal goals on this path. The positive charismatic leader is very optimistic and future focused. They use communication, which is their strong point, to mesmerize and attract followers. They are able to appeal to the emotions of others, stray away from the negative and focus on the positive. In determining charismatic leaders who have demonstrated positive influence, the following come to mind: Pope John Paul II, Mother Theresa, Winston Churchill, Dr. Martin Luther King, Mahatma Gandhi, Aung San Suu Kyi, Nelson Mandela and John F. Kennedy. This list is by no means exhaustive, but the examples given are clear representations of this type of leadership. All of these leaders were able to use charisma to inspire, serve others and demonstrate a passion for their vision.

Negative charisma

On the flip side, leadership charisma has been used in a negative light. Howell and Avolio (1992) discussed the dark side of charisma as "blind fanaticism in the service of megalomaniacs and dangerous values" (p. 43). The negative charismatic leader tends to thrive during times of crisis, turmoil, change or uncertainty. In events where there is chaos and fear, people look for a beacon of light. This type of leader will be viewed by followers as that beacon of light, or at least attempt to give off that impression. The dark charismatic leader will persuade a susceptible group by using missed messages that are interjected with fear, scare tactics and messages of how they are the only ones who can fix the chaos. As the leader delivers their message, followers begin to believe that the goals of the leader align with what is best for them. During this time, the leader will use tactics to persuade others to their advantage in order to win people over and make them think they are following someone who has their best interests in mind.

The negative charismatic leader has the ability to polarize others with rhetoric, drawing followers together against an imaginary force or outside enemy. The ability to stand up against these perceived evils or an enemy only heightens the leader's position and gives

16 Introduction to dysfunctional leadership

Table 1.2 Comparison of charismatic leaders

Positive charismatic leaders	Negative charismatic leaders
Winston Churchill	Fidel Castro
Pope John Paul II	Saddam Hussein
Nelson Mandela	Jim Jones
John F. Kennedy	Adolf Hitler
Mahatma Gandhi	Napoleon Bonaparte
Dr. Martin Luther King	Malcolm X

them a supernatural power. This is a common tactic used in political campaigns. The candidate demonizes the works of their opponents and highlights how they will stand up against the wrongdoings of that candidate throughout their campaign. It becomes an "us versus them" mentality in an attempt to unify the masses. Individuals have viewed the leader and follower relationship as hypnotic and manifesting in extreme self-confidence. Followers are asked to succumb to the leader's personal agenda and to suspend their better judgment. This is typically done using hypnotic terminology, which plays on the fears or goals of the followers.

When we look at the dark side of a charismatic leader, the perfect example is Adolf Hitler. When Hitler delivered a speech, he was passionate, hypnotic and offered a compelling vision of what Germany could be. He was able to inspire many to follow his vision, allowing him to quickly climb the leadership ranks. He was able to tell the German people that they were a superior race, to speak out against people who he viewed as the enemy, and he had a clear concept of what his followers at the time wanted to hear and to believe in. Other leaders who can be considered negative charismatics include Fidel Castro, Saddam Hussein, Jim Jones, Napoleon Bonaparte and Malcolm X.

As we look at both positive and negative charismatic leaders side by side, we can visualize how these leaders used charisma either positively or negatively

The structure of this book

The structure of this book aims to provide a basic foundation for understanding the different types of dysfunctional leadership characteristics and behaviors found within organizations today. As has been stated in this chapter, there are numerous dysfunctions that could be shared. For the purpose and structure of this book, only the most recognized and discussed behaviors in recent research will be addressed. This book was not designed to explore the psychological findings related to each of these characteristics. However, it does attempt to touch upon psychological components as a means of laying a foundational understanding. Examples are used to help to provide an understanding of each of the dysfunctional types of leadership in order to provide context for the reader.

The book has been structured by first examining bullying in leadership. Bullying has been a controversial topic in the mainstream media and research. It was chosen as the first dysfunction in order to examine and to provide the reader with a better understanding of the context of bullying. Next, the book discusses tyrant leadership. This chapter examines tyrants in the context of the political arena and their impact on society as well as looking at tyrants in the organizational setting. The book then moves on to unethical leadership and explores how each of the dysfunctions has components of unethical leadership. This chapter explores the ethical components of leadership and then seeks to understand unethical leadership behaviors and their impact on others. Part II of the book examines "The Dark Triad." This is followed by chapters that focus on each of the constructs of The Dark Triad, including narcissistic leadership, non-criminal psychopathy and Machiavellianism. Finally, the book examines the impact that dysfunctional leadership has on organizations and followers. In the final chapter, we examine what can be done to address dysfunctional behavior from a follower's, bystander's and organization's perspective. This chapter will explore potential interventions that can be employed to address these behaviors. In addition, we will examine how different countries are beginning to address these behaviors through legal means.

References

Barbuto Jr, J. E., & Gifford, G.T. 2009. Influence triggers and compliance. In D. Tjosvold and B. Wisse (Eds.), *Power and Interdependence in Organizations* (pp. 262–266). Cambridge: Cambridge University Press.

Bies, R. 2001. Interactional (in)justice: The sacred and the profane. In J. Greenberg and R. Cropanzano (Eds.), *Advances in Organizational Justice* (pp. 89–118). Stanford: Stanford University Press.

Bing, S. 1992. Crazy bosses. *Across the Board, 29*(7–8), 22–25.

Burns, J. 1978. *Leadership*. New York: Harper & Row.

Einarsen, S., Aasland, M., & Skogstad, A. 2007. Destructive leadership behavior: A definition and conceptual model. *Leadership Quarterly, 18*(3), 207–216.

Erickson, K., & Freud, S. 1962. Notes on the sociology of deviance. *Social Problems, 9*(2), 307–314.

Hackman, M., & Johnson, C. 2013. *Leadership: A communication perspective* (6th ed.). Prospect Heights, IL: Waveland.

Hogan, R., & Hogan, J. 2001. Assessing leadership: A view from the dark side. *International Journal of Selection and Assessment, 9*(1), 40–51.

Hogan, R., & Kaiser, R. 2005. What we know about leadership. *Review of General Psychology, 9*(3), 169–180.

Hornstein, H. 1996. *Brutal bosses and their prey*. New York: Penguin.

Howell, J., & Avolio, B. 1992. The ethics of charismatic leadership: Submission or liberation? *The Executive, 6*(2), 43–54.

Illies, J., & Reiter-Palmon, R. 2008. Responding destructively in leadership situations: The role of personal values and problem construction. *Journal of Business Ethics, 82*(1), 251–272.

Jacques, E. 1995. Why the psychoanalytical approach to understanding organizations is dysfunctional. *Human Relations, 48*(4), 343–350.

Johnson, C. 2015. *Meeting the ethical challenges of leadership: Casting light or shadow*. Thousand Oaks, CA: Sage Publications.

Kellerman, B. 2004. *Bad leadership: What it is, how it is, why it matters*. Boston, MA: Harvard Business School Press.

Kets de Vries, M. 2001. Creating authentizotic organizations: Well-functioning individuals in vibrant companies. *Human Relations, 54*(1), 101–112.

Kets de Vries, M., & Miller, D. 1985. Narcissism and leadership: An object relations perspective. *Human Relations, 38*, 583–601.

Klein, K., & House, R. 1995. On fire: Charismatic leadership and levels of analysis. *Leadership Quarterly, 6*(4), 183–198.

Kusy, M., & Holloway, E. 2009. *Toxic workplace! Managing toxic personalities and their systems of power*. San Francisco, CA: Jossey-Bass.

Lipman-Blumen, J. 2005a. Toxic leadership: When grand illusions masquerade as noble visions. *Leader to Leader, 2005*(36), 29–37.

Lipman-Blumen, J. 2005b. *The allure of toxic leaders: Why we follow destructive bosses and corrupt politicians – and how we can survive them*. New York: Oxford University Press.

Lovelace, J., & Hunter, S. 2013. Charismatic, ideological, and pragmatic leaders' influence on subordinate creative performance along the creative process. *Creativity Research Journal, 25*, 59–74.

Neuman, J., & Baron, R. 2005. *Aggression in the workplace: A social-psychological perspective. Counterproductive: Investigations of actors and targets*. Washington, DC: American Psychological Association.

Pellitier, K. 2009. *The effects of favored status and identification with victim on perceptions of and reactions to leader toxicity*. Doctoral Dissertation. Claremont Graduate University. UMI 3383643.

Popper, M. 2000. The development of charismatic leaders. *Political Psychology, 21*(3), 729–744.

Somech, A., & Drach-Zahavy, A. 2002. Relative power and influence strategy: The effects of agent-target organizational power on superiors' choices of influence strategies. *Journal of Organizational Behavior, 23*(2), 167–179.

Starratt, A., & Grandy, G. 2010. Your workers' experiences of abusive leadership. *Leadership & Organization Development Journal, 31*(2), 136–138.

Tepper, B., & Duffy, M. 2002. Abusive supervision and subordinates organizational citizenship behavior. *Journal of Applied Psychology, 87*(6), 1068–1076.

Weber, M. 1948. *The theory of social and economic organizations*. Translated by T. Parsons. New York: Free Press.

Wyatt, J., & Hare, C. 1997. *Work abuse: How to recognize and survive it*. Rochester, NY: Schenkman Books.

Chapter 2

Bullying

Introduction

We are all familiar with the bullies from our youth. The bully on the playground who targeted their victim through verbal and non-verbal abuse, pushing, intimidating and humiliating others to get what they wanted. They found out early in life that these tactics worked to gain power over others. The target had something that the bully wanted, they were smarter than the bully, they were liked by others, or the bully found someone that they perceived was weaker. They could exhibit their strength to others by pushing that person around. As we grew up, we hoped that those days on the playground were left behind. Unfortunately, that is not the case. The bully can be found in our adult lives and in our organizations. The bully in the workplace is no different from when we were younger and the results are just as vicious and devastating as they were when we were children. Children who were bullies on the playground tend to grow up to be bullies in the workplace. They find that the tactics used as a childhood bully have worked in the past and they continue these behaviors as they get older. In addition, children who were targets of bullies in grade school tend to grow up to be bullied as adults in the workplace, allowing for the cycle to continue.

Workplace bullying has been a major concern within corporations in many different countries. In the US, over 50 percent of workers have reported that they have been exposed to bullying in the workplace (Namie & Namie, 2009). Organizations downplay adult bullying as people not getting along or simple conflict between two or more individuals. In other cases, bullied individuals may deny being attacked or fail to recognize bullying behaviors. Another complication relates to understanding what bullying is and what it is not. Research has characterized targets of bullying as people who are weak and lack proper social skills or social networks (Einarsen & Skogstad, 1996; Mikkelsen & Einarsen, 2002; Harvey, Heames, Richey, & Leonard, 2006; Tepper, Duffy, Henle, & Lambert, 2006). Others have argued that targets are not weak. They find that the target may not be a poor performer, but instead is a person who the bully has determined is a threat to their self-esteem and status, and may cause the bully to question their own competencies and abilities. In either case, bullying behaviors are detrimental to the target and cause great distress.

Bullying in leadership is an increasing issue within the workplace. Research conducted by Lewis (2006) has found that a high percentage of bullies (over 90 percent of them) were in leadership positions. The 2007 Zogby study (Namie & Namie, 2009) found that in incidents of bullying, more than 75 percent of the bullies were in higher levels of management.

Bullying defined

Bullying in the workplace has become a focal point of scholarly research in the last few years. There are many different definitions of bullying in the workplace. The first study related to workplace bullying was conducted in the 1980s by Heinz Leymann (1990), who used the term "mobbing," which was used to designate situations that dealt with multiple individuals focusing on one single person. Later in the 1990s, Andrea Adams was the first to use the term "workplace bullying." She explained that this was any act that threatens the livelihood and credibility of an individual. Workplace bullying has been given various names, including workplace mobbing, workplace harassment, workplace victimization, workplace psychological terror, workplace aggression, workplace incivility, emotional abuse in the workplace and generalized terms of abuse (Einarsen, Hoel, Zapf, & Cooper, 2010; Keashly & Jagatic, 2000).

The first true definition of workplace bullying was given by Olweus (1993) as repeated, systematic, intentional, negative behavior of one or more individuals directed at another individual. In 1997, Einarsen and Raknes defined bullying as "intentional repeated actions that occur frequently over an extended period of time of at least six months by a person or a group directed against an individual in the form of verbal abuse, behavior that humiliates, threatens, and/or sabotages an individual's work production or status and there is a perceived imbalance of power" (2007: 48–49). Keashly defined bullying as "hostile verbal and nonverbal, non-physical behaviors directed at a person(s) such that the target's sense of him or herself as a competent person and the employee is negatively affected" (1998: 86). Fields (1999) defined bullying as a compulsive need to displace aggression that is achieved by the expression of inadequacy (whether social, interpersonal, behavioral or professional) by the projection of that inadequacy onto others through control and subjugation (criticism, exclusion and isolation). Bullying is sustained by the abdication of responsibility (denial, counter-accusations or the pretense of victimhood) and perpetuated by a climate of fear, ignorance, indifference, silence, denial, disbelief, deception, evasion of accountability, tolerance and reward (promotion) for the bully. Einarsen (1999) expanded upon the definition, defining it as repeated events and actions intended to offend, humiliate, harass, cause the victim stress and social isolation, negatively impacting an employee's work tasks and demonstrate hostile or aggressive behaviors. Yamada provided the following definition of bullying: "the intentional infliction of a hostile work environment upon an employee by others in the workplace typically through a combination of verbal and non-verbal behaviors" (2000: 480). Einarasen (2000) elaborated upon this by adding the requirement that bullying behaviors occur repeatedly and regularly over a period of time. In this definition the target is forced into an inferior position through isolation or menial work that diminishes their capabilities. In 2009, Namie and Namie, founders of the Workplace Bullying Institute, continued to expand upon the definition by adding that bullying is the repeated health-harming mistreatment of a person by one or more workers, taking the form of verbal abuse, conduct or behaviors that are threatening, intimidating or humiliating, sabotaging, or any combination of these behaviors. Barrow (2010) added that workplace bullying is repetitive, abusive behavior that devalues and harms other people on the job.

Workplace bullying is not physically violent, but relies instead on the formidable weapons of hostile actions and words. Bond, Tuckey and Dollard stated that "workplace bullying is a serious and chronic workplace stressor that negatively impacts individuals and organizations" (2010: 37). Bullying is also characterized as harassment toward another individual. In many cases bullying is an imbalance of power where the bully benefits by weakening their target. Bullying can be found at all levels of an organization. However, we find that bullies in positions of power are more prevalent in the workplace. Others have defined bullying as persistent exposure to interpersonal aggression and mistreatment from colleagues, superiors or subordinates that is a prevalent problem in contemporary working life, with devastating effects on both the target and the organization (Rayner & Keashly, 2005; Einarsen, Helge, Hoel & Notelaers, 2009; Einarsen, Hoel, Zapf & Cooper, 2010).

Clearly there is a level of complexity when trying to define what bullying is and what it is not. When we look at the definitions of "workplace bullying," we find that there is a pattern in them. Primary themes relate to psychological abuse inflicted on targets over a period of time. It is also behavior that is repetitive. The intention of these actions is to degrade, humiliate and isolate the bully's target. The bully identifies the target and proceeds to systematically bully that person until they are forced to move to another role or leave the organization. The bully may have one target or may have several targets at any given time. What is important to recognize within all the definitions is the common theme regarding the construct of workplace bullying. This relates to situations where an employee is persistently exposed to negative and aggressive forms of behavior at work, primarily of a psychological nature with the ultimate goal of humiliating, intimidating, punishing or frightening the target into submission. In order to be classified as bullying, the acts must be repetitive and must happen regularly over a period of time (i.e., weeks, months and/or years).

The characteristics of bullying

As we have just read, there are a number of different definitions of bullying in the workplace. Now that we have an understanding of the definitions of bullying, let's look at the dimensions related to bullying in more detail. Hutchinson, Vickers, Jackson and Wilkes (2006) explored the dimensions related to workplace bullying and pointed out that bullying is not limited to one individual. This behavior can include targeted groups, such as functioning organizational units. We understand that bullying consists of acts of verbal violence that deliberately seek to humiliate or withhold resources and information. The three identifiable characteristics of bullying include the following:

1   repetitive behavior that occurs at least twice a week;
2   long-term behavior that continues for a minimum of six months;
3   forms of behavior that occur in situations where the person who is targeted finds it difficult to defend themselves or stop the abuse.

(Felblinger, 2009)

The bully

Many people think that a bully is quite powerful and in some cases they are when it comes to controlling the situation. When the bully is the leader, they not only control the situation, but also possess a different level of power over followers and others in the organization. What is important to understand about the bully is that they are often very insecure, with a low level of self-esteem. They are the type of person who needs to control situations as well as being right all the time. Depending on the situation, they can be charming one minute and nasty the next. They lack social skills and are constantly seeking to protect their image, self-esteem and control of their world. Anyone who threatens any of these components can be targeted by the bully.

Bullies lack the insight to analyze their actions, or identify their own personal inadequacy or their own self-loathing (Namie & Namie, 2009). Their own lives are out of control in one area and as a result they compensate elsewhere in order to regain the control they are lacking. They project their flaws onto others, even if these flaws only exist in the bully and not in the target. For example, they will find a target who is extremely competent. The bully recognizes that the target has characteristics that the bully lacks. They hone in on the target and will begin to tear the individual down. Insults such as calling them "incompetent" or "stupid" are used while criticizing their work. The target starts to question their own abilities and competence, while the bully slowly starts to gain power over the target. While regaining power and control, they are able to compensate for what is lacking in their personal lives. The target continues to analyze what they are doing wrong and what they can do differently. They become self-conscious and paranoid in relation to their work. What was once considered competent and strong work is now being called incompetence. The target starts to become sensitive and overly cautious to ensure they are not making mistakes. However, because they have become overly cautious, mistakes begin to happen. The bully hones in on these mistakes, which perpetuates the problem further. It becomes a repeated cycle. Each time a mistake is made by the employee, the bullying leader calls out the mistakes publicly to others so that they can witness the "incompetence." In reality, the bully is only mirroring their own incompetence and faults. By attacking someone else, they are able to divert the attention away from their own ineffectiveness. In turn, the leader is able to gain control and power over the situation, confirming their belief that they are truly competent over the target. The cycle continues to the point where the bully has achieved complete domination over the target. Eventually, the employee will either give in to the abuse, ignore the behavior, eventually leave the situation by transferring out of the unit or department, or leave the organization. Only in rare situations is the target relieved of the abuse if the bully diverts their attention to someone else.

Types of bullies

The public bully or direct bully

This type of bully is focused on publicly humiliating, screaming, throwing tantrums, finger pointing, invading personal space, interrupting and publicly threatening job security. They love to be spectacles and the center of attention in public. The target often feels like a child who is being ridiculed or scolded in front of their siblings. The public bully wants people to witness their power through their actions. It is their hope that others will side with the bully or that they will witness what is occurring and will not challenge the bully. The target avoids interactions with the bully and they slowly begin to shrink away. In meetings, it is difficult for them to speak up for fear of being publicly ridiculed or embarrassed. The target moves into a self-preservation mode as a means to protect themselves. By doing so, the bully continues to see the target as weak and prompts them to lash out.

They have spotted the weakness in their target and the behavior continues. The goal of the public bully is to move the target into complete submission and to do so publicly in order to assert their dominance over others. The target becomes focused on the attacks, causing them to focus less on the work that needs to be done. As a result, the target begins to make mistakes and the bully escalates their efforts to go after the target, and now has the justification to publicly humiliate the target. The target starts to dread the career that they once loved. Self-doubt and depression starts to creep in and these feelings now invade not only their professional lives, but also their personal lives. They start to question their own abilities and career choices, and start to ask "What is wrong with me?", to which their answer is "Maybe I really am incompetent."

Example of a public or direct bully

John was the new leader in the department. Sam was an employee who was very competent and well-liked by leadership and peers. Sam even applied for John's position, but was told that he wasn't quite ready for leadership, although with the right experiences he would be in a few years. He understood that he needed more leadership development and experiences. He hoped that John would be a mentor to him. During a meeting, Sam paid attention to John and was interested in his leadership approaches and styles. About two months later, Sam met with John to tell him he was interested in leadership and had applied for John's position. He shared with John that leadership had felt he was not ready, but would be in a couple of years with the right experiences. Sam wanted to build his skills and leadership abilities. John smiled and said "Let me see what I can do for you." A few weeks later, John came to Sam with a new project for the supply chain department. Sam said this was an area that he was not familiar with and that he would be excited to learn about the project. John said it was a great opportunity for Sam and he would be happy to mentor him. At the first meeting, Sam sat quietly, listening and learning. John led the meeting effectively and delegated project work to Sam. He was excited about the new project and could not wait to get started. During a team touchpoint meeting, Sam shared his progress and what he was doing. John shook his head and said that this was not what he asked Sam to do and that he should meet with John as soon as possible to "Get back on track." After the meeting, Sam met with John and clarified what he was working on. "That is not what you said in the meeting" said John, raising his voice. "If you are going to say something, your thoughts should be clear, articulate and not jumbled." Sam took this as constructive feedback and went back to work on the project. At the next touchpoint meeting, Sam made a point of being very clear on the direction of the part he was working on. He asked if anyone had any questions; everyone in the room shook their heads, except for John. John stood up and towered over Sam. "I don't understand why you can't get this. At the last meeting I told you that you were off track and not doing what I asked. If you can't handle this project, then maybe you are on the wrong team." No one said anything and Sam left the meeting feeling confused and concerned. He met with John and stated there must be a misunderstanding. He shared with him what they had discussed at their last one-on-one meeting and made sure he was clear during the meeting. "Well, apparently you were not clear again. Honestly Sam, I don't know how much longer I can put up with your incompetence and inability to understand supply chain. I trusted you and gave you a part in this project and you have failed not once but twice. I don't think you are cut out for leadership." Sam left the office and went to lunch with his co-workers, asking for their help and what he should do. They didn't know what to say as they believed Sam to be extremely competent and a quick learner. Sam went back to the office determined to prove John wrong. As the weeks went by, Sam dreaded the touchpoint meetings and the follow-ups with John. Just when he thought he was on the right track, John would scream at him and tell him he was nowhere near the target. In the last touchpoint meeting John stepped in and said he would take over Sam's part of the project since Sam "just couldn't catch on." Others in the meeting started to question whether Sam was competent. In turn, Sam started to question his abilities as well. For him, it felt like everything was falling apart. He could feel that he was being isolated from others in the department, his work was less meaningful and his marriage was suffering. His wife did not understand what was happening and that very morning has said she didn't want to hear about it again. He felt like his life and career was in a tailspin. He decided to apply for a different position within the organization, hoping that he could try something new and get back on track. However, at this point he was known for being incompetent and "just not getting it." He went from being a competent employee with leadership potential to the employee no one wanted. He eventually left the organization and took an entry-level position. John continued to grow in his leadership position, but others shared that the behavior Sam experienced was something many others had experienced. Anyone who aspired to a leadership position was treated the same way as Sam.

The silent or indirect bully

The silent or indirect bully will attack their target in private. They don't want witnesses while inflicting harm on their target. In public, the bully will come across as kind, charming and pleasant to everyone. When the attack is in private, it may be difficult for the target to share what happened with others, since they already have a positive impression of the bully. In other cases, the bully might meet with others and focus on the target behind closed doors. The tactics employed by a silent bully involve spreading rumors, talking maliciously about the target and spending hours discussing how to sabotage the target. The target can usually hear the laughter that is happening behind closed doors and knows that something is wrong, but can't put their finger on what is happening. In other cases, the target does not know they are being attacked until they hear the rumors and gossip being spread about them. At this point, it is often difficult to pinpoint who the person is that is attacking them. People begin to believe the rumors and begin to isolate the target by excluding them from events, lunches, meetings or discussions that impact the target.

Example of a silent bully

As a leader, either Bob liked you or didn't like you. The problem was that he never showed his dislike, but his followers felt it. It seemed as though their interactions with Bob just did not seem right. There was no one thing that they could pinpoint, but they felt uncomfortable. He seemed like a good manager, but over time, targets would feel and experience indirect tactics that left them wondering. Slowly, they would be excluded from meetings or from events that were taking place. Information that was necessary for certain people to do their jobs was not funneled down to them. When followers would ask Bob what happened, he would just say that "I forgot to include them in the invite to the meeting" or "I forgot to send you that email. So sorry!" During promotion or performance reviews, his targets were often told that they were not ready to move forward or that their performance was not up to par. This was always a surprise for his direct reports; they never saw it coming. When asked how they could improve, Bob would have recommendations, but never followed through or helped in promoting his people in any way. Typically, the people Bob would target were high performers and it seemed to others that he was threatened by these individuals.

The critical bully

The critical bully is always looking for fault and to place blame. They are negative individuals and will find fault in whatever and whoever they can. They will mask their own insecurities with public boldness in order to impress or intimidate others. They use the performance management system as a lethal weapon to document false information about the target. This system is used to document incompetence, which may be true or made up. In either case, the performance is documented and it becomes a challenge to remove critical information from the record. If the target does push back on false claims, they are faced with blame and not taking ownership of their faults. The critical bully will demand unreasonable expectations. When these unreasonable demands are not met or mistakes are made in haste, the critic will be quick to point out the mistakes, faults or missed deadlines, pointing the finger back at the target and how incompetent they are. The critic will attack their target by flooding their inboxes with unnecessary emails, messages and work, leaving the target wondering what and what not to address. The target will receive late-night phone calls asking for last-minute deadlines. The critic will want updates on the smallest of issues, only to pile additional pressure and stress on the target. This type of bully lives to find the negative, to find fault in everyone and everything. They have learned this behavior from someone in their past. In order to be successful, they believe that they need to focus on the negative versus the positive in other people and situations. The critical bully will use their tone of voice and body language to convey criticism that makes the target uncomfortable.

Example of a critical bully

Shelby was one of those leaders who people just did not want to associate with. Within her department she was known for her attention to detail, which translated into being extremely critical. Every year she would pick someone within the department to focus on and would tear apart everything that the employee in question turned in. She bragged about her degree in English and her ability to spot errors from a mile away. Charlie was the target for Shelby this year. Everything that he turned in was wrong and she would red ink every single piece of his work. He told her to look at the content and that he would have the editing department look at the formatting, but she wouldn't listen. Charlie dreaded turning anything in and would sit as his desk waiting to hear her rip into his work. In team meetings she would always find the negative side of anything. She was called "The Office Joy Sucker" as she found something negative about everything. New and fresh ideas for innovation were shot down and she had 1,000 reasons why something would not work. People within the department just stopped bringing up issues, new ideas or talking about anything. Employees came into work at 8:00 am, and at 4:30 pm every day the office cleared out. The team stopped doing anything together because they found themselves talking about the negativity and they found that they were becoming bitter and negative. Work had become just that – work. There was no joy in the workplace and work had little or no meaning. Charlie began to use more vacation time and when he ran out of vacation days, he used sick time. Eventually, he filed for disability because of recurring migraines and GI issues. Charlie often told his family he was most happy when he was home with a migraine because that pain was much better than the job. When he was not in the office, he was migraine-free and when he thought of going back to the office, he would experience GI problems. In the mornings, the issues were so severe that he was unable to work. When he did not come into work, Shelby was on the phone calling him at home to pester him and to find fault with whatever work he had previously turned in. He just could not get away from her. The rest of the team learned not to answer Shelby's phone calls, which infuriated her and only made matters worse.

The friendly bully

This type of bully is just that – "friendly." They introduce themselves as someone you want to befriend. The friendliness of this type of individual causes the target to let their guard down. When this happens, the target becomes vulnerable, open and willing to share information. The goal of the friendly bully is to get as much information as they can from the individual. This information is used against the target when they least expect it. Friendly bullies will look for tidbits of gossip and information about others, including the target. They capitalize on the friendship in order to get inside information. Once this information has been obtained, they will use it to their advantage. During this time, the target will be thinking that they are friends with the bully, but in reality they are nothing but a pawn for the bully to use in order to advance their own personal agenda. The friendly bully will be the direct opposite of the critical bully. They will focus on telling the target how great they are to build them up in order to get them let their defenses down, while they are taking whatever information they receive and sharing it with others. The friendly bully is sure to tell others that they got this information from the target. They may twist, lie or embellish the information in order to cause conflict with others. This tactic is used to pit individuals against each other. Eventually, the target realizes that the bully is "two-faced" and usually by that time it will be too late. The one who will be cast in a negative light is the target, who is blamed for spreading malicious gossip and rumors. The friendly bully will also get on the right side of those higher up in the organization, showing themselves in a positive light and putting on a face that is friendly, cooperative, competent and one of a team player. Others will view this person in the same light until they are "burned" by that person. If the target complains to others about the friendly bully, they will be the ones who are viewed in a negative light. How can anyone say anything negative about this kind, loyal, team-playing person? "After all, aren't you the one who shared information with this person and aren't you the one who put the negative spin on the rumor?" They won't see the friendly bully doing anything wrong. In public forums, the friendly bully will sing the target's praises, coming across as kind, laughing at jokes and talking the target up. However, behind the scenes they will show their true colors. Targets will want to call the friendly bully out for their behavior and that is exactly what the friendly bully wants. They will remain cool and collected when the target is emotionally charged and angry. The target looks like they are the one with the problem. In their state, they will look emotional and erratic, while the friendly bully stands there and has tears in their eyes. In the end, it is the target who comes across to others as the bully. The friendly bully will then play the role of victim, stating that they have been nothing but kind, caring and considerate toward the individual. To others, that will be true and they will sympathize with the friendly bully.

Example of a friendly bully

Ben interviewed for the position as leader for the operations team. Everyone loved Ben and saw him as extremely kind and friendly. He was a great fit for the culture of the organization and the team. He came on board and started to befriend members of the staff. He wanted to get to know people and wanted to get a "lay of the land." Followers and peers believed that he was kind, considerate and a good listener. They felt that they could share anything with him. Ben always wanted to meet over coffee or during walks. During these meetings, he showed genuine interest in the person he was meeting. People felt comfortable with him and started to let their guard down. Ben started asking questions about co-workers and what their stories were. He assured whoever he was talking to that what was shared was confidential. Slowly people started to open up to Ben, sharing information about their co-workers. They started to notice that the talks with Ben and coffee meetings were scheduled more frequently. Slowly, conflict started in the department as people heard stories that others shared with Ben. Susan started to hear a story that she shared with Ben about Terry. Terry confronted Susan over the story and as they talked, Susan realized that Ben twisted the story in a negative way. The story was no longer the truth. When Susan went to confront Ben about what was said, he just smiled and said "I don't understand, I am not sure what you are talking about. I never said anything about Terry and would never break your confidence." He shared with others that Susan was accusing him of things that were not true. This created a larger void between Susan and her fellow team members. Susan started to put her guard up with Ben, but this came across to others as her being uncooperative and not being a team player. The team sided with Ben and Susan was ostracized. Later on in the week, Ben walked into Susan's office and lost his temper with her. He was talking about Terry and was "just venting." Susan realized that Ben was not the person they all thought he was. This was a side that no one had ever seen before. Susan mentioned this to a couple of other co-workers and shared what she experienced with Ben and the behavior she witnessed. No one believed her and they felt that she was trying to divert the attention away from her actions of spreading lies about Terry. Ben was always kind and considerate. His temper was on an even keel even under stress and they could not believe he would act in that way. Later that week, the department met and Susan shared information about productivity. Ben spoke up and said "I just want to publicly acknowledge Susan for the great work that she does. She has been working so hard to support me in my new role and I have learned so much from Susan. She is the best." All eyes turned in the direction of Susan. Susan could just hear them thinking, "This person sings your praises and this is the way you treat him." Susan looked at Ben as he smiled at her and understood what had

28 Bullying

just happened – she had been used by Ben. However, her reputation in the meantime had been damaged and the trust her team members had for her had been diminished.

The hoarder bully

The hoarder bully believes in the term "knowledge is power." They gain power by hoarding information and controlling resources. By hoarding resources, they control the knowledge and situation. They view their success as tied to the knowledge that they have and the resources they control. They do not want others to succeed and will withhold information. Examples of resources on which they may keep a tight hold include:

- budgets and funding;
- institutional knowledge on processes and procedures;
- time and scheduling;
- recognition and/or praise;
- staffing resources.

The hoarder bully will cut the target out of communication, meetings and emails. They want to be considered in the know and the keeper of information. They are well-connected to the grapevine and truly know what is happening. By keeping information to themselves, they gain control and power while others are left out of the loop. One tactic that they like to use is the silent treatment, ignoring the target and putting them into isolation and exclusion. Targets find that they are not in the know regarding their own work or department. The hoarder bully leader will begin to make decisions without input from key stakeholders. In many cases, they will create new rules, processes and regulations without input from key stakeholders. The hoarder bully leader will bypass current rules and regulations, creating new ones that will protect their knowledge base and build their power. This type of leader will ignore others, including their direct reports. These types of behavior make the target feel isolated, worthless and diminished. That is the ultimate goal of this type of bully. Eventually the person feels as though they have no self-worth and that they have nothing to offer the organization. Eventually they leave. Typically this type of bully finds the target to be a threat to their own existence. By hoarding information, the ultimate control is in the hands of the bully. They control the dissemination of information, the knowledge needed to do the job and the necessary resources. The goal of the hoarder bully leader is to preserve their job and status. They will withhold information from their targets, causing them to feel helpless. This bully creates an environment where they are the expert and the person with the power.

Example of a hoarder bully

Nickie had worked with the organization for over 20 years. As a leader, she was the one with most tenure and was viewed as the go-to person for information. She was also the finance controller, keeping track of financial and human resources. When people came to her for information or resources, she was extremely difficult to deal with. Since she had tenure in the organization, she was the only one who had the necessary information and getting this from her was always a challenge. What made matters worse was that Nickie decided who got the necessary information and when they got it. When a new employee came to work and needed information from her, she would always tell them how she had all the information they needed in order to be successful. She controlled what people should and shouldn't know. She even held information back from the executives of the organization. No one questioned her unwillingness to help provide resources or information. Frankly, many were afraid of her. They were afraid of what would happen to all the knowledge if she left. She always maintained the budgets and made sure the organization was fiscally sound. She viewed herself as the one who was ultimately running the organization rather than the CEO. In her mind, she had all the necessary information in order to be successful. She told employees that she knew where all the bodies were buried within the organization and was not afraid to share this information. The CEO of the organization seemed to be afraid of her.

The opportunistic bully

The opportunistic bully thrives on moving ahead. When an opportunity arises, they will do whatever is necessary to seize that opportunity as a way to position themselves for the next position. They can effectively separate themselves from work and their personal lives. In the workplace, they are cut-throat and will bully others in order to move ahead in the organization. This type of bully will walk over people they view as competition or will block others from achieving their goals in order to maintain control over others and the situation. They align themselves with senior leadership. They are extremely effective at finding a corporate sponsor who also believes in the bully's tactics. The sponsor sees nothing wrong with this type of behavior and views the opportunistic bullying leader as a "go getter," "ambitious," "strong" and "competent." In their eyes, the bully can do no wrong.

When the opportunistic bully is met outside of the workplace, they are a different person and will seem kind and caring. Friends and significant others who have heard horror stories of the antics of the bullying leader in the workplace are shocked when they finally meet them, as they do not seem like the monster that they have been portrayed as. This person will position themselves outside of the workplace as the volunteer at their kid's school and as supportive members of the community, volunteering their time to help others. They do this in order to build their public image in the eyes of others and to ensure that they are viewed positively by others outside the organization. In addition, they know that this feedback will get back to others in the organization, especially senior leadership.

Example of an opportunistic bully

Tom was always looking for an opportunity to improve and to move up the corporate ladder. Throughout school he was viewed as a "go getter." He was brutal in winning and would do anything at any time to get what he wanted. He took credit for everything, even if the idea was not his. As Tom moved into leadership roles, his behavior got worse and he became more cut-throat. "Anything to get ahead" was his motto. He loved to get his ideas from Mike and Shelly. They tried not to share ideas with him because they knew that eventually he would spin the ideas as his own. Shelly suggested that the group look to hire a Bryan from a local competitor. Bryan was looking for a new opportunity and was sending out feelers. Shelly thought that Bryan would be a great addition to the department and she sent an email to Tom. Weeks went by, nothing was said and Shelly did not hear anything. In a one-on-one meeting with Tom, Shelly mentioned the idea again to him. Tom said he had been thinking about hiring Bryan and bringing him on board. Shelly said she thought it was a great idea and mentioned the email. Tom said he had no recollection of the email and that he had just thought of the idea. Tom positioned himself well within the organization. At social events, he always made sure he was seated within vision of the CEO of the company. He made a point of being seen at work functions. When a position came up for a senior leadership position, he began to push for the role. He had lunch with the CEO and made sure other that the vice presidents knew about his interest. When he heard that Annie was interested in the position as well, he started laying the foundations to obstruct her movement. During his time with the CEO and the other vice presidents, he started to mention how he really liked Annie, but that frankly she was not ready for a senior leadership position. He would be happy to mentor her if they would like, but she was just not ready. During meetings with Annie, he would make comments about her and about how she just was not mature enough for a senior leadership position. In meetings he would call upon her to present on something that she was working on. Usually, Annie was not prepared to talk about the topic since she had not prepared anything. Tom used this opportunity to make comments about her not being prepared and that as a leader, she should be able to "Think on her feet" and "Why was she not prepared?" Then he would present on the topic and provide his insights, which were ultimately Annie's ideas. In the eyes of her peers, she looked unprepared and they did not have much confidence in her. Annie was always frustrated after these meetings. She would go home and tell her husband how angry she was and how she could not handle working with Tom.

During Tom's time away from work, he coached his son's football team and worked at the local homeless shelter, which was sponsored by his organization. He volunteered at every shift that he knew the CEO or upper leadership would be at. They were so impressed that Tom gave back to the community. During a social for the retirement of a person in their department, Annie introduced her husband to Tom. Tom was so gracious and kind. He even complimented Annie for her work and said that one day she would make a great leader within the organization. Annie's husband looked at her and said "I like this guy. I don't know what your problem is with him. He is kind and just complimented you on your work." After that day, Annie's husband never wanted to hear anything negative about Tom since he felt the guy was great. Tom moved into the senior leadership role and was focusing on his next opportunity to move forward.

Mobbing

Mobbing is a term that is used when a group of individuals collectively bully a person in the workplace. This concept in the workplace includes workplace terrorizing, pressuring, belittling or abstract violence (Yildirim & Yildirim, 2007). As was mentioned earlier in the chapter, mobbing was first identified by Leymann in 1984. At that time, he described the behavior as the presence of systematic, directed, unethical communication along with antagonistic behavior by one or more individuals directed at another (Leymann, 1992). The individual or individuals who participate in the psychological abuse are very organized and the behavior is systematic, long-term and frequently occurs. Others within the organization typically ignore the behavior. In other cases, others may participate in the behavior because of peer pressure. With more individuals involved, the target feels helpless when faced with many different people acting out toward them (Einarsen, 2000). There are several different interpretations regarding the meaning of mobbing in the workplace. Einarsen, Hoel, Zapf and Cooper (2010) defined "workplace mobbing" as anti-social behavior directed at a victim who finds it difficult to defend themselves. This type of behavior relates to psychological violence. Mobbing can happen at various levels within the organization, including top–down, horizontal and bottom–up. Research conducted by Erturk (2013) found that mobbing by leadership toward direct reports is most common, resulting in 57 percent of all mobbing situations in Europe and 87 percent of those reported in the US. Typically, this behavior is led by the leader, with several direct reports mobbing against one or more people in a unit or department. People involved in the mobbing hope that by partnering with the leader, they will be seen in a positive light.

Gender and bullying

Several studies related to bullying in the workplace have been completed. Research conducted by Einarsen and Skogstad (1996) reported that 49 percent of the victims were male and 30 percent were women. Studies by Zapf (1999) found that 26 percent of the bullies were male, while 11 percent were female. Rayner and Cooper (1997) conducted another study which found that two-thirds of the bullies were men. It appears that the gender of bullies is more male-dominated, although this is not a conclusive finding.

There are subtle differences related to gender and bullying. A survey in 2007 conducted by the Workplace Bullying Institute provided the following insights:

- Men prefer to bully in public, whereas women prefer to bully behind closed doors.
- Most bullies are men, while most victims are women.
- Women tend to bully other women; men tend to bully men and women equally.

Follow-up research conducted by the Workplace Bullying Institute in 2010 focused on key findings on bullying and provided the following research information on gender-related bullying:

- Gender of targets: 58 percent were women and 42 percent were men. This may be related to power differences between men and women.
- Gender of bullies: 62 percent men and 38 percent women.
- Female bullies targeted their own gender in 79.8 percent of cases.
- Women targeted men in 20.2 percent of cases.
- In 2007, the woman-on-woman bullying prevalence was 71 percent and in 2010, this increased to 80 percent.

Bullying by women can often be ignored or overlooked as women seem to prefer less aggressive forms of bullying such as gossip and rumors, and usually conduct such behavior behind closed doors. As a result, bullying may not be as noticeable as the direct aggression that their male counterparts tend to engage in. To further complicate matters, women tend to be viewed as nurturing and caring. Bullying behaviors in women may only be recognized once the extent of their actions has escalated.

The respective numbers given above show that men appear to be over-represented among bullies. Some researchers believe that there is a direct relation to aggressive behaviors such as shouting and public humiliation. This type of direct bullying is more aligned to male traits, whereas women tend to be less aggressive and prefer a more indirect approach. Studies of the past reflected a male-dominated workforce, with more men in leadership roles. In recent years, as women continue to enter the ranks of leadership, we are finding that these numbers may be increasing.

In recent years there has been an increase in bullying toward men focusing on men displaying non-masculine traits or men working in non-traditional roles (Berdahl, Magley & Waldo, 1996; Lee, 2001). Research finds that men are typically less likely to report that they are a target of bullying because of how it may be perceived by others. In contrast, women are more likely to come forward and report bullying (Salin, 2009). Because of the unreported claims of male bullying, there may not be a significant difference in terms of the reporting of bullying in the workplace between genders.

One noticeable difference in relation to workplace bullying is the way in which genders react to bullying. For example, men who are bullied are inclined to be confrontational or are likely to retaliate against the bully. This type of reaction is likely to escalate tension and conflict. Men are also less willing to seek help for bullying, as it relates to physical and/or psychological issues, while women tend to seek out professional help earlier. Seeking help earlier tends to address the psychological and physical impact of bullying. However, it is important to note that women are less likely to confront the bullying leader, which allows for the behaviors to continue.

Bullying tactics

The bully has an arsenal of tactics that they use to tear down their target. We have looked at some of the tactics that are most typically used. Let us examine in detail some of the tactics used:

- *Exclusion and isolation*: Exclusion or social isolation is often utilized in order take control or power away from the target. This is done through socially or professionally excluding the target. The target is omitted from key meetings that specifically impact their work. They are excluded from information sharing, which makes it difficult to do their job. Ideas that they bring forward are ignored or rejected as meaningless. Targets learn about decisions made that impact their work through rumors or others who are willing to share information with them. By withholding vital information, the target is left in the dark and is unable to effectively do their job. They are ignored during meetings and find that they are unable to provide input into the direction of their work, the team's direction or the organization. The bully will also socially isolate the target. When the target is isolated from social contact with others, they often suffer alone and do not have the social system in place to support them through these tactics. Some people refer to this tactic as being viewed as an outcast, treated like a pariah or being put in cold storage.

- *Creation of an uncomfortable work environment*: This type of work atmosphere is often referred to as a hostile work environment. Through gossip, rumors, public humiliation, isolation, lack of direction and feedback, the bully creates a difficult work environment. The target is unable to effectively perform their work duties. They often experience feelings of not wanting to go to work because the bully has made the environment too difficult or hostile.
- *Invasion of personal space*: The bully will often invade a person's personal space. For others, this comes across as a sincere gesture of a hug, handshake, leaning into or sitting close to a person. However, by being in someone's personal space, the bully is physically showing signs of exerting control and power. Invasion of personal space in scenarios involving conflict and tension often makes the target uncomfortable and this tactic is deliberately used for this reason.
- *Unfair or destructive criticism/feedback*: The bullying leader usually does not provide feedback. When feedback is given, it is typically negative in nature. The bully will provide feedback that is destructive and comes in the form of criticism. Bullies often use the words "stupid," "incompetent," "crazy," "lazy," "inadequate," etc. These words are unfair and destructive to the self-esteem of the follower. This tactic is used repetitively in order to chip away at the target's self-esteem. At first the target may laugh it off, but over time they start to believe these words since they are heard so often.
- *Blaming others for errors*: The bully never takes responsibility or accountability for their actions. They look to blame people or individuals for errors that occur; these errors are committed by the bully, but they will look for someone else to wrongly accuse. They are constantly looking for a scapegoat and to blame someone when something goes wrong. This tactic is used to divert the attention away from the bully and their faults. If need be, fictitious errors are fabricated in order to draw attention to the target's incompetence and the bully's competence. The bully will use this opportunity to step in and save the day.
- *Unreasonable job demands*: Unreasonable job demands or deadlines are imposed on the target. This can be a project given to the target at 3:00 pm on Friday with a 7:00 am deadline of Monday morning, requiring the target to work through the weekend. The bullying leader increases the target's workload without help or reasonable deadlines. Job requirements that are menial, above the skillset of the employee or not part of the target's job are assigned. The bully hopes that the target will fail at these tasks so as to provide an opportunity to point out their failure to others and the target.
- *Inconsistent application of rules and policies*: One set of rules and policies apply to one group of individuals who the bullying leader likes. These rules are flexible and are meant to be broken without consequences – for example, coming in late or leaving earlier. Another set of rules applies to the target or targets. They are held to a different standard in relation to rules and are required to be in on time or stay late, and there is not flexibility in the rules.
- *Threatening job or personal security*: The bully loves to hold job security over the heads of the target. A common threat tactic of a bully is to threaten the security of the target. Comments include: "I don't know why I keep you around," "If you don't do this project, then you better get your résumé sent out" and "You need to start looking for another job." Threats to personal security may also include threats to a target's personal income, benefits or basic needs.

34   Bullying

- *Name calling*: Name calling is another popular tactic of bullies. Their vocabulary is full of hurtful words used to diminish the target. They will find just the word or phrase that they know will belittle and tear down the target. In some cases they will use a derogatory nickname for their target and will share this with others, who will then also use this term when discussing the target.
- *Spreading rumors or gossip*: Rumors and malicious gossip are used to discredit the target. They will embellish and twist information to put the target in a bad light with others, including higher levels of leadership. Any information collected about the target will be used against them. The bullying leader will share personal information about the target from the target's personnel records, including previous performance reviews and personal information about medical leave or family medical leave. Whatever information the bully has on the target, they will use against the target. If they don't have information, they will make up stories, embellish stories or twist conversations in order to gain the upper hand with the target. Gossip is one of the most difficult things to approach in the workplace. A leader who engages in gossip sets a precedent for employees to engage in this type of behavior.
- *Verbal and non-verbal threats*: Threatening verbal comments made by a bullying leader include threatening to take work away, not promoting an individual and threatening the employee with termination. Forms of non-verbal cues include eye rolling, turning away, mocking, staring or glaring, smirking or shaking of the head.
- *Physical threats*: On very rare occasions, there may be physical abuse. This may include intimidating behaviors such as physically blocking a person, finger pointing, invasion of personal space, shoving, touching, hitting and throwing objects, and very rarely even physical assault. The use of physical assault is rare since leaders are aware of its consequences.
- *Demeaning individuals on the basis of race, age, gender, sexuality, weight and disability*: The bully will focus on the target's personal characteristics, such as demeaning a person for being a certain age, including the target being too young or too old to do the work. The bully may focus on the weight of an individual or they may focus in on other characteristics, including sexuality, disability and gender. In a recent bullying case, the bully commented how he was successful "in getting the two fat, old women out of the organization."
- *Derailment*: Derailment is a term used to sabotage a person's job. This can cover a range of approaches from placing obstacles in the way of the employee in order to prevent them from completing tasks to ending a person's career. Typically, when the leader is the bully, they cause an employee to be derailed by making it impossible for the employee to get work completed. Typically the role of leadership is to get the employee the resources that they need in order to complete their work. In the case when the leader is the bully, employees are not provided with direction, resources or the means of removing obstacles to the successful completion of their tasks. The leader becomes the one causing the interruption in the employee's work, resulting in accusations and humiliation as the leader accuses the employee of being lazy, incompetent or stupid. Another form of sabotage includes the derailment of a person's career – for example, where a person would like to be promoted to another position and the leader blocks that promotion, or where the employee would like to leave

the department and move to a different department and the leader stops this by making false allegations about the employee's performance. By preventing the employee from moving forward, it allows the target to stay within the grasp of the bullying leader. Eventually, though, the employee will exit the organization.

As we can see, all of these tactics are used to establish a pattern of aggressive behavior that is designed to inflict psychological destruction. The behavior is characterized by psychological abuse occurring over time that is intended to degrade, isolate and humiliate the target. The bully may use one or several different tactics in order to inflict harm on an individual.

Summary of the classification of bullying

All of the tactics we have looked at can be classified as either direct or indirect bullying. In some cases, the tactics may include one approach or both approaches. As discussed earlier in this chapter, direct actions relating to bullying include accusations, verbal abuse and public humiliation. These types of behavior may include publicly accusing someone of not doing their work, calling them derogatory names and screaming or yelling at them in public. Indirect bullying tactics are done behind closed doors where a group of people gather with the leader to gossip about the target. Through gossiping, rumors are started and circulated. Another form of indirect bullying actions includes isolation, where the target is not included in meetings that impact their work or social gatherings such as team lunches, or they are simply ignored. Indirect bullying is usually associated with mobbing tactics, which may turn into direct bullying as tensions and conflict escalate. Bullying can be targeted at both the person and the work in which that person participates. Person-related tactics include slandering an individual through gossip or rumors and social isolation, where the employee is excluded from the social structure

Table 2.1 Bullying factors from the Negative Acts Questionnaire-Revised (NAQ-R)

Direct actions	*Indirect actions*
Accusations	Rumors
Verbal abuse	Isolation
Public humiliation	Gossiping
Person-related	*Work-related*
Slander	Giving too much or not enough work
Social isolation (being ignored or excluded)	Menial tasks
Insinuation toward a person	Persistent criticizing of person's work
Humiliated or ridiculed in connection to work or personal life	Withholding information that impacts the employee's performance
Gossiping/spreading rumors	Being ordered to work at a level that is below the employee's capabilities
Having key areas of responsibility taken away	Unreasonable deadlines
Persistent ridicule	Micro-managing/excessive monitoring of work
Excessive teasing and sarcasm	Not allowing an employee to claim what is due to them (time off, sick time, pay, travel expenses)

of the organization. Work-related behaviors focus on other tactics, such as assigning a person menial tasks and making them feel as though they are less than adequate at their work, overloading a person with too much or too little work, or constant criticism of a person's work.

Incivility versus bullying

A common term used for bullying is incivility. Incivility can be defined as types of behavior that are rude, annoying or disrespectful and that may or may not be directed at one particular person in order to cause harm. However, it is important to understand that bullying is different from incivility. A possible cause of confusion in this respect is that incivility may escalate to bullying behaviors in the workplace. Andersson and Pearson (1999: 457) defined "workplace incivility" as "low intensity deviant behavior with ambiguous intent to harm the target in violation of workplace norms for mutual respect. Uncivil behavior is characterized as rude and discourteous, displaying a lack of regard for others." While the definition focuses on low-intensity behavior, it is important to recognize that it is not bullying. However, while it may not be bullying, it can be just as devastating to the target as the other dysfunctional leadership behaviors that have been addressed. What separates incivility from bullying is that it is typically a single event, such as rudeness or minor gossiping, which is done in isolation. Incivility is usually short term in nature. Bullying, which may also include rude comments or gossiping, is repetitive and is done over sustained periods of time. If we look at a spectrum, incivility would be at one end, while bullying would be in the middle and physical violence would be at the other end (Von Bergen, Zavalitta & Soper, 2006). Figure 2.1 demonstrates this spectrum.

In order to address incivility in the workplace, training programs are utilized. Organizations often believe that these programs help to prevent the escalation of bullying or that they actually address bullying behaviors, which often they do not. However, these programs do help to address the early onset of incivility.

The impact of bullying

Now that we have addressed bullying and the type of bullying tactics utilized, it is important to understand the impact of bullying. Bullying has a negative impact on the target as well as the organization. Table 2.2 identifies both the individual and organization impacts of bullying.

Let us first examine the impact that bullying has on individuals or targets.

The individual impact

Bullies inflict harm on individuals by inflicting emotional distress, which results in physical distress. The bully delights in humbling other individuals into submission and gloating

Figure 2.1 Spectrum of workplace violence

Table 2.2 The individual and organizational impact of bullying

Individual impact	Organizational impact
Physical illness	Increased turn over of staff
Psychological symptoms	Absenteeism
Social and professional isolation	Decreased commitment to the organization
Anxiety	Decreased productivity
Insomnia/sleep disturbances	Impact on rights in the workplace/lawsuits
PTSD	Target's reputation in the workplace

when they feel a sense of victory over others. Targets of bullying suffer from higher stress levels, resulting in stress-related illnesses. The individual being bullied is often on guard, wondering when the next attack will take place. They suffer from sleepless nights, reliving the last attack by playing the scene over and over in their minds, analyzing what they could have done to prevent the attack. Targets will experience feelings of frustration and anger. They may lash out at others. They experience negative feelings such as frustration, negative self-image, feelings of loneliness through isolation, and extreme emotional pain and anguish. Emotional feelings will cycle through shock, disbelief, shame, guilt, anger, fear and powerlessness. Depression and self-blame which can lead to a loss of self-confidence have also been reported by targets of bullying.

Targets who have experienced bullying trauma may be less likely to report this behavior to others for fear of how they may be perceived. They demonstrate a decrease in self-confidence. They also begin to develop a higher tolerance for this type of behavior, which allows bullying to invade other areas of their lives. They may experience higher levels of shame and post-traumatic stress disorder (PTSD) through reliving the trauma repeatedly.

The organizational impact

Bullying in the workplace impacts morale, lowers levels of job satisfaction in the target and those witnessing the bullying, decreases organizational effectiveness, increases the inability to attract as well as retain talent, and damages the reputation of the organization. Organizations are faced with increased financial costs, including turnover of staff, lack of commitment to the organization, an increase in grievances, safety issues and negative impacts on employee physical, mental health and well-being. The negative impact on employee physical and mental health has a big effect on the organization. Organizations face the cost of increased absenteeism, sick leave, increased hours of overtime to cover for absenteeism and lost opportunity costs. Poor performance, lost productivity and a loss of creative problem solving are also repercussions that may be experienced by the organization.

As we can see, the impact of bullying on the target and the organization is great. We will discuss the impact of dysfunctional leadership in further detail in Chapter 9.

The organizational role in bullying

We often ask ourselves how an organization can allow this type of behavior to occur. Organizational cultures at times encourage a culture of bullying. The higher up in the hierarchy the bully resides, the more likely it is that the organization will allow this behavior to continue. If the bully is the leader of a team that is producing results, has been with the organization for a long time or is respected by their superiors, their behavior is often excused or disregarded. Typically we only see this behavior change when the bully leaves the organization. If the target leaves the organization, the bullying behavior will shift and focus on a new target.

Like any dysfunctional leader, the bully thrives in work environments that are full of chaos and uncertainty. Research shows that organizations that demonstrate a lack of security due to layoffs, cultures that are highly chaotic and lower levels of job satisfaction demonstrate high levels of bullying. In addition, organizations that are related to the service sector or public services experience higher levels of bullying.

It is important to recognize that bullying can and does exist at all levels of an organization. Organizations that have tight controls in place, demonstrate transparency, hold employees and leadership accountable, and promote a zero-tolerance policy toward harassment were less likely to have a culture of bullying. Bullying in these types of culture is unable to flourish and typically these behaviors are addressed and eliminated quickly. Leadership can combat bullying behaviors within the organization. However, if the leader is the bully, then the chances are that bullying behavior will permeate throughout the organization. Followers see this behavior occurring at leadership levels and believe that this behavior is acceptable, and they will start to mirror the same behavior toward either the target(s) or others within the organization.

Organizations where bullying is prevalent often have a secretive culture where leaders or employees are not held accountable and loose systems are in place. When these organizations attempt to deal with a leader who is a bully, the organization struggles to address the behavior. More than likely, the leader will be moved to another unit or department. They will be offered a promotion in the hope that this will placate their behavior or they will be promoted to a higher level of leadership with no direct reports. For a short period of time, the move will placate the leader until they find their next target or they will simply continue the behavior when the dust settles and they feel as though attention has been diverted away from them. It is often easier for the organization to move the leader and placate them for a period of time than to challenge or address the situation. The bully is allowed to bully because the environment permits this behavior to occur. Most organizations do not have the mechanisms in place to address the behavior or to prevent it from happening.

Organizations that promote a competitive, cut-throat type of environment are those where the bullying leader feels right at home. In the competitive environment, the bully's goal is to beat their competition at all costs. For the bullying leader, it is a chance for them to flex their muscles and hold people accountable through bullying. This type of environment is seen in sales and services organizations.

How to recognize bullying

Targets of bullying will often question whether they are truly being bullied. They will question the behavior of the bullying leader. Meanwhile, the bully will focus on ensuring that they make their target questions themselves and their competence at all times. Eventually the target will become submissive and will believe the insults that the bully is hurling at them. The following is a list of feelings that the target will feel or experience when being bullied. This guide can be helpful in determining whether or not a person is being bullied:

1 At the end of a weekend or an extended period away, a feeling of dread starts to creep in. The individual starts to feel depressed and/or physically ill.
2 Loved ones and friends see the target obsessing over work or the individual bully. Conversations are monopolized by the actions of the bully or the negative experience of the workplace. No other conversation matters.
3 Vacation and sick days are used as a way to escape the bully. They are referred to as "mental health days."
4 Feelings of depression, isolation and hopelessness take the place of joy and career contentment.
5 The target starts to believe they deserve this negative treatment.
6 The target is socially isolated or ostracized from the workplace, social events or work interactions.
7 The bullying leader makes decisions about the target's work without consulting the target. The target is removed from all decision making related to their work.
8 Surprise or last-minute meetings are called to discomfort the target and are used to humiliate them in front of others.
9 The bullying leader openly criticizes the target's work. There is constant criticism. The target is told to redo their work until they "get it right."
10 The target feels as though they are on constant edge waiting for the next attack.
11 The target addresses the bully, only to be accused of bullying.
12 The target is blacklisted by the bully from applying for other positions or movement within the organization.

All of these examples relate to bullying behavior and actions of the bully. If any of these are observed, it is important to seek professional assistance to help address the situation.

Why targets are bullied

Targets often wonder "Why me?" or "Why is this person going after me?" There are many reasons why a bully will choose their target. The bully identifies and moves in on their target very quickly. They are able to scan a group and pinpoint who they want to focus on. If the bully feels resistance from the target, they will back off. The goal of the bully is to find someone who they feel will be easy to manipulate and who they can control.

The bully does not want to have a relationship with the target. They may say they are friends or equals, but this a ploy used to lull the target into a false sense of security. If the bully truly believed they were equals, this would mean that there is no reason to have control over their target. There would be no power advantage. If a relationship is of equal status, that would mean that others could push back and they would be able to challenge the bully's behavior. This in turn makes the bully very uncomfortable, as it may show that they are incompetent or that they are not a willing adversary.

It is important for the target to recognize that if they are being bullied, it does not mean that they are weak or incompetent – if anything, it is actually the exact opposite.

The bully wants the target to feel this way and when the target does the bully has been successful. The bully will focus in on the target who they find is very competent, is liked by others, is a perceived threat or is viewed as having a positive attitude. The target may be recognized by those higher up as a person with growth potential, which may threaten the bully. The bully is forced to take power and control over the target to make them look and/or feel as though they are incompetent and not liked by others, and to ruin the positive attitude that they might have. This is done in order to get the person out of the picture and for the attention to be focused positively on the bullying leader. The target is a threat to them.

When a bully identifies a person to target, they look for specific signs that they perceive as weakness. This does not mean that the target is weak; it is merely a perception held by the bully. Here are some behaviors that the bully may hone in on:

- *Non-verbal and verbal cues*: Voices that are hesitant or sound uncertain will come across to the bully as displaying weakness. Non-verbal cues can indicate insecurity, lack of confidence or weakness. Self-effacing comments is another sign for a bully. Someone who diverts attention away from themselves, deflects compliments or praise, or makes self-defeating comments can all signal to the bully that they lack confidence and may be an easy target.
- *Tone of voice*: The bully listens to the tone of voice used by an individual. A quiet voice and rapid or slow speech can be indicators that the target is insecure. Someone who demonstrates a tolerance for being interrupted also highlights that they may be a potential target to the bully who perceives that they can dominate in conversations.
- *Body language*: The use of body language, including the way in which the target carries themselves, eye contact or lack of eye contact, sitting, staring, the use of hands and personal space, are all cues for the bully. The way that a person carries themselves can be a perceived indication to the bully of that person's self-esteem or lack of self-esteem. People who have confidence in their body language send a signal to the bully to stay away.
- *Identifying weakness*: The dysfunctional leader typically hones in on the weakness of their target. They look for cues that are unintentionally sent out by the target. When a target is approached by a dysfunctional leader, there are times when their distress is on display. Signs of outward distress include flushed skin, shallow or rapid breathing, tearfulness and sweating. In other cases, the target will be flustered, stuttering and unable to think or speak. The dysfunctional leader sees these signals, viewing them as a weakness, and will move in for the kill. These behaviors are difficult for the target to control and yet they are signals for the dysfunctional leader. Then the behavior and the cycle of abuse continue.

Dealing with a bully

Addressing a bully is not easy, especially if the bully is a leader within an organization. The bullying leader is focused on ensuring that the target questions their own abilities, making them feel insecure. It cannot be stressed enough that it is important to recognize that in reality, the one who is insecure is the bullying leader – they are the one with the issue. This is not about the target, it is about the fact that they have something that the bully either wants or is threatened by – talent, intelligence, a strong work ethic or being well-liked by others in the organization. The target is usually more competent than the bully and frankly the bully is afraid of the target. Recognizing that the person with the problem is the bully is the first step toward regaining power over the bullying leader.

Next it is important for the target to find individuals that they can confide in. Talking to others who are trusted colleagues or friends is important. Finding individuals who are supportive and believe in them is also important. For the target, finding someone that they can talk to about the situation can help to restore some sanity to the situation. If necessary, the target should seek professional help in order to bring the situation into perspective.

When the target finds someone they can talk to, they will ask "Am I really incompetent?" Then they will say "I feel like I am going crazy." This is normal as people have a certain level of respect and expectation when dealing with leadership. When a leader starts to attack a target, criticizes their work or calls them incompetent, it is easy to believe them. Asking others for their insights is important in order to get grounded. It is important to ask individuals for honest feedback and not to rely on the feedback from the bully or to over-analyze the information. Instead, the target should go directly to others for support and feedback. They may provide feedback that is positive or on areas that can be focused on for development. But it is worth remembering that they are coming from a place of positive intent.

There are times when the target feels the need to address the bully. When doing so, it should be done early on in the process, before the bully has gained complete power and control over the individual. The following list highlights tactics that can be used when addressing or dealing with a bully:

- *Set boundaries*: Set boundaries early on and address behavior that is not acceptable. For example, if a bully lashes out the first time, it is critical to address that behavior quickly. Discuss what acceptable and unacceptable behavior is and what will and will not be tolerated. This needs to be done early on with the bully.
- *Wait to talk to them*: Immediately after a bully lashes out is not the time to address the behavior. Emotions at this point are running high for the target. More than likely, any response will be emotional and will only fuel the bully further. Wait to talk to them and walk away from the confrontation. Address the bully during a time when the bully does not expect it and without an audience for the bully to play to.
- *Frame statements*: When speaking with the bully, open the discussion by outlining what needs to be discussed before beginning the conversation. By framing statements, the speaker is able to set the "scene," explain the goal of the conversation and avoid jumping into the conversation if they are in an emotional state. The bullying leader may display their emotions, but it is important for the target to stay grounded and not to become emotional. Focus on the conversation. If the discussion gets derailed, refocus the conversation. By framing the statement, it will help to clarify the situation and the purpose of the conversation.
- *Address the behavior quickly*: Don't wait too long to address the problem or issue. Ask for clarity on the agenda of these attacks. "What are your intentions?" By asking them what their intentions are, they will be confused as they believe that the target does not realize that there is an agenda. The bully will respond that they don't know what

42   Bullying

is meant by this, but keep asking and asking for clarification. Why are they acting in this way? It is also important to recognize that the bully will more than likely deny that they have an agenda. That is OK – the key is that the bully knows that the target is aware that there is an agenda and will not tolerate it. Keep emotion out of the situation. If the target feels their emotions rising, they should walk away and re-address the behavior when they are calm. It is vital not to get into a fight or argument with the bullying leader; this may cause a negative situation for the individual.

- *Stay focused and rational*: When addressing the bully, stay rational and focused on the problem, not the person. If the bully feels they are being attacked, they will fight back. The bully may already feel incompetent or insecure. Focus not on the person, but on the problem and what the behavior is doing to the team, the organization, etc.
- *Document the conversation*: Document what was said during conversations. Note time, date, location and whether anyone witnessed the conversation. Next, identify any actions that were identified in the discussion and be sure to document everything that was discussed. This information may become important and require follow-up from the target.

Conclusion

This chapter has focused on the characteristics and behaviors of the bullying leader. We have also discussed a variety of different types of bullying leaders and the tactics that they deploy. As we can see, there are many different definitions regarding bullying in the workplace, so it can be a challenge to clearly define what bullying is. What we do know is that bullying is repetitive behavior that is meant to inflict psychological harm on others. Bullying can last weeks, months and even years. The bullying leader may use the tactic of involving others in the attack, which is called "mobbing." By involving others, the target feels outnumbered and does not feel able to confide in others. During incidences of bullying, the target often feels helpless, depressed and isolated from others. Often the bullying leader will purposely isolate their target from information that impacts their work or they may socially isolate the target so that they feel weak and vulnerable.

It is crucial for the person who is targeted by the bully to understand that the one with the problem is the bully. They are the ones who have a low level of self-confidence and low self-esteem. By attacking others, they are able to build themselves up. They feel best when they are attacking someone else. Often the person they target is someone who they are threatened by and they regard as a threat to their own security and status. By tearing them down, they are able to subdue that person into submission in order to gain ultimate power over them.

A target can address a bully. It is important to set the boundaries quickly and to address the problematic behavior as soon as possible. Do not allow the situation to fester. Too many times the target will think that this behavior will be a one-time incident. They hope that by ignoring the behavior, it will go away, but that is not the case. The behavior will continue and by the time the target is ready to address the behavior, it will be difficult to do so. For the target, it is critical to focus the situation quickly and address what is and is not acceptable. In Chapter 10 we will discuss in further detail how to address dysfunctional behavior as well as the impact of these types of behavior.

References

Adams, A. 2014. *Bullying at work: How to confront and overcome it.* London: Little Brown Book Group.

Andersson, L., & Pearson, C. 1999. Tit for tat? The spiraling effect of incivility in the workplace. *Academy of Management Review, 24,* 452–471.

Barrow, L. 2010. *In darkness light dawns: Exposing workplace bullying.* Port Colborne, Ontario: Purple Crown.

Berdahl, J., Magley, V., & Waldo, C. 1996. The sexual harassment of men? Exploring the concept with theory and data. *Psychology of Women Quarterly, 20,* 527–547.

Bond, S., Tuckey, M., & Dollard, M. 2010. Psychosocial safety climate, workplace bullying, and symptoms of posttraumatic stress. *Organization Development Journal, 28*(1), 37–56.

Einarsen, S. 1999. The nature and causes of bullying at work. *International Journal of Manpower, 20*(1/2), 16–20.

Einarsen, S. 2000. Harassment and bullying at work: A review of the Scandinavian approach. *Aggression and Violent Behavior, 5*(4), 379–401.

Einarsen, S., Helge, Hoel, H., & Notelaers, G. 2009. Measuring exposure to bullying and harassment at work: Validity, factor structure and psychometric properties of the Negative Acts Questionnaire—Revised. *Work and Stress, 23*(1), 22–44.

Einarsen, S., Hoel, H., Zapf, D., & Cooper, C. (Eds.) 2010. *Bullying and harassment in the workplace: Developments in theory, research, and practice.* Boca Raton, FL: CRC Press.

Einarsen, S., & Raknes, B. 1997. Harassment in the workplace and the victimization of men. *Violence and Victims, 12*(3), 247–263.

Einarsen, S., & Skogstad, A. 1996. Prevalence and risk groups of bullying and harassment at work. *European Journal of Work and Organizational Psychology, 5*(2), 185–202.

Erturk, A. 2013. Mobbing behavior: Victims and the affected. *Educational Sciences: Theory and Practice, 13*(1), 169–173.

Felblinger, D. 2009. Bullying, incivility, and disruptive behaviors in health care setting: Identification, impact and intervention. *Frontiers of Health Services Management, 25*(4), 13–24.

Fields, T. 1999. Bully in sight. How to predict, resist, challenge and combat workplace bullying. Overcoming the silence and denial by which abuse thrives. Retrieved from http://bullyonline.org/old/successunlimited/books/bistress.htm.

Harvey, M., Heames, J., Richey, R., & Leonard, N. 2006. Bullying: From the playground to the boardroom. *Journal of Leadership and Organizational Studies, 12*(4), 1–11.

Hutchinson, M., Vickers, M., Jackson, D., & Wilkes, L. 2006. Like wolves in a pack: Predatory alliances of bullies in nursing. *Journal of Management and Organization, 12*(3), 235–251.

Keashly, L. 1998. Emotional abuse in the workplace: Conceptual and empirical issues. *Journal of Emotional Abuse, 1,* 85–117.

Keashly, L., & Jagatic, H. 2000. The nature, extent, and impact of emotional abuse in the workplace: Results of a statewide survey. Paper presented at the Academy of Management Conference, Toronto, Canada.

Lee, D. 2001. Gendered workplace bullying in the restructured UK civil service. *Personnel Review, 31*(1/2), 205–222.

Lewis, S. 2006. Recognition of workplace bullying: A qualitative study of women targets in the public sector. *Journal of Community and Applied Social Psychology, 16*(2), 119–135.

Leymann, H. 1990. Mobbing and psychological terror at workplaces. *Violence and Victims, 5,* 119–126.

Leymann, H. 1992. The content and development of mobbing at work. *European Journal of Work and Organizational Psychology, 5*(2), 168–184.

Mikkelsen, E., & Einarsen, S. 2002. Basic assumptions and symptoms of post-traumatic stress among victims of bullying at work. *European Journal of Work and Organizational Psychology, 11*(1), 251–275.

Namie, G., & Namie, T. 2000. *The bully at work: What you can do to stop the hurt and reclaim your dignity on the job.* Naperville, IL: Sourcebooks.

Namie, G., & Namie, T. 2009. US workplace bullying: Some basic considerations and consultation interventions. *Consulting Psychology Journal: Practice and Research*, *61*(3), 202–219.

Olweus, D. 1993. *Aggression in schools: Bullies and whipping boys*. Washington, DC: Hemisphere.

Rayner, C., & Cooper, C. 1997. Workplace bullying: Myth or reality—can we afford to ignore it? *Leadership and Organization Development Journal*, *18*(4), 211–214.

Rayner, C., & Keashly, L. 2005. Bullying at work: A perspective from Britain and North America. *American Psychological Association*, *329*, 271–296.

Salin, D. 2009. Organizational responses to workplace harassment. *Personnel Review*, *38*(1), 26–44.

Tepper, B., Duffy, M., Henle, C., & Lambert, L. 2006. Procedural injustice, victim precipitation, and abusive supervision. *Personnel Psychology*, *59*(1), 101–124.

Von Bergen, C., Zavalitta, J., & Soper, B. 2006. Legal remedies for workplace bullying: Grabbing the bully by the horns. *Employee Relations Law Journal*, *32*(3), 14–41.

Yamada, D. 2000. The phenomenon of workplace bullying and the need for status-blind hostile work environment protection. *Georgetown Law Journal*, *88*, 475–536.

Yildirim, A., & Yildirim, D. 2007. Mobbing in the workplace by peers and managers: Mobbing experienced by nurses working in healthcare facilities in Turkey and its effect on nurses. *Journal of Clinical Nursing*, *16*(8), 1444–1453.

Zapf, D. 1999. Organizational, work group related and personal causes of mobbing/bullying at work. *International Journal of Manpower*, *20*(1/2), 70–85.

Chapter 3

Tyrant leadership

Introduction

The term "tyrant" was first used in the seventh century BC to describe the King of Lydia, the first foreign ruler to bring Greece under complete control. This term was used to describe a wealthy leader who used extreme power to exert control. At that time, the word "tyrant" did not have a negative connotation and was used to provide meaning to this person's actions. As Greece continued to fall under the rule of many powerful men, the word "tyrant" came to have new meaning as a leader who breaks all the rules (Foss, 1892).

Tyrants are individuals who have been described as pushing the limits of extreme power. Typically they use power, in the form of brutality, torture and violence, beyond what is acceptable by social standards. Tyrants have been a part of history since the time of organized government. Ambitious and aggressive leaders have used tyrant power to achieve individual goals for the advancement of their personalized agenda and not for the well-being of society or humankind.

Tyrants in ancient times were linked more to nobility and royalty. It was typically easier to understand the evolution of a tyrant during these times since there was a link to birthright. However, over time, tyrants have emerged in every circle of life. Tyrants in modern society range from being highly educated to having no formal education, and come from both impoverished, broken homes and wealthy families. Today's tyrants move up through the ranks of the military or through the government hierarchy. These are the tyrants who we are most familiar with. Such leaders include Kim Il-sung, Hitler, Mussolini and Saddam Hussein, to name just a few. This chapter will explore tyrants through history in governmental roles and nobility, and will then address organizational tyrants. Typically the tyrant is more subdued in the corporate world. They do not use torture or execution in the workplace, but their actions, which usually involve psychological terror, can be swift and equally destructive. They will use power and extreme control over others to achieve their goals.

Tyranny

Tyranny consists of many different behaviors. Themes related to organizational tyranny include micro-managing, distrust and suspicion of others, interactions that are cold and lack emotion, severe and public criticism, emotional outbursts, coercion, boasting, rigid and inflexible behavior, making random decisions, blaming others for mistakes and failing to collaborate with others (Ashforth, 1994).

Dysfunctional behaviors related to tyranny include: belittling, lack of consideration, forced conflict resolution, discouraging others from taking initiative, and punishment (Ashforth, 1994). In the research of Ashforth (1997) he found that tyrannical leadership is a broader form of dysfunction within leadership and may lead employees to think they are defenseless. Hornstein (1996) described tyrannical leaders as distrusting, condescending, patronizing, arrogant, boastful, and inflexible. Tyrannical behaviors include belittling, discouraging initiative, and forceful conflict resolutions (Ashforth, 1994). Tyrannical leaders are known to cause low-esteem, low performance, lack of work team cohesiveness, higher levels of frustration, stress, helplessness and alienation of followers. They are typically known for reaching organizational goals while at the expense or abuse of followers. Pellitier (2009) expanded upon the definition of tyrannical leadership as taking credit for the efforts of others, blaming subordinates for mistakes, discouraging informal interaction and creating dissent in the work environment.

Petty tyranny

Ashforth (1994, 1997) defined petty tyranny as a manager's use of power and authority too cruelly, erratically, and to be unkind to others. Ashforth (1997: 126) began to explore the negative leadership style referred to as "petty tyranny," which was defined as "the tendency to lord one's power over others." He went on to define tyranny as the abuse of power and authority by managers in a manner that is oppressive, capricious and vindictive. Tyranny is often interconnected with the term "abusive leadership." However, abusive leadership focuses on personal attacking behaviors, including ridicule, negative comments, and rudeness and lies (Tepper, 2000), and is not linked to the target's work task as it is to the actual person themselves. Petty tyranny is focused on the use of power and authority of leaders who includes both hostile and non-hostile behaviors.

Tyrannical leadership

Adorno, Frenkel-Brunswick, Levinson and Sanford (1950) stated that tyrannical leaders fear weakness, whether in themselves or in others. They cannot face or tolerate weakness. Leaders demonstrating this type of leadership style will often attack those perceived as weak or considered social outcasts. These leaders are highly punitive and reject anyone portraying any level of weakness (Adorno et al., 1950).

Glad (2002) stated that rule of the tyrant is reliant on inflicting fear on others. Hitler, Stalin and Saddam Hussein accentuated fear though extreme cruelty toward their allies, supporters and civilians. The following provides further insights into the actions and beliefs of tyrants:

- *They are convinced they are unique and "God"-like*: Often they believe that they are the only ones who have the power to fix whatever they are facing and that they were chosen to do so by a higher power. In some cases they will refer to themselves as the one who can save a company, a nation or a society. Followers begin to worship this individual until they realize that this person is not at all that they seem to be. We have seen this behavior many times in historical leaders as well as cult leaders. In organizations this is the type of leader who is hired to save the organization from its downfall or to pull the organization back from the brink of disaster. They will portray themselves as a leader who has been chosen by a higher power to lead the people.

- *They are above the rules of law and societal norms*: Because of their thoughts of being unique and "God"-like, they believe that they are bestowed with special powers and rules. As a result, tyrant leaders of countries believe themselves to be above the laws and norms that society has issued. They will circumvent these laws and norms to fit what they believe will justify their actions. Organizational tyrants will either ignore or change the organizational culture, norms and values to allow them to achieve their goals and agenda in order to promote their behavior. They will re-create rules in order to fit and allow for their behavior. They will ignore rules and expectations in order to achieve their goals and vision. The use of unethical tactics will be used to ignore tax codes, financial reporting or employment laws. In some countries, unethical practices will be used to control societies, ethnic groups and financial controls, along with controlling the media.
- *They reject any advice or criticism from others*: The tyrant will believe that they are correct and that their judgment is always the right one. Advice or criticism is not appreciated. When this is given, it will be ignored or will be heard, tucked away and turned into the tyrant's own ideas. When feedback is given, it will also be ignored, unless it is positive feedback, in which case they will listen to the praise of others toward them. If the feedback is constructive and focused on development, the tyrant will ignore it and will take it as a threat against their abilities and capabilities. Criticism is also viewed negatively in their eyes and they will seek to stifle any criticism directed toward their leadership. In some cases, this is done through targeting an individual and insulting, ridiculing, micro-managing and, in extreme cases, termination. In relation to political tyrants, the stifling of individuals can result in penalties, arrest, torture and execution.
- *They do not take responsibility for their actions and will silence critics or blame others for their misfortunes*: The tyrant will take credit for anything that shows them in a positive manner. Rather than accepting blame, they will place it on someone else. If misfortune is something that comes their way, it will not be because of anything that they have done – it will be someone else's fault. They believe that they can do no wrong and that others are to blame for their mistakes and mishaps.

The historical tyrant

Throughout history we can identify many different tyrants, from Caligula to Henry VIII to the most famous tyrant of all, Adolf Hitler. All of them have made a name for themselves as being leaders who led by using abusive, amoral and tyrant behaviors. While history has many historical tyrants to choose from, the following will look at the rule of Joseph Stalin and provides a historical account of his behavior and how his tyrant leadership style impacted millions of people under his leadership. Many are familiar with the tyrant behaviors of Hitler, but fewer are able to identify the tyrant behaviors of Joseph Stalin. Over the course of history, Stalin has been viewed either as a national hero or a cruel dictator and master of iron rule. The following section provides insights into his leadership.

Joseph Stalin

"There are no fortresses that Bolsheviks cannot storm"—Joseph Stalin

Joseph Stalin was born on December 18, 1879 in Gori, Georgia in the Russian Empire. His name at the time of birth was Josif (Joseph) Vissarionovich Dzhugashvili. His father was a cobbler and his mother worked in a laundry. His father was an alcoholic and was extremely abusive to his son. When he was seven, Joseph suffered from smallpox, which caused a deformity to his left arm and scarred his face. Because of this deformity and the scarring, he was the target of school bullies. He believed that he had to prove himself to his father as well as the bullies at school. His mother was a religious woman and her dream for her son was to become a priest. He was sent to the Georgian capital of Tiflis, where he was to attend seminary and prepare for a life as a priest. However, he had other ideas and rebelled against his mother's wishes. In secret he studied the works of Karl Marx and joined a socialist group. During seminary, he declared himself an atheist and did not show up for his final exams, causing him to be thrown out. He then devoted his time to the revolutionary movement. He earned the nickname "Koba" and joined the Marxist Socialist movement referred to as the Bolsheviks. He chose as his profession to work as a clerk while still focusing on activities of the revolution. He worked behind the scenes organizing strikes and protests. Word of his work with the revolution was reported to the Tsarist secret police and he was forced into hiding. During this time, he met Vladimir Lenin during a conference in Finland and the two developed a mutual admiration for each other. In order to help with the revolution, Joseph robbed a bank and stole approximately US $3.4 million, which was used to aid the revolution. He later married his first wife, who gave birth to their son Yakov. The young family was constantly on the run because of the robbery along with Joseph's work in the revolution. His wife died of typhus and he left his son to be raised by his wife's parents. His main focus turned to the work of the revolution. It is believed that he loved his wife greatly and he often stated at her passing that his last warm feelings for humanity died with her. He changed his last name to Stalin, which in Russian meant "steel." In 1910 he was arrested and sent to Siberia. During his time in exile, Lenin organized the Russian Revolution and promised "peace, land, and bread" for all his followers. Meanwhile, Stalin was instrumental in heading up the Boleshevik newspaper *Pravda*.

Lenin was wanted by the Tsar's army and Stalin assisted him in escaping to Finland and later in helping him to move to Switzerland. Because of his ability to help Lenin, Stalin was now a member of Lenin's inner circle and was appointed to serve on the Central Committee. The Tsar was removed from power and the country faced civil war. Anyone trying to flee or members of the opposition were executed in public for all to witness. Lenin gained power and asked Stalin to serve as General Secretary of the Communist Party. In his new position, Stalin was able to appoint his own people to government positions while building his political power base.

In 1924, Lenin died and Stalin began to position himself as Lenin's successor. His campaign was ruthless. Many believed that Leon Trotsky would be the one to succeed Lenin, but his ideas were not aligned with those of the Communist Party. Stalin developed his own brand of Marxism and focused on strengthening the Soviet Union. Trotsky criticized Stalin and was exiled. With the aid of his supporters and the power base that he had built up, he was named as the dictator of the Soviet Union.

At the start of his leadership, Stalin focused on the ideology of turning the Soviet Union into an industrialized country. He believed that there was a need for the country to modernize and that if it failed to do so, communism would fail. If communism failed, then the country would be destroyed by capitalism. During his time in power, he was able to transform Russia into an industrial and military power. Under him, the country began to experience economic prosperity. While this was taking place, Stalin initiated strict productivity targets which many found extremely difficult to meet. Any employee who did not meet these targets was either imprisoned or executed. It was believed that they were sabotaging progress and they were viewed as enemies of the country.

In the agricultural realm, farming was dominated by small landowners who could not keep up because of inefficient farming methods. Stalin moved his focus to modernizing agriculture. Farms became state-owned. In response to this idea, farmers began hoarding food and killing livestock. During this time, it is believed that over five million people died because of famine. Stalin believed in his plan and anyone who opposed the idea was to be punished. Millions were killed or arrested. By the 1930s, farming was owned by the government and productivity rose.

During his time in power, Stalin tried to show others that he was a caring and compassionate leader and wanted to be viewed as a national hero. However, he became paranoid and started to look for people who opposed his views. He purged the Communist Party along with the military forces of anyone who showed signs of opposition. It is assumed that 93 of the 139 members of the Central Committee were executed and another 81 of the 103 generals or admirals from the military were also executed. Secret police forces were used to enforce Stalin's rules. Citizens were asked to spy and inform on each other. During this time, over three million people were accused of opposition and were sent to labor camps or executed.

Stalin married his second wife and had two children with her. He physically abused her and she committed suicide. Stalin reported that she died from appendicitis rather than suicide. His son Yakov by his first wife served in the army and was captured by Germany. Germany proposed freeing him in a prisoner exchange, but Stalin refused and believed that his son surrendered voluntarily, viewing him as a traitor. His son died in a concentration camp.

Stalin agreed to partner with Hitler and they determined that they wanted to divide Eastern Europe and especially Poland, and split power between them. Hitler's army defeated France, and Britain began to back down. Stalin was warned by his generals that Hitler was hungry for power and wanted to increase his empire. Stalin ignored these warnings and was not prepared when the Nazis attacked Poland and the Soviet Union. The surprise attack impacted the Soviet Army and they suffered heavy losses. Stalin was enraged by Hitler and his betrayal. As a result, he retreated to his office and was unable to make any decisions. As the Nazis moved forward into Russia, the country was paralyzed. Stalin was prepared to sacrifice as many lives as possible in order to claim victory over Germany. In December 1941, the German army moved closer to Moscow, but Stalin refused to leave. As Germany moved into Stalingrad, which was named after Stalin, Hitler's goal was to humiliate him. Stalin did not budge. During the Battle of Stalingrad, over a million people lost their lives, but Russia was able to defeat Germany, pushing its forces back toward Berlin. Stalin focused his military strategy on claiming large sections of Eastern Europe, including East Berlin. He wanted these territories to be a part of the Soviet Union. America and Britain, once allies of Russia, now become its rivals. Stalin

50 Tyrant leadership

blocked entry to Allied-occupied Berlin, which became divided. The US responded with an 11-month airlift of supplies to the people trapped there. In 1949 the Soviet Union tested its first atomic bomb and the Cold War began.

During Stalin's last years, he was in a state of constant paranoia and continued to purge his enemies within the party. In March 1953, he suffered a stroke and passed away. His supporters mourned the passing of a person who they believed was a great leader, but the millions who were arrested for opposing or showing signs of opposition were happy to see the end of his tyrannical leadership.

Stalin led the Soviet Union on his own terms. Anyone who demonstrated any type of independent thought, opposition or was not a supporter was eliminated. He ruled not just with an iron fist, but with a tyrannical grip. Through the use and power of the secret police, citizens were encouraged to turn against one another, resulting in millions being killed or sent off to forced labor camps. In the 1930s a campaign was initialized that focused on the "Great Purge." The Great Purge eliminated anyone who threatened Stalin's agenda and vision. He surrounded himself with people he believed worshipped and honored him. Cities were named after him. Books were written about him, giving him even more power and more influence in relation to the Russian Revolution than had actually been the case. He commissioned artwork, literature and music in which he was the central focal point. He also controlled all media outlets, and controlled what was and was not reported to the people of the Soviet Union.

Modern-day tyrants

Today, modern-day tyrants in history are often referred to as dictators, fascists, autocrats and despots. These rulers lead with tight reins and use any means necessary to achieve ultimate power, domination, status and influence. They strive for complete dominance and will use any method necessary, including the imprisonment, torture, death and destruction of followers. Several of these leaders focus on the removal of whole ethnic groups or nations that they feel threatened by. Similar to the motives and tactics of Hitler, modern-day tyrants are no different, they will focus on execution, genocide, torture and alienation of whole groups of individuals in order to promote their vision of domination. Some make the argument that these leaders can be viewed as national heroes, while others may view them as cold-blooded murderers, manipulators and masters of terror. This section discusses several leaders in history who used these tactics in their leadership style and approaches.

Robert Mugabe

Born in 1924 in Katuma, a Jesuit mission station, Robert Mugabe's father was a carpenter and his mother belonged to the prominent Shona ethnic group. In 1945 he graduated from college, but wanted to continue his education and trained as a teacher. In 1960 he was the publicity secretary of the National Democratic Party (NDP). In 1961, the NDP was reformed as the Zimbabwe African People's Union (ZAPU). Mugabe was imprisoned and served 11 years as a political prisoner. During his years of incarceration, he received a number of graduate degrees from the University of London and taught inmates how to speak English. After serving his term, he was exiled to Zambia and Mozambique.

He helped to lead a civil war against the government. In 1977 he was able to gain domination over the ZAPU's political and military control. It was during this time that he adopted Marxist and Maoist views. In 1978 four black moderates announced that they had reached a settlement with the white regime, beginning the start of democratic elections. One of these leaders dispatched 39 envoys to meet the representatives of Mugabe and Joshua Nkomo, another guerrilla leader. However, these envoys were captured and murdered. To send a message to others, the bodies were laid out along the side of the road as a warning to the locals. Mugabe was named President of Zimbabwe and has served in this role since the 1980s. He is one of the longest-serving African leaders. During his early years as a leader, he showed great promise, but over time he became corrupted by power. He was once compared to Nelson Mandela; however, their views differed greatly. He did not believe in a multi-party system and if citizens did not embrace Marxism, then they should be re-educated. During the 1980s, he implemented a campaign focused on terror and killed up to 30,000 individuals of the Ndebele tribe. In the early 2000s he encouraged forces to take over white-owned farms. Many farm owners fled the country, which led to an economic collapse as well as inflation and food shortages.

It is rumored that Mugabe's leadership was tainted by fraud, voter intimidation, rape and murder. In 2008 he stated that he felt that elections were polarizing for the country and stated that there were to be no elections for 30–40 years. This new rule meant that he could not go up for re-election and thus would remain in power unchallenged. Individuals who have criticized him are considered traitors, a label which is punishable by death. Torture camps were used to beat and torture people who spoke out against Mugabe's regime. Under his leadership, his country has suffered from high inflation rates and some of the lowest life expectancy rates in the world. He has received several honorary doctorate degrees, some of which have been revoked. In 1994, he was given an honorary knighthood by Queen Elizabeth II. All of these honors were bestowed upon him while his country was experiencing genocide and murder under his tyrant leadership.

Bashar al-Assad

The Assad family has run Syria like a family business since the 1970s. Hafez Assad gained control in a Baathist coup and ruled with ruthless brutality. An example of his brutality was seen in 1982, when he stopped a rebellion by the Muslim Brotherhood in the city of Haman, killing approximately 20,000 people. His son, Bashar al-Assad, a former eye doctor, was elected in 2000 after his more charismatic brother Bassel, who was designated as his father's successor, was killed in a car accident. It was not expected for Bashar to be his father's successor. In his early years as a leader, he came across as awkward and nervous during interviews, yet he was thoughtful and eager to engage in conversation. He seemed genuine in his claims to seek political reform. At first he seemed eager to want to seek peace talks with Israel and intended to pull all Syrian troops out of Lebanon. Many believed that he would be a leader who would take Syria in a peaceful direction.

Assad's early leadership talked about transparency and democracy. He released political prisoners and focused on economic reform. However, in 2001 his policies changed.

Some say that the change was brought about by his father's advisors. It is claimed that his father's leaders and advisors suggested that he revert back to the old style of government and enforce repression along with utilizing the secret police to uphold his rule. Over time he morphed into a tyrant leader whose brutality surpassed that of his father, killing over 126,000 people. It is estimated that 1,000 individuals, of which 400 were children, were killed by chemical weapons. Hundreds of thousands were wounded and more than two million refugees have attempted to flee to neighboring countries. This number grows each day as war continues to ravage his country. His philosophy is that if he keeps killing, eventually people will give up. During his more than 15 years in power, he has been accused of human rights violations and the displacement of millions of Syrians. Yet he continues to remain in power. During the last decade, his leadership has focused on repression, human rights violations and the detaining, torture and murder of political opponents.

Other countries have turned on him and have wanted him to be deposed after launching chemical assaults on his own people. He has been able to placate the US, although barely, by complying with the minimum rules imposed on him. Under his leadership, the media is controlled, with internet censorship and a one-party system. A rise in anti-government rebels led to civil war in 2011 with hundreds of thousands of people killed, tortured and held prisoner. It is believed that he has used cluster bombs along with chemical weapons on his own citizens. His regime has been responsible for attacks on Syrian hospitals, medical personnel and bombs to destroy infrastructure. The acts committed under his regime have been likened to the war crimes of Nazi Germany. Syria has partnered with Russia for support and President Vladimir Putin continues to support the Assad regime. Other countries supportive of his regime include China and Iran. Assad has been able to gain control and support of his country by urging Western countries to aid Syria in the fight against Islamic State, thereby playing the role of working to stop terrorism while allowing acts of terror to continue in his own country.

Saddam Hussein

Saddam Hussein was born in 1937. His father, a shepherd, disappeared before he was born. A few months later, his eldest brother died of cancer. With the loss of her oldest son and husband, Saddam's mother was severely depressed and could not effectively care for her newborn son. At the age of three, he was sent to live with an uncle and later returned to live with his mother. During his absence, his mother remarried. His stepfather was abusive toward him and later he chose to leave the abusive situation and moved back in with his uncle, who had a profound impact on his life.

At the age of 20, Saddam joined the Ba'ath Party, which focused on the unity of the Arab States within the Middle East. In 1959, Saddam and members of the Ba'ath Party attempted to assassinate Iraq's President Abd al-Karim Qasim. During the attempted assassination, Qasim's driver was killed and the President was shot several times, but survived. Several of the members of the failed assassination team were captured, tried and then executed. Saddam and others were able to escape and found their way to Syria and then to Egypt, where he attended law school. In 1968 he participated in a coup which resulted in Ahmed Hassan al-Bakr becoming the next President of Iraq, while Saddam was named his deputy. In his new role, Saddam proved himself to be politically astute; however, he was also viewed as ruthless and ambitious. His goal was to modernize the infrastructure of the country. Prior to the energy crisis, he was able to nationalize the oil industry, which provided a great deal of wealth to the country. During this time, he began to work on the country's chemical weapon program. To prevent further coups from happening, a strong security force was implemented which used torture, rape and assassination to instill fear into the people and to prevent uprisings.

In 1979 al-Bakr tried to unite Iraq and Syria. Saddam viewed this move as detrimental to his own power and forced al-Bakr to resign. In July of that year, Saddam became President of Iraq. A week later he called the Ba'ath Party together, where a list of 68 names was read off. These individuals were rounded up, arrested, tried and found guilty of treason. Of these 68 individuals, 22 were executed. A month later, hundreds of Saddam's enemies were executed. In the meantime in Iran, the Ayatollah Khomeini led a successful Islamic revolution. Saddam worried that this could branch out into a similar uprising in Iraq. Saddam made a move on the oil-rich area of Khuzestan located in Iran. This military maneuver led to war and many countries of the Arab region, along with Western nations, which were fearful of Islamic radicalism, found themselves supporting this move, even though this act was against international law. Genocide and chemical weapons were used while a nuclear program was under development. In 1988 a ceasefire was declared; however, hundreds of thousands were killed during this war.

After the war, Saddam turned his focus to rebuilding Iraq's economy and infrastructure. He was interested in Kuwait, which possessed the wealth that he needed in order to rebuild his country. In 1990 he ordered the invasion of Kuwait. The UN Security Council did not agree with this move, imposed strict economic sanctions on the country and demanded that Iraq leave Kuwait. When the deadline to leave Kuwait came and went, a UN coalition headed by the US confronted the Iraqi troops and a ceasefire agreement was signed. In the agreement it was laid out that all biological and chemical weapons were to be dismantled. Economic sanctions that were imposed before the Gulf War remained in place afterwards. However, at the end of the war, Saddam claimed victory.

The rest of the world feared another war, but ignored what was happening. The force of Saddam's repressive security forces was felt by many citizens. His military forces continued to taunt other countries. Iraqi forces became brazen and violated no-fly zones imposed by the UN. In 1993, the US launched a missile attack on Baghdad. Violations continued in 1998, along with the alleged continuation of chemical weapons development. All of these violations led to further missile strikes on Iraq until 2001.

It was believed that Saddam had links to Osama bin Laden, who was the mastermind behind the 9/11 attacks on the US World Trade Center and the US Pentagon. US President George W. Bush claimed that Saddam was developing chemical weapons, which were referred to as weapons of mass destruction, and accused him of supporting terrorist groups. The UN inspections group was asked to go in to determine if these weapons existed. While they suspected there were weapons, no evidence was found. Under the pretense that weapons did exist, the US invaded Iraq and the government of Iraq was overthrown. Saddam was able to escape. While in hiding, he condemned the US and called for his citizens to resist. In December 2003, he was captured and moved to a US-held base in Baghdad. He was handed over to the Iraqi government, where he was tried for crimes against humanity. He was found guilty and sentenced to death. He was hanged on December 31, 2006.

54 Tyrant leadership

During Saddam's rule, he was viewed as ruthless and calculating, and was believed to have derived great pleasure from other people's pain and suffering. He made it law that if anyone was caught criticizing him, they would have their tongues cut out. Proof was not needed in these circumstances – if a person was suspected or if there was a level of suspicion, there was no trial and punishment was handed out. No one was off limits from his tyranny, including family members. His sons-in-law were not immune from his wrath – they were exiled to Jordan and when they returned, they were dragged away with meat hooks through their eyes. When prisoners were executed, their family members were told to supply coffins and bring these with them to the execution.

Tyranny ran within Saddam's family as well. His son Uday would identify a woman he was interested in and she would be kidnapped, raped and tortured. If the woman pleased Uday, she was allowed to return home, but if not, she was left for dead. Saddam would take his sons to view the prison camps that were established to torture and execute hundreds of thousands of citizens of Iraq.

Vladmir Putin

Vladmir Putin was born in 1952 in Leningrad, Russia. He was no stranger to suffering. His father went off to battle, as a result of which he was disabled and disfigured. During the war, his mother almost died of starvation. In addition, he lost two siblings during this time. When he was born, both of his parents were 41 years old. Because of their age, it was rumored that he was adopted, but there was no proof of these rumors. After the war, his parents worked any jobs that that they could find. In turn, he was cared for by an elderly Jewish couple who lived across the hall from the Putin family's home. He spent his spare time in the courtyard of the building and the streets, which were filled with drunks and gangsters. He became enamored with these people and prided himself as being one of the thugs that he hung out with. If anyone spoke out against him or started a fight, he would attack and do whatever needed to be done to prevent that person from ever humiliating him.

During this time, Leningrad was in ruins from the Second World War. Living conditions were deplorable and citizens were both angry and resentful. Putin attended school and excelled in sports. He went on to study law at Leningrad State University. Upon graduation, he served as a member of the KGB as an intelligence officer in East Germany. In 1990 he retired with the title of lieutenant colonel. He returned to Russia and worked in an administrative position at the University of Leningrad. After the fall of communism, he worked for the Mayor of Leningrad, Anatoly Sobchak. Putin was named the first deputy director and served in that role until Sobchak was not re-elected. He moved to Moscow, where he worked as the deputy head of management under Boris Yeltsin. In his new position he oversaw the Kremlin's relations with regional governments. He was later appointed the head of the Federal Security Service, while also overseeing Yeltsin's Security Council. In 1999 Yeltsin dismissed his Prime Minister and appointed Putin to the role. Later that year, Yeltsin resigned from his presidency and Putin stepped in as acting President until elections could be held in March 2000, when he was officially elected as President. During this time, he promised to reform both the economic and political sectors of the country. In 2004 he was re-elected President. The law stated that he could not run for re-election in 2008, so he allowed Dmitri Medvedev to run for President. In turn, he stepped into the role of Prime Minister, where he was allowed to continue to exercise his power and influence. In 2012 he ran for his third term as President and was re-elected. He then appointed Medvedev as his Prime Minister. Many believed that the elections were riddled with fraud and protests broke out. Protesters who were against Putin were arrested. In 2012, he banned US citizens from adopting orphaned children from Russia. In that same year he granted asylum to Edward Snowden, who was wanted by the US for sharing classified information. He also implemented anti-gay laws and it was now illegal for gay couples to adopt children in Russia.

As tension escalated in Syria over the use of chemical weapons, the US threatened military action if these weapons were not destroyed. Russia and the US partnered together to make a deal with Syria ensuring that these weapons would be destroyed. Later, Putin condemned the US for making military threats against Syria and stated that these acts would be considered unilateral and would only increase violence and tension in the Middle East. He then said that the claims that Syria had used chemical weapons were unfounded and blamed Syrian rebels.

In 2014 Russia hosted the Winter Olympics. It spent over $50 billion preparing for the events. Many protested the games because of the anti-gay legislation that had been passed. Security measures were put into place to focus on Muslim extremists. Saliva was collected for DNA profiling, focusing on Muslim women who were known as "black widows" and were associated in their role as suicide bombers.

After the Olympics, the President of Ukraine was removed from power. Putin quickly sent troops to Crimea, where over 16,000 troops invaded. In a referendum vote, the Crimean people voted to secede from Ukraine and reunite with Russia. The vote was questionable as it was believed that it was prompted by military violence. Putin argued that the troops were used to boost military defenses and were in no way connected with war in Ukraine. He assured others that he had sought permission from Russia's upper house to use force if need be, but he felt that this measure should only be used as a last resort.

Russia provided support to the Syrian government and began airstrikes on the rebels in Syria. The claim was made that the airstrikes were targeting Islamic State extremists. Others argued that these attacks were focused on rebel forces who were attempting to overthrow President Assad's regime. Anyone speaking out against Putin was targeted by the police and local authorities. Journalists who have been openly critical of Putin have been executed. These executions are not investigated and reports of wrongdoing are ignored. Anyone supporting Putin's agenda is richly rewarded, while his opponents are punished. Media outlets are controlled by the wealthy as a means to gain political power. Anyone who opposes him is either arrested or killed. It is believed that in 2016 Putin spent $1.3 billion on propaganda. Personal websites were launched that provide background information on him, promoting his personal interests in sports, animal protection, his car collection and what he likes to do in his personal life.

Putin controls journalists as well as political opposition. Individuals who have criticized him have been arrested, tortured and executed. Anyone who opposes his rule is considered a criminal. His rule is one of fear and intimidation and his actions have violated human rights and social justice. His ultimate goal is to bring back the former Soviet republics in order gain unlimited power.

Kim Jong-un

Kim Jong-un was the third and youngest son of Kim Jong-il, who was the leader of North Korea for over a decade. His father recognized leadership traits in Kim Jong-un and saw many of his own qualities in his son. Because of these same qualities, Kim Jong-il prepared his son as his successor, but passed away in 2011. After his father's death, Kim Jong-un was named the Supreme Leader of North Korea. He possesses totalitarian control over the North Korean government. In his early years he had little military or political experience to draw from. Instead of drawing upon the experience of senior leadership, he instead viewed them as a threat. Anyone who was loyal to his father was removed from office or executed. A close advisor to his father was his uncle, Jang Song-thaek. His uncle mentored his nephew during his transition to power. During a very public display, Jang Song-thaek was removed from a public meeting in full view of his colleagues. He was arrested and then executed for being a traitor for plotting a coup to overthrow the government. He was also charged with abuse of power, womanizing and drug abuse. It is rumored that members of Jang Song-thaek's family were also executed. Some believe this move was taken in order for Kim Jong-un to assert his independence and establish his right of leadership. Others believed it was his way of instilling fear and dominance into the older leaders who felt that they were more qualified to run the country.

During a speech in 2012, Kim Jong-un stated that the era of his nation being threatened by other powers was over and that the superiority of military technology would no longer be monopolized by imperialists. He made it clear that he would actively pursue the development of nuclear weapons. In 2012 he was appointed the highest military rank of Marshall. He agreed to stop nuclear testing and long-range missile launching; however, in April 2012 the country tried to launch a satellite that failed shortly after takeoff. Later that year the government launched a long-range rocket that did put a satellite into orbit. It is believed that these launches were used as a cover-up for testing and launching missile technology. In 2013 North Korea conducted its third underground nuclear test. Testing was condemned by many of the super-powers including China, Japan, Russia and the US. Sanctions were placed on North Korea. Later, in 2016, a fifth underground nuclear test was conducted.

North Korea has experienced poverty and economic problems with a devastating famine and food shortages in the 1990s. Citizens have been executed for watching illegally imported movies, soap operas or Western television shows. Opponents and defectors are publicly executed. Anyone who is viewed as a threat or opposition is sent to prison or labor camps, which have been set up to punish anyone questioning or going against the rules of the government. The camps are not just limited to those believed to be guilty; North Korea has implemented a guilt by association rule, which punishes members of a person's family and succeeding generations for one person's perceived misdeed, whether they are guilty or not. These camps have been accused of violations of human rights. Conditions in the camps are considered deplorable, with many survivors looking for any food available. A concentration camp system has been established that utilizes torture on thousands of prisoners, as well as horrific conditions. People have been sent to these camps for being found guilty of stealing food to feed their family members. Meanwhile, parts of the capital city Pyongyang, called Pyonghattan, are now restricted and only citizens who are the most loyal to his leadership are allowed in. Here citizens can enjoy designer labels from Western countries and are able to dine in the finest restaurants. This elite group makes up about one percent of the population.

Summary of political tyrants

Once in leadership, political tyrants will exercise and abuse the power they are granted. Some believe war is a way to demonstrate and flex their power. For others, it is the domination of world power that motivates them. Those who oppose these leaders, along with people who do not follow them, are executed, tortured, raped and/or imprisoned. In many of these cases the deaths of millions of people is a means to achieving their goals. Anyone who gets in their way is removed. Many of these leaders have believed that divine intervention is what guides their destinies and that they have been chosen by a higher power to implement their rule and power. They share this divine power with their followers, who either believe or follow them in a cult-like following or rally against that leader.

Organizational tyrants

Ashforth (1994) shared that for many years, social psychology, leadership and political sciences have all focused on tyranny, providing many examples. Common traits of organizational tyrants are given in Table 3.1 below.

Primary themes related to tyrant leaders include micro-managing the work of employees, treating employees in an illogical way, and being uncaring and punitive in nature. While we do see organizational tyrants, they are not as prevalent in organizations as one might think. This may be because there are other more suitable titles for their dysfunction, including narcissistic, bullying, abusive or psychopath leadership. Typical thoughts associated with a tyrant connect back to despots, dictators and rulers of countries. The following section highlights some people who have been considered tyrants within their organization and through their leadership.

Leona Helmsley

Leona Helmsley made her career in residential real estate. In 1972 she married real-estate tycoon Harry Helmsley, who was her fourth husband. It is estimated that Harry Helmsley had a $5 billion empire that consisted of hotels and apartment buildings along with commercial properties, which included managing the Empire State Building. Leona was named President of the Helmsley Hotels in 1980. In 1987 she was tried for tax evasion. It was during her trial that stories were leaked about her behavior and the media gave her the title "Queen of Mean." It was reported that she once said that "Only

Table 3.1 Characteristics of organizational tyrants

Micro-managing	High levels of distrust	Cold and aloof
Public criticism of others	Condescension	Emotional outbursts
Coercion	Boastful behavior	Inflexible
Random and illogical decision making	Takes credit from others	Places blame on others
Fails to consult with others	Does not inform others of decisions	Discourages interactions with others
Suppresses initiative, creativity and innovation	Obstructs the development of others	

58 Tyrant leadership

little people pay taxes" (Kellerman, 2004). It was during her trial that her tyrant-like behavior emerged. Several disgruntled employees testified against her, sharing stories of her behavior and actions.

During Leona's leadership, she appreciated the finer things. Luxuries included a 100-seat jet with a bedroom suite, a penthouse suite that included a swimming pool overlooking Central Park, an $8 million estate in Connecticut, a condo in Palm Beach and a mountaintop hideaway in Phoenix. In advertising campaigns she was often pictured in gowns and tiaras, and referred to herself as royalty. The family was very generous in its philanthropic efforts, giving millions to research in health care. In business Leona was less generous and more frugal, including not paying contracts, terminating employees for no reason or just plain terrorizing them. When she was convicted of tax evasion, she served 21 months of her sentence. After she was released, she was assigned community service. She asked employees to serve her community service hours for her. The judge found out and then sentenced her to an additional 150 hours. During the trial, it was revealed that she and her husband had evaded paying taxes and billed personal expenses as business expenses. The following are further examples of her actions:

- A painting contractor shared that she would not pay an $88,000 bill for work he had completed since she felt she was entitled to a "commission" for the $800,000-worth of jobs that he had worked on related to other Helmsley properties. She thought he had earned enough money from their businesses.
- Her son died of a heart attack in 1982. Following this, she sued the estate for money and property that she claimed she had lent to her son and then served an eviction notice to his widow, Mimi, and her grandchildren. Mimi later stated that the legal costs resulted in her becoming destitute and that she never understood why Leona went after her and the estate.
- During a breakfast meeting with her attorney, the waiter spilled a small amount of water from the cup he was carrying. She picked up the cup and threw it down, shattering it on the floor. She then demanded that the waiter get on his hands and knees and beg for his job.
- Upon her death, she left $12 million for the care of her dog and the rest of the trust, which was estimated to be worth billions of dollars, was used to care for dogs. She excluded two of her grandchildren from receiving any money from the estate. Her will stated that her tomb must be acid washed or steam cleaned once a year.
- She demanded perfection in everything, yet treated her employees poorly. She led by instilling fear into employees along with misuse of power. She was known for unexpected inspections of rooms and would look for spots on bedspreads, wrinkles, lint on the floor, dust or crooked lampshades. If the inspection was not up to par, she would demand that the maid was fired immediately (Kellerman, 2004).
- She would often walk into one of her restaurants and fire waiters, bus boys and chefs on the spot, often for no reason. She was known as a perfectionist and provided harsh criticism, and had little patience.
- A secretary spilled something on her dress and sent it to one of Helmsley's dry cleaners. When Leona found out, she felt that the woman was deliberately cheating the organization and fired her (Kellerman, 2004).

- She openly discriminated against employees and barred African Americans from working in her Tri-Plex Apartments, along with banning openly gay individuals from her hotels. A former manager filed a suit against her, stating that she created a "hostile work environment" and used the term "gay" as an all-encompassing insult. He reported that he was approached by one of her bodyguards, who demanded to know if the manager was gay. On the manager's birthday, he was fired and later that day he was evicted from his apartment, despite having had excellent performance reviews and Leona often complimenting him on his efforts. An Asian florist was also fired by Leona, who said "She was not even an American."

Kellerman (2004) gave Leona Helmsley as an example of a tyrannical leader; her abusive language and ranting made her employees fear for their positions and physical safety. She lashed out at employees who she considered weak and under her control. Her dysfunction ultimately led to her downfall.

Albert J. Dunlap

The focus of Albert J. Dunlap's leadership was on one thing only, which was shareholder value. In the 1990s he was known as the head of Scott Paper Company. He was able to increase stock prices by 225 percent, but did so by cutting over 11,000 jobs. Other financial cuts were in the areas of Research & Development, plant improvements, company charitable campaigns and cutting everything he was able to cut. After the financial cuts were made, he sold Scott Paper to Kimberly Clark, netting him a personal profit of $100 million for his work during his 18-month tenure. Next he moved on to Sunbeam Corporation. Once it was announced that he was the new CEO, stock prices jumped 79 percent. He used the same tactics he had used at Scott Paper and he continued to make cuts. He laid off approximately 6,000 employees at all levels of the organization. During his first seven months, the company's stock price rose over 284 percent. This rise was too good to be true and it was discovered that these numbers were fraudulent. He was released from Sunbeam having been accused of accounting fraud. He was fined $500 million payable to the Securities and Exchange Commission (SEC). During this time, Sunbeam dropped in trading to two cents per share. He was never to be a CEO in his career because he was forbidden from serving as an officer or a director of any publicly traded company.

During his tenures of leadership, Dunlap often referred to himself as having celebrity status. His nicknames ranged from "Rambo in Pinstripes," "The Shredder" and "Chainsaw Al." He was also referred to as the "Turnaround Specialist." For media campaigns he was pictured with automatic weapons and wearing an ammunition belt. During his career, he jumped from organization to organization, focusing his obsession on the profits or financials performance of the organization, but at the expense of everyone and everything else. He capitalized on his own fame by writing a book entitled *Mean Business* which focused on corporate brutality.

Mark Pincus

Zynga's culture under the leadership of its CEO, Mark Pincus, is one where employees were tracked by excessive metrics and analytics, harsh deadlines that were difficult to meet and his aggressiveness in pushing employees to meet these goals. His leadership style was referred to as micro-managing and as struggling with delegating. Employees who were chosen to work as his right-hand person were often moved into powerful positions, only to be removed from these positions. When Pincus stepped down as CEO, *New York Magazine* announced the appointment of a new CEO of Zynga and that Pincus' reign of terror was over (Roose, 2013). Pincus' management style has been referred to as that of a "control freak" and "fearsome." He issued company stock to employees and later believed that the company had been too generous. He demanded that employees either give the stock back or they would be fired. He later changed his mind and decided to give the stock back based on performance, but his employees felt that this move was an insult. He eventually left the organization that he founded, but returned a few years later.

Larry Ellison

Larry Ellison, CEO of Oracle, was known for his extravagant lifestyle. Extremely aggressive and ruthless, he has been called the "modern-day Genghis Khan." This nickname originated from his use of the quotes of Genghis Kahn, including the line "Everyone must fail" (Southwick, 2003). During Oracle's takeover of PeopleSoft in 2003, 5,000 employees were fired and he repeatedly insulted its CEO. During the hostile takeover, he made the following statement: "If Mr. Conway and his dog were standing next to each other and I had one bullet, trust me, it wouldn't be for the dog" (Pimentel, 2014). However, it is reported that he has developed great talent in the technology sector. Many of the businesses in Silicon Valley are run by former Oracle employees. Ellison was named by *BusinessWeek Magazine* as one of the most competitive people on the planet (Finkelstein, 2016). He was credited for being able to motivate people and to articulate the strategy of the company; however, much of his motivation was created through fear and greed. He was unable to tolerate executives who stood up to him and would often purge senior-level leadership (Southwick, 2003).

Other organizational tyrants

Through the years, there have been a number of leaders who have been viewed as tyrants. However, it is also essential to recognize that many of these leaders have been successful and in some cases are viewed as possessing the hallmarks of great leaders, having built strong empires and successful businesses. JP Morgan CEO Jamie Dimon would interrogate direct reports for hours over numbers and strategize possible scenarios. He is considered a bad listener and often interrupts people by finishing their sentences. However, others have focused on his leadership, stating that he is a visionary, leads with humility and fosters collaboration. Rupert Murdoch built a strong empire and has been able to demonstrate his leadership through delivering on grand strategies. However, he has earned the reputation of being ruthless. He claimed that when he heard that his employees were hacking phones, he was shocked and appalled. He has maintained that he did not know about the scandal and was not responsible for the actions of his employees. While he may not have been involved in the scandal, others argued that he created a culture that was one of extreme competition. During company acquisitions, there was extreme pressure for new leadership to conform to their new culture. The internal environment created a culture of doing whatever needed to be done to meet expectations. When print union workers went on strike, they were handed a letter stating that their employment had been terminated.

What leads to the ultimate downfall of the tyrant?

The tyrant leader eventually falls. As they build their empires, their inner circle diminishes. They question their followers and become paranoid, wondering when the next person will attempt to overthrow them. Their downfall is often caused by getting caught bending the rules through unethical acts, including tax evasion, falsifying numbers or stock reporting. They experience extreme paranoia and tire of constantly looking over their shoulder, wondering who they can and cannot trust. In the end, the tyrant leader does not regret their choices. They have built an empire, whether it is a company or a nation. They don't regret the number of lives destroyed as this is just a means to an end to get where they need to go in order to develop their fortune, power and status.

References

Adorno, T., Frenkel-Brunswick, E., Levinson, D., & Sanford, R. 1950. *The authoritarian personality.* Oxford: Harper.

Ashforth, B. 1994. Petty tyranny in organizations. *Human Relations, 47*(1), 755–778.

Ashforth, B. 1997. Petty tyranny in organizations: A preliminary examination of antecedents and consequences. *Canadian Journal of Administrative Services, 14*(2), 126–140.

Finkelstein, S. 2016. Secrets of super bosses: Larry Ellison, Glorious Bastard. *Fortune Magazine.* Retrieved from http://fortune.com/2016/03/02/secrets-of-the-superbosses-larry-ellison-glorious-bastard.

Foss, C. 1892. Politics and the pulpit. *North American Review, 155*(432), 536–544.

Glad, B. 2002. Why tyrants go too far: Malignant narcissism and absolute power. *Political Psychology, 23,* 1–37.

Hornstein, H. 1996. *Brutal bosses and their prey.* New York: Penguin.

Kellerman, B. 2004. *Bad leadership: What it is, how it happens, why it matters.* Boston, MA: Harvard Business School Press.

Mugabe, R. 2016. It's true, I was dead. Robert Mugabe laughs off rumors of his death as the dictator arrives back in Zimbabwe capital Harare. Retrieved from https://www.thesun.co.uk/news/1720580/robert-mugabe-slaps-down-rumours-of-his-death-as-the-dictator-arrives-back-in-zimbabwe-capital-harare.

Pellitier, K. 2009. The effects of favored status and identification with victim on perceptions of and reactions to leader toxicity. Doctoral dissertation. Claremont Graduate University. UMI 3383643.

Pimentel, B. 2014. Oracle's Larry Ellison was the "bad boy" of tech. *Market Watch.* Retrieved from http://www.marketwatch.com/story/oracles-larry-ellison-was-the-bad-boy-of-tech-2014-09-19.

Roose, K. 2013. With New Zynga CEO, Mark Pincus's reign of terror is over. *New York Magazine.* Retrieved from http://nymag.com/daily/intelligencer/2013/07/mark-pincuss-reign-of-terror-over.html.

Southwick, K. 2003. Everyone must fail. *Forbes Magazine.* Retrieved from http://www.forbes.com/2003/11/26/1126southwick.html.

Tepper, B. 2000. Consequences of abusive supervision. *Academy of Management Journal, 43*(3), 178–191.

Chapter 4

Unethical leadership

Introduction

Leadership plays a dominant role in shaping the culture and ethical tone of an organization. The values and ethical behaviors of leadership help to determine how organizational goals and outcomes are met within the organization. Scholars have found that there are similarities between ethics and morality and that the two are synonymous (Ciulla, 2005; Boatright, 2007). In recent years, the news has been occupied with reports of corporate scandals, unethical leadership and the questionable morality of executive leadership. These scandals highlight the role that leadership plays in influencing these scandals.

Understanding ethical leadership

In order to understand unethical leadership, it is first important to understand what ethical leadership is. Ethics in leadership is what defines the leader's ability to influence others through beliefs, values and behaviors to achieve organizational goals. Trevino and Brown (2005: 120) defined "ethical leadership" as the demonstration of normatively appropriate conduct through personal actions and interpersonal relationships, and the promotion of such conduct to followers through two-way communication, reinforcement and decision making. They further stated that ethical leaders engage in demonstrating integrity and high ethical standards, considerate and fair treatment for all employees, and holding employees accountable for ethical conduct (Trevino & Brown, 2005: 130). Other researchers believe that in order to understand the ethical components of leadership, it is important to understand leadership. Ethical leaders are able to make decisions in the best interests of others and not for their own personal or financial gain. These types of leaders have the ability to motivate and encourage ethical behavior or normative behavior in the workplace. Ethical and effective leaders not only work to fulfill their obligations toward an organization, but have to also worry about how their interactions with others have the potential to alter the outcomes of all their decisions (Eisenbeiß & Brodbeck, 2014). Burns (1978) placed ethics at the core of leadership. Leadership is responsible for driving behaviors that are acceptable within the organization, defining what the norms and values are of the organization.

Ethical leaders have a positive effect on the work environment by enhancing employee autonomy and feelings of significance in the workplace. Work that is seen as fair and balanced – along with leaders who are concerned with the well-being of their employees – is essential to ethical leadership. Strong ethical leaders will use their position power to serve others instead of pursuing self-serving agendas. The role of the leader is to demonstrate to their followers the values and behaviors that the organization believes are acceptable.

In order to understand ethical leadership, it is crucial to understand that it is simply not bounded by the theory of what is right versus what is wrong. When researching ethics, it is important to understand both the good and the bad. It is not about good leadership versus bad leadership, it is about understanding what differentiates an ethical leader from an unethical leader. In many cases there is a tipping point for leaders where the focus shifts from serving the greater good to an agenda that is self-serving.

An ethical leader can be classified as one who demonstrates integrity, honesty and trustworthiness. In addition, these behaviors are focused on doing the right thing, having concern for others, being open and personal morality. Decision making is focused on the concerns of others, holding true to their values and beliefs, being fair and objective, and following ethical rules (Trevino, Hartman & Brown 2000).

Ethical principles

There are seven principles that can be used to see if policies, policy makers and all other staff are ethical. The first principle is selflessness. This indicates that "holders of public office should take decisions solely in terms of the public interest. They should not do so in order to gain financial or other material benefits for themselves, their family or their friends" (Millar, Delves & Harris, 2010: 117). The second principle is integrity, which indicates that "holders of public office should not place themselves under any financial or other obligation to outside individuals or organizations that might influence them in the performance of their official duties" (Millar et al., 2010: 117). The third principle is objectivity, where "in carrying out public business, including making public appointments, awarding contracts or recommending individuals for rewards and benefits, holders of public office should make choices on merit" (Millar et al., 2010: 117). The fourth principle is accountability, where "holders of public office are accountable for their decisions and actions to the public and must submit themselves to whatever scrutiny is appropriate to their office" (Millar et al., 2010: 117). The fifth principle is openness, where "holders of public office should be as open as possible about all the decisions and actions that they take. They should give reasons for their decisions and restrict information only when the wider public interest clearly demands" (Millar et al., 2010: 117). The sixth principle is honesty, where "holders of public office have a duty to declare any private interests relating to their public duties and to take steps to resolve any conflicts arising in a way that protects the public interest" (Millar et al., 2010: 118). The last principle is leadership, where "holders of public office should promote and support these principles by leadership and example" (Millar et al., 2010: 118). Implementing all seven principles will not only help an organization improve the working environment, but will also help to increase the public's trust in the organization and to build a better reputation.

Unethical leadership

Leaders who display unethical behaviors do not consider their stakeholders and how their decisions will impact others. A common quality found in dysfunctional leaders is their

64 Unethical leadership

lack of consideration for ethics, which then relates to unethical behavior. Dysfunctional leadership is found to be associated with unethical behaviors in the workplace, whether it is the psychopath who is purposely sabotaging employees, the Machiavellian leader who is focused on trying to bend the rules and not getting caught, or the tyrant who will do anything to get what they want. All of these dysfunctional leadership behaviors show a lack of respect and responsibility toward others by violating workplace standards of appropriate conduct (Stouten et al., 2010). Unethical leaders use power for personal gain and for self-promotion (Conger, 2005). The use of control and coercion is used to impose their goals while incorporating censoring of opposing views or the opinions of others. Chandler (2009: 71) defined "unethical leadership" as "the organizational processes of leaders acting in a manner inconsistent with agreed upon standards of character, decency, and integrity, which blurs or violates clear, measurable, and legal standards, fostering constituent distrust because of personal self-interest." Brown and Mitchell (2010: 588) defined "unethical leadership" as behaviors conducted and decisions made by organizational leaders who are illegal and/or violate moral standards, and those that impose processes and structure that promote unethical conduct by followers. They go on to explain that unethical leadership goes beyond the leaders' own behavior. In seeking to accomplish organizational goals, leaders can encourage corrupt and unethical acts within their own organizations. They also add that an unethical leader possesses weak moral character (Brown & Mitchell, 2010).

Leaders who engage in unethical behaviors violate the core values, morals and standards of the organization, and have the potential to put the company at risk of failure (Miao, Newman, Yu & Xu, 2013). Unethical leaders counteract objectives and strategies that are defined by the organization. The unethical leader can quickly damage the culture and systems of the organization.

To date, there is little clarity in relation to a true definition of "unethical leadership." Quite a lot of research exists relating to ethical leadership, but little research has been undertaken on definitions of unethical leaders. The literature associated with unethical leadership can also be termed corrupt leadership when the leader and at least some followers lie, cheat or steal to a degree that exceeds the norm. They put their own self-interest ahead of public interest. The lack of a clearly defined definition is a challenge for organizations, as there is increasing demand for promoting organizational ethics. There is an increased demand for regulations due to the rise in the number of scandals involving government, religious institutions and organizations. As a result, more rules and regulations are in place to clearly identify ethical behavior versus unethical behavior and to address the latter.

Often the unethical leader will invite others to share in their behavior and will extend their unethical approaches to followers within the organization. Simply stated, they encourage unethical behavior from their followers. In some cases, the unethical leader does not have to act unethically; they may think unethically and ask their follower(s) to implement the unethical behavior. Followers learn behaviors within the organization through observation. Behaviors that are observed often lead to follower action. Popper (2001) proposed that unethical leadership is comprised of three elements: (1) the leader; (2) the follower; and (3) the environmental circumstances. When these three interact in unique situations, the context allows for unethical leadership to occur. However, it is argued that there needs to be a tipping point that helps to escalate or fuel the unethical behavior. We will discuss this in detail shortly.

Unethical leadership crossover

There are many crossovers between various dysfunctions and unethical leadership. Recent literature focusing on unethical leadership has also been referred to as destructive and tyrant leadership. Destructive leadership styles have been linked to recent scandals in financial and economic disciplines, such as those involving WorldCom and Enron. Kellerman (2004) referred to destructive and tyrannical leaders as unethical and ineffective leaders. These types of leaders are viewed as corrupt liars and cheaters, whose goals include moving ahead at any cost. Viewed as unethical and physically destructive, these leaders are emotionally harmful to their followers. While destructive and tyrannical behaviors and traits are similarly compared in the literature, it is important to identify the two separately (Illies & Reiter-Palmon, 2008).

Characteristics and traits of an unethical leader

The unethical leader is unable to distinguish between what is right and what is wrong. Ethical leaders exercise leadership in the interests of the common good. They always put the needs of their followers first and exemplify virtues such as courage and temperance (Burns, 1978). The unethical leader is motivated by power or greed, along with the desire to acquire more. They do this by accepting bribes and favors and evading taxes, exaggerating corporate earnings and participating in insider trading/fraud. In many cases, the leader can feel powerlessness and in order to increase their feeling of power, they will act out in an unethical manner. By adding more to their portfolio, building their empire and focusing on monetary greed or power, they are able to increase their power base. The unethical leader will participate in corruption and will encourage some of their followers to do the same to a degree that exceeds the norms. They put their own self-interest ahead of public interest (Kellerman, 2004).

Temptation and greed

For leaders, temptation is great. Lying, cheating and stealing are easy to follow and fall into. Think of political leaders who make promises that they know they cannot or will not keep – they will not raise taxes, they will address crime, they will increase employment, etc. They know that these are promises that are attractive to the voters, but in the long run, they know that they cannot be kept once they are in office. This philosophy also applies to leaders who come into organizations promising workplace joy, job satisfaction and no job cuts. The reality is that they know that this is only what their followers want to hear. At the end of the day, they will do whatever is necessary to keep their jobs, status and power base intact.

Often leaders begin their leadership journey with the best of intentions. They believe in a noble cause, vision or strategy. They believe that they can change an organization or change the world, and have dreams of being the person who can make things happen. However, at some point, there is a level of temptation that is presented to the leader. The temptation may be a taste of power, achieving monetary status, recognition, a boost to their ego or whatever fulfills their needs at that time. This results in the leader taking a step into a new territory and slowly the focus on doing noble work turns inward to a focus on oneself and on personal satisfaction.

When their victims or targets are faceless, it makes it easier for leaders to be unethical. This can be seen through scandals related to corporate fraud. Shareholders who lose money because of corrupt business practices, employees who lose their jobs and families that are impacted by these job losses do not have a face. For unethical leaders, at times it is easier to disassociate themselves from followers, customers, stakeholders and employees when they are not seen and a face cannot be attached to them. They are more readily able to act in an unethical manner when their victims are unknown.

Unethical leadership behavior/tipping points

Leaders who are shown to be unethical tend to be oppressive, abusive, manipulative and calculating (Tepper, 2007). Their interactions are perceived as intentional and harmful, and may be the source of legal action against organizations. In order to achieve their organizational goals, leaders tend to engage followers in unethical behavior. In many cases, there is a tipping point where the leader, the follower and the environment provide a unique situation that allows the unethical behavior to happen:

- *Deliberate deception*: Taking credit for work that is done by others or sabotaging work, such as sales, numbers, misrepresenting products and services. Ultimately the leader uses the trust that they have established within the organization and followers, and uses that trust as a weapon to deceive others. The tipping point for the leader is the need to build their self-esteem and to be recognized by others.
- *Violation of conscience*: Being held to higher expectations and demands for meeting exceedingly difficult goals. These leaders will often believe in violating their conscience and asking others to do the same. They feel as though they have no choice and will ask their followers to do likewise in order to meet goals, budgets and timelines. Stress, lack of resources, strict guidelines and protocols create the tipping point. The leader is asked to violate their conscience in order to achieve the goals of the organization.
- *Self-interest*: Ethical leadership looks at the interests of others and past individual self-interest. In the context of unethical leadership, the leader only looks after their own interests. This focus results in the leader wanting to achieve their own goals and not those that will be for the greater good. They are focused on monetary gains primarily and will do whatever it takes to address their own needs. Another term for this type of driver is individualism and focusing on self-serving rather than serving the group as a whole.
- *Conflict*: When unethical leaders act, there is a conflict between moral right and wrong. Typically that conflict is overwritten by what needs to be done for the good of the leader. In addition, the unethical leader often fosters conflict within the organization or team members. By fostering an unethical environment or culture, a conflict of norms comes into play. By destabilizing the environment, conflict escalates as followers get caught up in the issue of distinguishing between right and wrong.
- *Self-enhancement*: Unethical leaders focus on building their own sense of self. By building power, wealth and success, they are able to focus on their self-enhancement and to provide an opportunity for their own recognition and growth. This self-enhancement may be deep-rooted, going back to the need for recognition in their early childhood to other unresolved issues in their life.

- *Conformity*: Depending on the environment, the leader may be asked to conform to the unethical behavior that has existed for many years. In other cases conformity may occur because of a highly competitive environment. In some cases the leader may no longer be authentic to themselves and may conform to the pressures of the organization. This may result in the leader utilizing unethical methods in order to achieve either personal or organizational goals.
- *Pressure*: As has been mentioned in previous chapters, leadership today is full of pressures and stressors. From reduction in headcount to decreased resources, accelerating technologies, rapid change and less time and money, leaders experience extreme pressure and stress. In some cases they may cave in to the pressures of the organization, followers, shareholders, market demands and customer needs. In order to achieve unrealistic goals and expectations, they may feel the need to utilize unethical acts. As these needs and demands increase, the pressure increases as well. As goals are achieved, the ease of acting in an unethical manner becomes a little easier, but the fear of being caught is always in the back of the leader's mind.

Examples of how unethical leadership impacts organizations

Looking at the US, we find many top CEOs are amongst the highest paid in the world, with an average salary of $14.5 million, which includes stocks, bonuses and other perks. During the 2007 financial crisis, nine banks paid out over $32 billion in bonuses, while collecting more than $175 billion in federal government bailouts. In 2011, New York Security firms paid out over $20 billion in year-end compensation and in 2014, bonus pools equaled $28.5 billion, increasing by three percent compared to the previous year, with average bonuses paid out at $172,800. The challenge for many organizations, especially during an economic downturn, is watching executives being rewarded while underperforming. In other cases, organizational leaders feel compelled to demonstrated increased profits and higher productivity, and may adjust numbers so that they can earn corporate bonuses. These numbers may continue to be falsified until they are caught. As time goes by, the leader believes they are smarter than others within the organization and that they can get away with unethical behavior. Eventually, followers begin to see the unethical behavior of leaders. They question the differences between unethical leaders who are held to one set of rules and followers who are held to a higher standard of ethics. The following provides insights into some of the largest corporate scandals and unethical acts:

- *Andrew Fastow, CFO at Enron*: Enron, the seventh-largest company listed on the Fortune 500 list, went bankrupt. A committee was created to investigate its CFO, Andrew Fastow. During this time, it was discovered that Fastow broke regulations and created a special purpose entity used to keep debts off the books of Enron. Enron overstated income by over $586 million. The loss to investors was equivalent to $60 billion.
- *Jeff Skilling, CEO at Enron*: Jeff Skilling, the former CEO of Enron, was convicted of 18 separate counts of fraud, insider trading, and lying to investors and employees along with the government regarding false accounting practices, which brought about the downfall of Enron in 2001. He had been employed at Enron since 1990 and was CEO for only six months when he abruptly quit the organization shortly before the collapse of the company.

- *John Thain*: Merrill Lynch and Company CEO John Thain spent $22 million in 2008 decorating his offices during the financial meltdown while the company was losing $27 billion.
- *EduCap, Inc*: EduCap, Inc, a multi-million-dollar student loan charity, took advantage of its tax-exempt status by charging excessive interest rates on student loans while the CEO enjoyed perks including the use of a $31 million private jet for family and friends.
- *Martin Shkreil*: Former CEO of Turning Pharmaceuticals Martin Shkreil raised the price of a drug to treat life-threatening infections by more than 4,000 percent. It is believed that he ran a Ponzi-like scheme for several years and lost investors while continuing to provide inflated and false performance updates to investors. He used funds from one company to pay off bad market debts to another company. The drug Daraprim is used for cancer treatment along with treatment for AIDS and its cost went up from $13.50 a pill to $750 a pill. The drug is also an essential drug used to treat parasitic infections in pregnant women with compromised immune systems and the elderly. Infection can cause blindness, seizures, birth defects and in some cases death. While testifying to Congress, he pleaded the Fifth and rolled his eyes at Congressmen. Afterwards he called them imbeciles. He compared himself to John D. Rockerfeller, who never apologized for his actions as long as what he did was legal. Shkreil said he did nothing wrong since his actions were legal and had only wished that he had increased the price even more. He used social media to Tweet labels of $1,000 bottles of wine and selfies of helicopter rides over Manhattan, all the while lying about his investments. Instead of telling investors he had lost their money, he told them that he in fact doubled it. Investors were told that there was $35 million in reserve when in reality there was only $750.
- *Dennis Kozlowski*: Dennis Kozlowski worked for Tyco for the majority of his career. During his time at Tyco, he was viewed as an effective leader. In 2001 he was featured on magazine covers as "The Most Aggressive CEO." Not only was he an aggressive leader, he was also very calculating and cunning. He was eventually indicted for evading over a million dollars in taxes. Further investigations found that he and two other executives at Tyco were accused of embezzling over $600 million. With the help of his accounting team, it was decided that he deserved an $81 million bonus. In addition, he spent approximately $15 million of company money purchasing art, a $6,000 shower curtain, $15,000 for a dog-shaped umbrella, $2,200 for a gold-plated wastebasket, $2,900 on coat hangers and $5,900 on sheets, to name but a few of the extravagant items he purchased. For his wife's birthday, he threw her a $2 million party and asked the company to cover half the costs. Board members were treated to "shareholder meetings" on an Italian island where they were treated to luxuries. He continued to maintain his innocence and felt that he was wrongly accused. He felt that jurors viewed him as someone who was making $100 million and that they were envious of his wealth, which was why he was wrongly convicted and served close to seven years in prison. Tyco on the other hand did not fare well at all. Kozlowski made several wrong business decisions that impacted the organization, resulting in a $90 billion drop in Tyco's stock.
- *James McDermmott, Jr. CEO of KBW*: James McDermmott, Jr. did not embezzle millions of dollars; instead his unethical behavior focused on inappropriate behavior. He would share secrets of the boardroom in the bedroom. During his affairs, he shared

insider information with his mistress, who used this information and shared it with others for personal gain. He was convicted of insider trading, served five months in prison and paid fines of approximately one-tenth of one percent of his annual salary.

Why people follow the unethical leader: What is in it for the follower?

There are many reasons why followers follow unethical leaders. In many cases it is through fear, retaliation or how they themselves can gain from the unethical behaviors. One reason is the challenge of obedience – following orders or policies, resulting in blindly following the leader and sometimes engaging in illegal and immoral activities. For some, they are simply following the rules. For others, they are afraid of challenging the leader. The second is the challenge of dissent – expressing disagreement, fear of speaking up because of a lack of psychological safety, or a fear of retaliation, retribution or putting oneself in harm's way. The follower fears telling the unethical leader something they don't want to hear. Dealing with a leader who may lash out can be a challenge. The follower fears the leader and may hide information in order to protect themselves.

Conclusion

Many of the dysfunctional leaders traits discussed in this book do align with unethical behaviors. Throughout the course of the book, we will examine dysfunctional leaders who utilize unethical practices to promote themselves, along with providing self-enhancement. Overall, when we look at ethical behavior, we are able to identify that an ethical leader focuses on the greater good of their followers and others. Unethical leadership behaviors are focused on the good of the leader and their personal goals and agendas.

References

Boatright, J. R. 2007. *Ethics and the conduct of business* (5th ed.). Upper Saddle River, NJ: Pearson.

Burns, J. M. 1978. *Leadership*. New York: Harper & Row.

Brown, M., & Mitchell, M. 2010. Ethical and unethical leadership: Exploring new avenues for future research. *Business Ethics Quarterly, 20*(4), 582–616.

Chandler, D. 2009. The perfect storm of leaders' unethical behavior: A conceptual framework. *International Journal of Leadership Studies, 5*(1), 69–93.

Ciulla, J. B. 2005. Introduction. In J. B. Ciulla, T. L. Price, & S. E. Murphy (Eds.), *The quest for moral leaders: Essays on leadership ethics* (pp. 1–9). Northampton, MA: Edward Elgar.

Conger, J. A. 2005. "Oh Lord, won't you buy me a Mercedes-Benz": How compensation practices are undermining the credibility of executive leaders. In J. B. Ciulla, T. L. Price, & S. E. Murphy (Eds.), *The quest for moral leaders: Essays on leadership ethics* (pp. 80–97). Northampton, MA: Edward Elgar.

Eisenbeiß, S., & Brodbeck, F. 2014. Ethical and unethical leadership: A cross-cultural and cross-sectoral analysis. *Journal of Business Ethics, 122*(2), 343–359.

Illies, J., & Reiter-Palmon, R. 2008. Responding destructively in leadership situations: The role of personal values and problem construction. *Journal of Business Ethics, 82*(1), 251–272.

Kellerman, B. 2004. *Bad leadership: What it is, how it happens, why it matters*. Boston, MA: Harvard Business School Press.

Miao, Q., Newman, A., Yu, J., & Xu, L. 2013. The relationship between ethical leadership and unethical pro-organizational behavior: Linear or curvilinear effects? *Journal of Business Ethics, 116*(3), 641–653.

Millar, C. M., Delves, R., & Harris, P. 2010. Ethical and unethical leadership: Double vision? *Journal of Public Affairs, 10*(3), 109–120.

Popper, N. 2001. *Hypnotic leadership: Leaders, followers, and the loss of self.* Westport, CT: Praeger.

Stouten, E., Baillien, E., Van den Broeck, A., Campes, J., De Witte, H., & Euweman, M. 2010. Discouraging bullying: The role of ethical leadership and its effects on the work environment. *Journal of Business Ethics, 95*, 17–27.

Tepper, B. 2007. Abusive supervision in work organizations: Review, synthesis and research agenda. *Journal of Management, 33*, 261–289.

Trevino, L., & Brown, M. 2005. *The role of leaders in influencing unethical behavior in the workplace: Managing organizational deviance.* London: Sage Publishing.

Trevino, L., Hartman, L. P., & Brown, M. 2000. Moral person and moral manager: How executives develop a reputation for ethical leadership. *California Management Review, 42*(2), 128–142.

Part II

The Dark Triad

Chapter 5

The Dark Triad

Introduction

The Dark Triad is a topic in psychology that centers on three personality types, which include narcissism, psychopathy and Machiavellianism. Narcissism is focused on feelings of grandiosity, dominance and superiority as defined by Paulhus and Williams in 2002. Psychopathy features traits of impulsive behavior, thrill seeking, low empathy and low anxiety (Paulhus & Williams, 2002), while Machiavellianism is focused on the manipulation of others (Stead & Fekken, 2014). These three personality types are the most widely studied of all the dysfunctional leadership traits. Research has found that individuals who possess these traits share tendencies to be callous, selfish and spiteful in their dealings with others. Another component of these three constructs is that these individuals thrive in environments that are chaotic and lack structure, and cultures that do not have clear expectations or accountability. These personality types will exploit these types of environments to their advantage.

While the three personalities are interconnected with each other and share several themes, they do manifest differently and produce different patterns. Where they intersect is in the areas of low agreeableness, impulsive behaviors and the use of interpersonal manipulation. All three characteristics entail characteristics of self-promotion, emotional detachment and aggressiveness. While the three constructs are very distinct, we find overlaps between Machiavellianism and psychopathy, narcissism and psychopathy, and Machiavellianism and narcissism. It is important to distinguish them from each other because of their uniqueness. The following provides behavioral insights into each of the three personality types that make up the Dark Triad.

Table 5.1 Dark Triad traits (Paulhus & Williams, 2002)

Narcissism	Psychopathy	Machiavellianism
Persistent attention seeking	Selfishness	Self-interest
Extreme vanity	Remorselessness	Pragmatic
Superiority	Superficial charm	Cynical
Arrogance	Exploitation	Dishonest
Exploitation	Arrogance	Self-interest
Entitlement	Anti-social	Interpersonal manipulation
Self-absorption/admiration	Impulsive	Cold
Feelings of superiority	Irresponsible/thrill seeking	Deceptive
Manipulation of interpersonal relationships	Deceitful/manipulation	Calculating toward own agenda

74   The Dark Triad

Leaders who possess these behaviors demonstrate various traits. The narcissistic leader tends to be arrogant, self-centered, consistently self-enhancing and is characterized by cynicism. Psychopath leaders are characterized as cold, detached, emotionless, impulsive, interpersonal manipulators and have a tendency to engage in anti-social behaviors. The psychopath is associated with deviant behaviors in the workplace and, although this only occurs rarely, they can be considered violent. The Machiavellian leader tends to be more in touch with reality and is rooted in their own sense of self. In turn they are highly deceptive, cunning and manipulate others in order to get done what needs to be done.

The following chapters go into detail on each of these dysfunctional leadership traits in order to help the reader understand how these characteristics are connected, while at the same time distinguishing the unique, yet subtle differences in each of these styles. While there is an overlap between these three personality types, each one is very distinct in its own right. The one common trait across all three personalities is low agreeableness. Low agreeableness on the surface is demonstrated as the leader appearing to be warm, welcoming and engaging. However, in actuality, low agreeableness manifests itself as being skeptical of other people's motives, suspicion and unfriendliness. These personality types have a tendency to manipulate others in social relationships. They are highly competitive and will win at all costs.

References

Paulhus, D., & Williams, K. 2002. The dark triad of personality: Narcissism, Machiavellianism, and psychopathy. *Journal of Research in Personality, 36*(6), 556–563.

Stead, R., & Fekken, C. 2014. Agreeableness at the core of the dark triad of personality. *Individual Differences Research, 12*(4), 131–141.

Chapter 6

Narcissism

> When the healthy pursuit of self-interest and self-realization turns into self-absorption, other people can lose their intrinsic value in our eyes and become mere means to the fulfillment of our needs and desires.
>
> (Forni, 2008)

Introduction

Narcissism defined

The term "narcissism" comes from the mythological story of Narcissus. Narcissus was an extremely handsome hunter who was admired by many. One day, whilst walking past a stream, he caught sight of his reflection in the water and was mesmerized by the beauty he saw. He fell instantly in love with his reflection and could not stop staring.

The definition of narcissism has evolved through the years. In 1898, Havelock Ellis (1927: 129) provided the following terms to define narcissism: "self-love" and "unhealthy self-absorption." Kets de Vries defined narcissistic individuals as "troubled by their being by a sense of deprivation, anger, and emptiness" (2001: 101). Later, Morin (2013) further defined narcissism as attention-seeking individuals, with inflated demands of entitlement and denial of weaknesses. Others have summed up narcissism as a personality trait that encompasses grandiosity, arrogance, self-absorption, dominance, superiority, entitlement, fragile self-esteem and hostility (Paulhus & Williams, 2002).

The narcissistic personality is the most researched of the three constructs of the Dark Triad. Early research indicates that Freud recognized narcissism as having a clinical or psychological element. Later, he determined that there were two components to narcissism: a positive side as well as a dark side. He stated that dark narcissists are emotionally isolated and highly distrustful (Maccoby, 2016). Scholars such as King, Rosenthal and Pittinsky (2007) and Kets de Vries (2001) have defined narcissism as a "personal form of admiration" or "perverse self-love." Others have defined narcissism as a "personal form of admiration (as cited by King, Rosenthal and Pittinsky, 2007: 184). Others have defined narcissism as individuals who are troubled by their being followed by a sense of deprivation, anger and emptiness. Morin (2013) further described narcissism as "attention seeking, inflated demands of entitlement and denial of weakness." The narcissistic leader demands attention from everyone they come into contact with.

The common themes related to narcissism demonstrate that narcissistic individuals are self-centered and over-confident in their abilities. Narcissism should not be confused with individuals who possess high levels of self-esteem. People with high self-esteem are confident and charming, but they also possess a caring component that is lacking in the narcissist. In contrast, the narcissistic personality style has an extreme need to build up their low self-esteem. They will seek ways to improve their self-esteem by increasing their status, seeking attention or admiration from others. They are driven by a need for power along with prestige, possess weak self-control and show indifference to the needs and/or well-being of others. The narcissist has an inflated view of their talents and abilities. Their primary driver is arrogance, self-absorption and a personal need for fulfillment related to power and the admiration of others.

In the corporate world, narcissism is demonstrated in many different areas of the organization and at many different levels of leadership. The corporate narcissist will say that they are committed to the organization and the goals of the organization; however, in reality they are committed to their own goals and personal agenda. Organizational decision making is centered on the narcissist's own self-interest rather than on the interests of the organization as a whole.

The strength of corporate narcissists is that they have the capacity to create compelling visions, have high levels of ambition, self-efficacy and the ability to attract followers. Because of these strengths, it would appear natural that organizations would want them in a leadership role. However, in a leadership role some narcissists are found to be poor listeners, are sensitive to criticism, possess a lack of listening skills and demonstrate low levels of emotional intelligence.

Overview of corporate narcissism

Most narcissistic leaders tend to move into leadership roles based on their ability to sell themselves, including their visions and concepts to higher leadership. Narcissists tend to be highly motivated, energetic, assertive and very competitive. This definition can apply back to many successful leaders. It can be argued that a healthy level of narcissism can be found in many of the world's most powerful leaders. Narcissistic leaders are motivated by their need for power and admiration. This need may overshadow any empathy or concern for their followers. But that is not the case for all narcissistic leaders.

One can agree that in order to be an effective leader, there needs to be a level of narcissism. Freud (1910) defined the narcissistic personality as an individual whose main interest is self-preservation, is independent and is impossible to intimidate. This personality style has an extreme need for esteem in the form of status, attention or admiration, and a need for power or prestige. The narcissistic leader is able to see the big picture, is able to envisage a grand future and is able to get others to buy into this vision along with the possibilities that it brings. On the flip side, as they build upon their successes, these leaders begin to feel as though they are invincible and start to take risks. They will listen to advice and information that will align with what they want to hear and begin to dominate others, viewing them less favorably than they see themselves. They then become insensitive to any form of criticism. They demand that others should be empathetic to their cause, but in turn they lack empathy toward others. Finally, they have an immense need to compete with others. As success continues, they crave more and will view others as a threat that they need to take down (Maccoby, 2016).

The two faces of narcissism

Just like everything in life, there is a positive and a negative reaction. In the case of narcissism, there are two forms of narcissism: constructive or proactive narcissism and destructive or reactive narcissism. It is important to understand each of these types of narcissism and how they apply to positive as well as dysfunctional leadership.

Research conducted by Kets de Vries and Miller (1985) found that there are positive and negative aspects to narcissistic behaviors. Research has noted that there are several different types of narcissism, including constructive/proactive and destructive/reactive. The most common forms of narcissism include the constructive, proactive or productive narcissist, who focuses on the positive attributes of corporate narcissism. In contrast, the reactive, destructive or unproductive narcissist focuses on the negative attributes of corporate narcissism. The following section discusses each of these in a bit more detail.

Proactive/constructive/productive narcissism

It is significant to recognize that not all narcissistic behaviors are considered negative. The constructive, proactive, or productive narcissist demonstrates a healthy component. Productive narcissists are gifted and creative individuals who are able to see the big picture and are focused on changing the world while leaving a legacy. Kets de Vries and Miller (1985) explained that all individuals display some level of narcissistic behavior. In the majority of cases, a narcissistic leader is aware of their abilities and has a realistic understanding of their traits and achievements. Kohut (1996) did not use the term "constructive narcissist," but instead used the term "mature narcissism," meaning narcissists were able to work productively through their personality type by utilizing humor and creativity. They are in touch with their narcissism. They will use their power and status to achieve a positive impact; lead by empowering, enabling and establishing a positive vision for the organization and their followers. In addition, they are viewed as being extremely creative, having the ability to generate innovative ideas, and have a very positive impact on the people who follow them. Often this type of narcissistic leader possesses charismatic traits, enabling them to effectively sell their vision to others. Because of their ability to sell their ideas, they are able to gain followership and to inspire others to buy into their ideas. They are not afraid to ask questions, often playing devil's advocate. Because of their high level of confidence and creativity, they are able to push through change and transformation easily. Using their charm, personality and the ability to effectively communicate, they are able to get followers on board to accept the change that is needed. Constructive narcissism is a characteristic of leaders who grew up in a stable and supportive environment. They are often regarded as positive and pleasant individuals who are assertive and goal-oriented, yet are not self-centered. During times of change and transformation, these types of leaders are willing to take risks and undertake transformation while selling their ideas to others.

Reactive/destructive/unproductive narcissism

The other face of narcissism is the destructive characteristic which occurs when an individual is unable to face their idealized beliefs with reality or acknowledgment of their

78 Narcissism

actual strengths and weaknesses. The reactive, destructive or unproductive narcissistic leader is extremely independent, highly distrustful, self-involved, and will eventually cause self-destruction to themselves, their followers and the organization (Maccoby, 2005). Reactive narcissistic leaders behave abusively due to a sense of denial and feelings of worthlessness, and in an attempt to cover up their own insecurities. They are preoccupied with their vision and self-importance. These individuals will over-estimate their abilities and exaggerate their sense of self. Easily enthralled with the spotlight, they will take credit for success, even if that success is achieved by others. They are only interested in their own gain and focus on promoting their personal agenda with little thought for the organization or their followers.

In order to cope with their insecurities, reactive narcissistic leaders often become fixated on power, status and superiority. The higher the leadership level that they achieve, the more insecure they become. They are driven, relentless and ruthless in getting what they want. When something goes wrong, they are quick to place the blame on someone else or divert the attention to other issues. They will exploit and take advantage of others, and will disregard the rights of their followers in order to achieve power and control (Kets de Vries, 2001).

A negative trait of a reactive narcissistic leader is that they possess high levels of distrust toward others. In reality, a reactive narcissist is psychologically fragile, resulting in high levels of suspicion toward others. They are often afraid that they will be discovered to be fraudulent or that others will question their abilities. Their lives are often exaggerated or fabricated in order to create a façade that will allow them to be viewed as more than what they truly are. They create these façades to protect themselves from others. Through fabrications, it can be difficult for the reactive narcissist leader to distinguish between fact and fiction. In a sense these fabrications are their own perceptions of false results and become their reality. To provide protection, they will surround themselves with individuals they view as weak, soft-spoken and who will not pose a challenge, or they surround themselves with people who will help them fuel the façade they have built. These people do not recognize the façade and believe that what the narcissist has created is in fact real. If they do recognize these falsehoods, they hide their knowledge in order to protect themselves. These individuals will praise the narcissist and demonstrate admiration, which continues to build the narcissist up. The term used for these types of individuals is sycophants. The sycophant flatters others in power in order to position themselves in a positive light.

It is important to realize that the narcissist will not give their trust easily. They may act as though they trust someone, but this is often a ploy to find that person's motives and weaknesses to use against them when necessary. The narcissist will never truly trust others, resulting in an inability to build lasting and emotionally healthy relationships. If others criticize or disagree with the narcissist, or let on that they know that the narcissist is putting up a façade, the narcissist will turn on them quickly. In the inner circle of the narcissist, the follower must demonstrate that they are loyal. Payment for this loyalty results in the narcissist promoting or extrinsically rewarding their inner circle. It is crucial to note that at any given time or in any given situation, the narcissist can turn on followers with little to no warning. The person may find themselves on the outside of the inner circle.

Another characteristic of a reactive narcissist is envy toward others. They are constantly comparing themselves to others. They are frequently assessing other people's strengths and weaknesses. They are very effective in judging the capabilities and abilities of others. If a narcissist sizes up a person and believes them to be less than the narcissist, then they invite them into the inner circle. In turn, they ask that the person fuel their ego and self-esteem. That person will do so because they believe in the greatness that the leader will bestow on them. However, if the person is perceived as a threat, then the narcissist will become aggressive toward that person. They will become envious of others who are perceived to have strong abilities, are well respected or are viewed as highly intellectual and capable individuals. Such a person is viewed as a threat and the reactive narcissist will do what they can to eliminate that person swiftly. To give them a false sense of security, the reactive narcissist will invite that person into their inner circle to observe them. They will work to gain that person's trust and, once achieved, they will swiftly isolate them. The narcissist views that person as having something that they cannot obtain and will fight and block that person at all costs.

How a narcissist becomes a reactive narcissist

Typically, reactive narcissists have experienced some sort of trauma in their lives. They are left with feelings of deprivation, insecurity and inadequacy as they grow up to be adults. Due to a lack of empathetic experiences, they typically lack empathy and are unable to experience how others feel. They will develop a sense of entitlement as a way of overcoming their feelings of insecurity and inadequacy. Some believe they will make the world a better place through their actions or that they will right the wrongs that were inflicted on them during the course of their lives, whether these wrongs are real or imagined. They become exploitive, vindictive, self-centered and treat people as objects rather than human beings with a complete lack of empathy. They fantasize about power

Table 6.1 Comparison of constructive and reactive narcissism

Characteristic	Constructive	Reactive
Self-confidence	High outward self-confidence in line with reality. Able to grasp reality of abilities and talents	Grandiose. Views self as highly talented and competent. Develops a façade to protect their confidence. Actually demonstrates low self-confidence
Relationships	Real concern for others and their ideas; does not exploit or devalue others. Able to draw followers to them for trusting relationships. Views people as humans	Concerns are limited to expressing socially appropriate responses when convenient; devalues and exploits others without remorse. Relationships do not last long. Is distrustful of others. Views people as objects
Power	May enjoy these elements. Will use power for the good of the organization and others	Pursues power at all costs and lacks normal inhibitions in its pursuit. Uses power for their own gain
Consistency	Has values, follows through on path, and is consistent with vision and goals	Lacks values, easily bored and often changes course. Is not consistent in their vision or goals
Foundation	Healthy childhood with support for self-esteem and appropriate limits on behavior toward others	Trauma at some point in childhood, undercutting true sense of self-esteem and/ or learning that they do not need to be considerate of others

80 Narcissism

and success, and their self-importance and their lack of empathy lead to manipulation and exploitation of others for their own personal gain and enhancement. They view situations as either good or bad and people are either supporters or betrayers – there is no in between for them.

Table 6.1 outlines the differences between the constructive and the reactive narcissist to provide a better understanding of the two constructs.

Summing up the two faces of narcissism

Higgs (2009) explains that the constructive narcissist provides a core assumption that they are indeed self-aware of their tendencies and work to control their behavior. They demonstrate high levels of emotional intelligence. This particular narcissistic type is productive when guided by reason and can effectively understand their situation. This results in a leader who is self-aware and does not get lost in their delusions. The reactive narcissist, on the other hand, displays negative traits such as self-importance, exaggerated achievements, preoccupation with fantasies of power and success, hostility toward criticism and intolerance to compromise. These behaviors become particularly dominant in stressful situations. They are not self-aware and tend to demonstrate low levels of emotional intelligence.

Whether one is constructive or reactive is a matter of what degree an individual's narcissism presents itself and how well the individual can practice self-awareness to combat the negative aspects of their narcissism. In addition, there is a level of leadership maturity that manifests itself in narcissism. A reactive narcissistic leader's style is smoke and mirrors. Eventually, what appears to be success is just an illusion that is self-created. When the illusion is discovered as a falsehood or threatened, they will be angered and will turn on their followers and inner circle in rage and contempt. For the purposes of this book, we will explore the negative aspects of narcissistic leadership in order to gain a better understanding of these traits and behaviors in leadership.

Understanding the characteristics and traits of a reactive narcissist

In the previous section we explored the negative or reactive side of the narcissist. In this section we will explore each of the characteristics and traits of the reactive narcissist in further depth. The characteristics and traits of a narcissist are somewhat interesting to pinpoint. Identifying a narcissist can be difficult because of the deceptive façade that they construct. Because they are protecting themselves, they are often not what they portray themselves to be. They are constantly changing and hiding who they are, along with their abilities. In a sense, they are providing a mask or a false picture of themselves and people do not really know the person whom they are dealing with. Many are deceived by a narcissist when they first meet and it may take time to actually identify their negative characteristics and traits.

Narcissists have a gift for communication and a commanding presence that allows followers to become enamored with them. Followers are easily pulled into the leader's magnetic charisma and will be blinded by them. However, in time they will start to see the cracks in the façade. When interacting with a narcissist, there will be a time when there is a realization that something is different about that person. Conversations will focus on that person and talk is focused primarily on their talents, abilities, connections, the great work they do and their importance. Facts will be distorted and lies will not connect. Soon, others will realize that these conversations are one-sided and focused on the narcissist. When suggestions are made or the conversation shifts to another topic, the approach is ignored and the narcissist will steer the conversation back to their agenda and ultimately to themselves. In the case of the narcissistic leader, they will talk about their vision and their accomplishments, often bragging, taking credit for work and positioning themselves so that they are at the forefront.

The following list looks further at the traits of the reactive narcissist and how they position themselves in relation to others:

- *Visioning*: Rosenthal and Pittinsky (2006: 622–623) explained that the narcissistic leader has grand visions based on their need for power and status, further bolstering their confidence and conviction in their vision. They have a strong view of their abilities and believe that they can do anything they set their mind to. Their visions are elaborate and enthralling to others, especially followers and upper leadership.
- *Lack of empathy*: Empathy is the ability to recognize and appreciate the feelings that others may be experiencing. There are two types of empathy. The first focuses on cognitive empathy, in which a person is able to identify that another person is experiencing emotion and to perceive what that emotion is. Emotional empathy is the ability to share in the emotional experience of others. Narcissism is not about being vain or difficult to work with; narcissists are individuals who are just unable to understand empathy. In order to protect themselves from being criticized by others, they are constantly seeking affirmation from others and are looking for what can bolster them up. They tend to ignore the feelings, words and behaviors of others, and therefore cultivate underdeveloped feelings of empathy. In their interactions with followers or other members of the organization, the narcissist is unable to see what others bring to the table; they are only concerned with themselves.

  Empathy is by far one of the most important characteristics of leadership and is an aspect of emotional intelligence. Many reactive narcissistic leaders lack many of the components of emotional intelligence and are often unaware of how their behavior impacts others. Because the leader does not possess empathy or a view of other perspectives, their decision-making skills are often hindered as well. Decision making by a narcissist is often self-centered and one-sided, and feedback that is viewed as differing from the narcissist leader's agenda is ignored.
- *Focus on the narcissist*: The narcissist will bring every interaction back to themselves. If the conversation is about someone or something else, they will become very uncomfortable and impatient until the conversation refocuses on them. Because of their lack of empathy toward others and their belief in their own self-importance, they will often interrupt conversations to redirect the attention back to their agenda. They need to control and dominate each interaction.
- *Difficulty maintaining lasting relationships*: Because the narcissist spends much of their time focused on themselves, they do not realize the importance of others. Eventually in relationships, people tire quickly of the narcissist taking center stage and the focus being on them. The narcissistic will not ask their followers how they are doing. If

they do ask how a person is doing, they are generally not interested in the response. They only ask to give the perception that they care when in reality they don't. There is no personal interest shown in others. They will not talk to peers about projects that the peer is leading or struggling with. The narcissist does not find this important to their goals and will not waste their time focusing on other people's issues or problems, unless of course it can benefit them in some way. The only time it may feel that there is a strong interpersonal relationship is when the narcissist needs an individual. However, two things will happen. The first is that as soon as the other person has met the needs of the narcissist and there is no longer a need for that individual, they will move on. Second, as soon as the target recognizes the negative intentions of the narcissist the relationship will turn negative. They will start to lay blame on others, take credit and accolades from others, or once they have no need for that person, the relationship will end. Remember, the ultimate goal of the narcissistic leader is to promote their personal vision or goals. They will use and manipulate anyone who can help them achieve their goals. In most cases, people will eventually see through the mask of the narcissistic leader and will begin to recognize this negative behavior. In many cases, the narcissist will sense when the other person is getting suspicious or that they have been discovered and will quickly move away from that person. If they feel threatened, they will lash out so that their façade is not exposed to others. The tables will be turned and the narcissist will set the other person up so that they will come out looking bad.

- *Distain for others*: The narcissist "loves to be loved." The narcissistic leader expects and believes that they are entitled to constant praise. They will surround themselves with people who will demonstrate constant admiration, praise and worship for them. They will hire people who are enamored and charmed by their vision, are like-minded, are easily persuaded or are presumed to be weak in their eyes.

When a follower, peer, or upper leader challenges the narcissist, they will lash out toward that individual. They do not like to be challenged because it tests their self-esteem. They believe their own thoughts, their worth and abilities, and buy into these beliefs about themselves. When challenged, they feel that they are no longer in control of the situation. Once the narcissist perceives that power and control is gone, then their guard is down, which is followed by feelings of inadequacies, which then fuels their low self-esteem. In turn they will start to continue to build up that façade bolstering their perceptions of themselves, will work to improve the perceptions of others toward them and will find a way to get others to change their minds or will sabotage them in order to regain control or power.

For many followers, showing admiration can be a difficult task. If they don't show admiration for the narcissist leader, then they risk being subjected to abuse or misconduct when the narcissistic leader lashes out. The narcissistic leader will make life difficult for the follower. Depending on the level of threat perceived, the reactive narcissist will ostracize the follower, have them moved to another unit or even terminate their employment on a simple technicality. For many followers, in order to survive a narcissist, they learn to show admiration and act as though they admire the leader until they are able to get out from under their control. However, this can be an extremely dangerous tactic as the narcissistic leader may deploy others as spies to find out if the admiration is true or false. In addition, since the follower is not being authentic to themselves, they will eventually become stressed, cynical and bitter about the situation.

In addition to admiration, the narcissist demands loyalty from others. There is an expectation that followers must ensure that others show respect and admiration toward the leader. If a follower hears someone talking negatively about the narcissistic leader, it is expected that the person in question is reported to the narcissist, who will address that individual's transgressions against them. In some cases, followers will be asked to be hostile toward anyone who criticizes or questions that leader. This demonstrates loyalty to the narcissistic leader.

- *Positioning*: The narcissist will always positon themselves and work to put themselves into the best possible situation. This is why we see so many reactive narcissists in leadership positions. They know when and where to position themselves for the most opportune times. Many people will ask themselves "How did that person get into a leadership position?" More than likely, that person was skillful in positioning themselves so that those higher up could see them and notice them for opportunities. Through positioning, they are quick to point out what they have done, their successes and how the organization needs them. Without them, the organization will surely fail. In leadership roles, they will portray themselves as the "knight on the white horse" who can and will save the organization. Reactive narcissists have been known to create a problem where there was no problem – either they will solve the problem or will bring the problem to the attention of others as something that they have discovered.

  Unfortunately, the narcissist is also quick to take credit for the work of others, even when they had little to do with the project. Many of their ideas and behaviors are taken from other people who they know or who they assume are in a position of authority (Thomas, 2010). They draw upon the successes of others and package these ideas as their own and in the line of sight of executive leadership. They will always be within sight of the powers that be. By doing this, executive leadership provides the narcissist leader with the necessary platform to position their personal agenda and goals. In turn the narcissist appears to executive leadership as innovative, extremely invaluable to the organization and quite capable of taking on more. They will subtly brag about their accomplishments and will most certainly make sure that everyone knows what they did, even when they had no part in the work.

- *Teamwork*: When working in a team, the focus will be on the narcissist. They are disruptive, counter-dependent, combative and resentful of others who are in a position of authority. The narcissist will come across as being an asset to the team and will draw attention to all that they have to offer the team. They will monopolize team meetings and will draw the attention away from the focus and goals of the team toward what the narcissist believes will benefit them. They will not notice the discord and conflict that they create in the team setting. They will also not be willing to listen to the perspective of other team members, which may result in team members shutting down and not contributing. While it appears that the narcissist leader has shot down ideas, in reality they are filing this information away to be used later. The idea will later be repackaged as their idea and concept. They will disregard the views of others unless of course that view will benefit them. The team will eventually move into a group-think mode, will give up and will follow the goals of the narcissist leader.

  It is essential to note that while working on a team with a narcissist, they will not help with the day-to-day activities. The narcissist feels as though they are too important for what they believe is menial work and will delegate this work to others. If the team is successful, then the narcissist will be quick to jump in and accept the credit. When working in a team, they will never highlight the team's contributions or the contributions of their direct reports. The only time they will highlight the team's contribution is when it makes them look good: "Under my direction and guidance, the team was able to complete the project on time and under budget." If failure occurs, the narcissistic leader is just as quick to point the finger and blame other members of the team who did the work. Or they will label other team members as indecisive, difficult to work with and resentful toward them. These are the reasons why the team was not successful – it was not because of a lack of leadership on the part of the narcissist.

When working in a team, the narcissistic leader may want to be in a position to ensure that nothing goes wrong that might make them look bad. They will take on the role of the puppet master and will spend their time controlling the situation and the events taking place. If necessary, they will move into a micro-managing position. They will exert control over the littlest of things and will control every part of the situation, along with the people on the team. In a position of control, the leader will become patronizing, condescending and critical of members of the team. They will set unrealistic goals and their expectations will be unclear. They will be vague in their direction for two reasons: (1) if the project fails, they will blame the person who was assigned a particular role or task and will claim that they are incapable of the work; and (2) they may not know what to do. This task might be something that they have no understanding of, but they do not want others to know that they are not capable. They hope that others will be able to figure things out. They need to preserve the perception that they are more capable than they really are. In their minds they are infallible, superior and skillful. Others need to believe this as well. Their behavior on the team will also be inconsistent. At one moment, they may devalue team members, then they will offer exaggerated praise in order to motivate others.

- *Emotional situations*: The narcissist is often very uncomfortable addressing emotions, whether their own or those of others. They are uneasy with anything that has to do personally with other people or sharing their inner thoughts and feelings. They do not make good teachers or coaches and have little time or patience for developing others. If a follower is looking for development, more than likely they will not get development from the narcissistic leader. Instead, the reactive narcissist wants to control their followers. They also want to ensure that their followers are not learning too much, as this may be pose a threat to them.

The narcissistic leader is extremely sensitive to any form of criticism. They will over-estimate their personal and professional capabilities. They are blind to any faults that they might have and are even more reluctant to have others point out their faults to them. They view any form of criticism as slowly chipping away at their façade. When criticism is focused on the reactive narcissist, they will become angry, which is one emotion that they are comfortable sharing with others. It is important to note that they do not show anger in the same way that others do. They are able to control their anger and do not demonstrate it outwardly, or at least not right away. The anger will slowly simmer under the surface. It will remain hidden until it can be used at a strategic time. Then in a calculated way, the narcissist will use that anger in order to regain control over a situation or person. Since the narcissist is afraid of their faults being discovered, they will not display irrational anger in public. They will hide their emotions until the right time and it will be in a very controlled manner. Once discovered, their anger will surface in the form of malicious and vindictive behavior that is focused only on the person who has discovered the façade of the narcissist (Thomas, 2010).

- *Unable to show gratitude*: The narcissistic leader is unable to show gratitude and will only reluctantly say "thank you." They view anyone who provides them assistance as a means to an end. The person who is assisting them is not there to be thanked, but for service to the narcissist; after all, they are viewed as objects and not as individuals with emotions. The only time narcissists will recognize others is if they find themselves in a public platform that requires them to thank or praise others in order to make themselves look good. While the narcissist struggles with showing gratitude, they are very quick to point out fault and blame. They are unable to show any type of remorse when something goes wrong. It is never their fault and they will put the blame on others. This is demonstrated by a quote from a recent research study conducted by the author:

> I always knew I was doing an OK job when nothing was said to me. So in this case no news was good news! But boy when something went wrong; even the most minor of issues, the [narcissist] leader would come down on me and would come down hard on me. I was blamed for everything that went wrong . . . even when it wasn't my fault. But when I did something right and saved his butt . . . well nothing was ever said to me and he strutted around making it sound like he did something great. He loved to take credit for my ideas or my work. Eventually, I just shut down and didn't offer anything to him. When I had nothing to offer him, he made my life hell and wanted me out. He replaced me with someone that gave him fresh ideas and suggestions.

- *Distrust of others*: The narcissistic leader possesses a high level of distrust toward others. They are constantly looking over their shoulder and wondering if they will be found out. They will become suspicious and will always wonder what the person across from them is thinking and what their motivation is. They are waiting for someone to find them out and to point out their faults. They will never let their guard down. Instead, they look for information that might be used against others in case a counterattack is needed. Much of their distrust is rooted deeply in paranoia. Glad (2002) stated that the narcissist will often create enemies where there are none. In order to protect themselves from any type of perceived threat, they will often cause an argument as a distraction. At any given time, the narcissist will turn against even the most loyal of followers and will focus on destroying that person. When the narcissist does strike, the other person is often caught off guard

> Sally returned to work after a well-deserved vacation. Prior to the vacation, she had landed a large account which the executive team had been trying to land for several months. The leader of the team, Lacy (a reactive narcissist), set up a meeting with Sally the morning after her return from her vacation. Sally assumed it was a follow-up to landing the account and to discuss strategy. Sally was surprised to find out that was not the agenda for the meeting. Lacy started the conversation by stating that she was disappointed in Sally's work. While on vacation several team

members had complained about Sally. Lacy felt that Sally needed to be demoted to a junior sales position in order to learn the basics of sales. Lacy was looking to promote another team member who was more in tune with the direction that she wanted to take the department. Sally was completely shocked at this turn of events and was even humiliated. She never saw this coming. After landing a major account, it was now being handed over to Lacy, who ended up downplaying Sally's involvement on the account with the Executive Leadership Team. The Executive Leadership Team stated that they were surprised that Sally had taken credit for the account and how noble it was that Lacy showed such integrity and humility in allowing Sally to take credit for the account. Lacy told the Executive Team that it was her vision, direction, mentoring and sales pitch that had won the sale. This was not the case and Lacy was nowhere to be found when working on the account presentation. Sally was left with no other choice – knowing the truth, she knew she had to leave the organization. That evening, she submitted her resignation. She reported Lacy to Human Resources and after an extensive investigation, nothing was found. Lacy had covered her tracks well. Lacy had positioned her people against Sally while she was on vacation and was prepared for the attack. When Sally had her exit interview, she called Lacy out on what had happened. Lacy stated "No hard feelings, after all it is just business," smiled and ended the exit interview. Lacy received the commission for the account that Sally had landed along with the admiration of the Executive Leadership Team for landing such a prestigious account.

Now that we have looked in depth at each of the traits or behaviors of the narcissist, let's take a look at the narcissist in the role of leadership.

Narcissism and leadership

It is difficult to understand the role of narcissism in leadership. Rosenthal and Pittinsky (2006: 628) supported this by stating that: "The contrast between the harmful impact that narcissistic leaders can have on their constituents and institutions and the fact that narcissism is a key trait of some of the world's most creative and generative leaders seems to suggest these concepts need to be further studied and refined." Other scholars and researchers have pointed out that narcissism is indeed a fundamental element of leadership effectiveness.

The narcissistic leader displays a pervasive pattern of grandiosity (in terms of fantasy and behavior), a need for admiration, a sense of entitlement and a lack of empathy. Narcissists are extremely self-centered and will take action in social situations to ensure that they are the center of attention, even at the cost of belittling others, or to control the situation. They struggle to pay attention to the needs and wants of others, since they view their own needs and wants as paramount. When it comes to their lack of empathy and sense of entitlement, this is viewed as anti-social behavior and destructive. When this happens, it is difficult to differentiate between a narcissist and a psychopath.

Reactive narcissistic leadership behavior will often manifest when leaders "lose control" and become self-absorbed. Eventually they will lose all sense of control and are unable to determine the boundaries of acceptable or unacceptable behavior. Once they lose control of their boundaries, they will believe that normal rules and norms no longer apply to them. They will only hear what they want to hear, will not want to be controlled and will retreat into their fantasy or façade that they have created to survive. They are of the opinion that the only ones they can trust are themselves and look toward themselves for their own gratification. They will come across as highly independent, but in reality are highly dependent on their inner circle for the admiration and affirmation they so desperately seek. In addition, their inner circle needs to help them to keep the façade fueled and to protect the reality they will have spent so many years developing.

Narcissism and gender

Narcissistic traits across gender do display differently. We find that only 25 percent of narcissists are female, while 75 percent are men (Higgs, 2009). It is critical to understand that the behaviors discussed earlier may not always hold true by gender. The female narcissist needs to be the center of attention with other women and needs to be the alpha female in groups where women are gathered. They also tend to demonstrate a desire for money and status through material items. Male narcissists may lean toward sexuality and status in marriage, such as a "trophy wife," in order to appear successful in the eyes of others. They thrive on power and aggression to assert their narcissistic tendencies. When interacting with men, female narcissists tend to use their charm, sexuality and physical attributes to gain an advantage over them. Table 6.2 demonstrates the differences between male and female narcissists.

The impact of narcissism

Organizational impact

The world is changing quickly and there is a constant demand for change in order for organizations to survive. Because of the rapid changes that are occurring, environments are ripe with ambiguity and are a breeding ground in which the reactive narcissist is able to step in and exploit the situation. The narcissistic leader will jump on the latest leadership fad and is politically astute, they will have the ability to position themselves in order to demonstrate how they are able to positively bring about change for the good of the organization. They will state that they can provide a new strategy or direction for the organization, giving upper leadership what they need and what they are hungry for.

Table 6.2 Gender traits of narcissists (Vaknin, 2001)

Male narcissists	Female narcissists
Intellect	Competition
Power/status	Charm/sexuality
Aggression	Sexuality/marital status
Money	Arrogance
Competition	Self-centeredness

Given the large numbers of narcissistic leaders running businesses and corporations, the challenge is to ensure that these leaders do not lead the organization toward disaster or destruction (Maccoby, 2005). Research is finding that narcissism is rampant in today's corporate cultures. In recent years organizations have featured many reactive narcissists, including Kenneth Lay, Bernie Madoff, Jeff Skilling and Fred Goodwin (Thomas, 2010). All were instrumental in the downfall of their organizations. While these leaders engaged in unethical behavior, their reactive narcissism led to their ultimate downfall. When asked if they felt any remorse for their actions, they said that they did not. Rampant narcissism puts the organization as well as the leader's followers in harm's way and can be detrimental to both parties.

Narcissists perceive greater benefits derived from risky behaviors and this in part fuels their tendency to engage in risk-taking behavior (Foster, Shenesey & Goff, 2009). Because of these precarious behaviors, the organization is at risk of poor judgments being made that can be costly, ultimately dangerous and negative to the organization. Reactive narcissists are known for their risky behaviors, as well as for creating a competitive internal environment. Unhealthy competition results in employees picking sides in order to win, which may result in a chaotic environment. The organization becomes divided between followers who continue to support the narcissistic leader and others who understand the narcissist's dysfunction and rebel against it. It is important for organizations to recognize that the narcissistic leader is unable to put the needs of followers or of the organization before their own egos or personal gain.

Narcissism has the ability to change the culture of the organization. This is demonstrated in the higher levels of leadership where the narcissist resides; as a result, the chances are that the corporate culture will morph to one of corporate narcissism. For example, when a narcissistic leader moves into the higher ranks of leadership within an organization, they bring with them their inner circle that they have cultivated over the years. These followers continue to enable the reactive narcissist's behavior and inflate their ego. The narcissistic leader will appear loyal and dedicated to the organization and will appear to be supporting it. However, most certainly the narcissist is not loyal to the organization. They are committed to furthering their own power base and control. Decisions and judgments are not based on the strategy of the organization; instead, they are based on the narcissistic leader's judgments, whether these are right or wrong. The narcissistic leader will manipulate and coerce others in order to continue to build up their self-esteem as they continue to grow in their leadership role.

Followership impact

Maccoby (2005: para. 15) stated that narcissists "have compelling, even gripping visions for companies and they have an innate ability to attract followers . . . Constructive narcissists understand the vision concept particularly well. By nature they are the people who see the big picture." In contrast, the reactive narcissist is only fueled and motivated by meeting their personal needs for power, control and ego. From their followers they demand excessive admiration and attention, along with affirmation.

The narcissistic leader cannot survive unless they have followers who are willing to inflate their egos, to drive them further or to assist them in carrying out their vision. Followers at first will become enamored with the charismatic ways of the narcissistic leader. In many cases they are happy to carry the load to help the narcissist reach their goals. They will work long hours and will push unhealthy boundaries to satisfy the demands of the narcissistic leader. In some ways the relationship can be considered a co-dependent relationship, with the narcissist craving power and the follower seeking security. Both support each other's needs. The two will work hand in hand until something happens to break that bond. Once the bond is broken, it will be the reactive narcissist who will come out on top, leaving the follower behind to pick up the pieces.

Working with a reactive narcissistic leader can be extremely stressful for the follower. This is especially true when the follower recognizes the leader's dysfunction or has been exposed to their anger and wrath. Followers will experience many different behaviors. Once the narcissistic leader feels threatened, the person posing the threat may experience abuse, rage, character assassination and intimidation. These behaviors can take the form of name calling, talking down to employees, sexual harassment, misuse of information, the silent treatment and ostracizing the target (Thomas, 2010). All of these unhealthy behaviors will be felt by the employee, as well as any bystanders who witness the behavior. Because of this treatment, bystanders will sit back and watch, but will seldom step in for fear of retaliation from the narcissistic leader. Eventually the employees will comply with the manipulations of the reactive narcissist in the hope that executive leadership will address the behavior or the leader will eventually leave the unit or the organization.

Why people follow narcissists

The sense of self-confidence and talk of grandeur is appealing to a follower especially if there is an unmet need for the follower. In the case of the follower, the narcissistic leader can be viewed as superhuman, a person they want to be, even god-like. The narcissistic leader believes in the power of words and using them to engage as well as intrigue followers (Maccoby, 2016). The power of their speech is mesmerizing to followers. The follower is blindly lured into believing the statements of the leader, resulting in the follower complying with the leader's directives for action. The follower will provide the leader with emotional support, loyalty and anything else that the leader needs.

The narcissistic leader is dependent on their followers. Without followers to fuel them, they would not be able to exist. The follower's role for the narcissist is to focus on bringing the leader's agenda to fruition. Followers supply the narcissist with what they need to further their agenda. The role of the follower is to adore, admire, agree and provide attention, while providing an approving audience. The narcissistic leader will surround themselves with people who can carry the load and who can cover up their own inabilities. The narcissistic leader is a natural delegator and will delegate the bulk of their work. Once the work has been delegated, the leader will then move into a micro-managing phase. The leader does not want followers who are independent; instead, they want people who they can consume and control. As the narcissistic leader becomes more confident and self-assured, they will start to isolate themselves from others. As their lack of empathy increases, their need to listen to others will decrease. However, the follower will continue to strive to be in the good graces of the reactive narcissist, feeding off of their energy for status, power and ego. They hope that the leader will reward them and provide them with extrinsic rewards and opportunities to move up within the organization.

New recruits are usually the main target of the narcissist. When someone new enters the organization, the narcissistic leader will turn their focus and attention on this person. The narcissistic leader will be very attentive, demonstrating compassion and being flexible and helpful, and will try to court the person in order to get into their good graces. Once that person has been recruited as a follower, the narcissist will begin to change their behavior, showing themselves as opinionated, demanding and aggressive. This will often throw the follower off and leave them questioning what is happening. Some may try harder to please the reactive narcissist in order to get back on their good side, while others will struggle with pleasing the leader.

Another view of followers is that by supporting the narcissistic leader, the follower is able to foster their own narcissistic behavior in some ways by being in the good graces of a leader who may be perceived as confident, attractive, intelligent and dynamic. They are viewed as members of the leader's inner circle. Many narcissistic leaders are viewed as being different. They are viewed as risk takers willing to push the envelope by saying what others would like to say and by standing up to others.

As mentioned earlier, most dysfunctional leaders thrive on chaos and in unstable environments. The narcissistic leader will purposely create chaos or step in during a time of crisis; they will be admired for their ability to save the situation. Followers will be impressed by their charm, connections, abilities and confidence during times of crisis or uncertainty. In turn the reactive narcissist will appear to restore order, end the chaos and allow followers to feel secure (Lipman-Blumen, 2005). Followers admire leaders who have a perceived sense of high self-confidence, blindly believing them and providing them with the support that they need (Rosenthal & Pittinsky, 2006). It is during times of crisis, change and chaos that the reactive narcissist will create an environment where followers want to follow that leader. During this time followers will not see through the mask or façade of the narcissist; instead, they will display admiration and awe at how great the leader truly is.

Followers will eventually identify a narcissist. The identification may be quick or it may take time. Once they discover the dysfunction, in order to survive, they will align themselves with the narcissist. It becomes a *quid pro quo* type of scenario. The follower will praise the leader and will continue to bolster their self-esteem while being rewarded. At other times, followers are lured in by the charismatic ways that a narcissist will use to push their agenda and goals. They will come across as genuine, persuasive and making a difference. In the 2016 US presidential campaign, people were drawn to Donald Trump because of his charismatic, self-assured presence. He was not afraid to speak his mind, saying and doing what many Americans wished they could do. In the meantime, he created chaos by creating small chaotic scenarios that drew followers and the media away from the real issues. He has been successful in attacking media outlets, reporters, politicians and other candidates in a self-assured manner, allowing him to gain ground in the media along with his followers. He has been able to draw upon the fears of terrorism and the economy, and how he is the only one who can save the US from the problems it is experiencing. However, the real issues never surfaced and other candidates were afraid to push these issues for fear of how Trump would lash out at them. One female candidate, Carly Fiorina, slowly gained ground in numbers and was soon a target for Trump. He attacked her physical appearance, stating: "Look at that face! Why would anyone vote for that?" Fiorina responded by stating "I'm not going to spend a single second wondering what Donald Trump means. But maybe, just maybe, I'm getting under his skin a little bit because I am climbing in the polls." She did not allow the negative comments thrown at her to draw her away from the topic of the political arena. She did not engage with the negative comments, understanding that if she had, it would only fuel the fire. However, only a few months later, she dropped out of the presidential race as Trump continued to gain followers. Slowly, he began to pick off other candidates by attacking them personally until he was the Republican nominee for President and later elected as the President of the United States. He continues to degrade others and to demean people who he perceives as less than he is. His followers continue to follow while others are gaining an understanding of his behaviors and actions.

Addressing the narcissist

It is extremely difficult to address the reactive narcissist. Of all the personalities covered in this book, there are two leadership styles that are the most difficult to tackle. The first is that of the psychopath, which will be discussed in the next chapter, and second is the narcissist. Narcissists when threatened will become aggressive and hostile. They have spent many years fine-tuning their powers of deception and have fabricated a world that they have come to believe in. This fabricated world has become the narcissist's reality. It is not likely that they will be willing to let the grand illusion of their reality go. They are not willing to expose their imperfections to others. It is very unlikely that the narcissist will ever change their behavior as it has become ingrained into their personality and their life.

It is extremely difficult for the reactive narcissistic leader to work through their behavior. They never want to feel shame. Instead of internalizing this shame, they will externalize it by blaming others. Surely, the narcissistic would never admit to fault or blame as this would be damaging to their ego, persona or self-esteem. If they are called out, the narcissist will weave a tale, point the finger at others or turn failure into potential success. If the person does not buy into the story or façade, the narcissist will take control of the situation through the use of rage, projections, abuse and character assassination (Thomas, 2010).

Organizations may address the narcissistic behavior of leaders by suggesting counseling or coaching. However, in most cases the narcissist will not notice or even be aware of their dysfunctional behavior. Because of this, they will not be aware of how their behavior is impacting others. They need to be open to any type of behavior modification if they are hoping to change their behavior. Yet this is difficult, as they are used to praising their own accomplishments along with accepting praise and admiration from others. They will ask "How can something be wrong when everyone thinks I am so great?" In some ways this will be confusing to them. They will have surrounded themselves with people who are like-minded and are busy supporting their vision.

As a means of addressing or understanding the issues related to the narcissistic leader's behavior, organizations may use a 360-degree feedback instrument to collect data on the leader. Research has found that narcissistic leaders do not score well based on 360-degree feedback instruments. When the feedback is reviewed and it is negative, the narcissist will react with anger and aggression, and will try to work out who would have reported negatively against them. When they are compared to others who are seen as more capable, the same reaction will occur. It is important that while this feedback may be helpful for the organization in gaining insights into the narcissistic leader, it will not change the narcissist.

92 Narcissism

If the narcissistic leader is successfully achieving their agenda and personal goals, they will see no reason to change. After all, they are successful and are able to meet the goals set in front of them. If they are not meeting their goals and the feedback is negative, they will start to work on their exit plan quietly and covertly.

Eventually, the narcissist will start to crumble. They will become overly confident and eventually will expose themselves for who they really are. Ultimately, people will see through the façade and the narcissist will pick up on these cues. Quietly, they will plan to leave the organization or will position themselves to move up in order to gain more power. It is their view that it is best to leave on their own terms. If the narcissistic leader is let go from the organization, they will have difficulty with this action. The reality of the situation will never occur to them and they will not take ownership for their actions. If they do, their self-esteem will be damaged. It is safer for them to lay blame on others or on the organization and they will spin the story back to finger pointing and blaming others.

Survival guide: Dealing with the narcissistic leader

There are ways to address or survive a narcissistic leader. It often feels uncomfortable for people and may go against their belief systems. The following list provides some tips on surviving a narcissistic leader:

1 Never disagree with or contradict the narcissistic leader. You won't win and you won't gain their trust. In the long run, you will only make them angry. It is better to show empathy toward them, but don't expect it in return. Support them, but not to the point of looking as though you are a sycophant (Maccoby, 2016).
2 Show admiration toward the leader: This can be extremely difficult as you might start to resent or hate this person, but for the time being until the problem with the narcissist is resolved, it may allow you to survive the narcissistic leader.
3 Do not bring the real world into the situation. Since the narcissistic leader has fabricated their reality, their mind and sense of the world is also fabricated. When real-life problems start to enter the narcissistic leader's life, they become uncomfortable and will resist the reality that is presenting itself.
4 Give them ideas, but realize that they will take credit for these. Find out what they think before presenting your viewpoints. If the leader is wrong, provide other solutions or alternatives that may benefit them and let them make the decision on what should be done (Maccoby, 2016).
5 Don't ever place blame on the narcissistic leader. In their mind they are always correct. If something is done incorrectly or they have made a mistake, they don't want to know about it. Focus on fixing the problem or finding a solution.
6 Manage your time effectively. The narcissist leader will place many demands on others. Be available to that leader at any time, but also prioritize their requests. Place high priorities at the top and move ideas that are not clear or don't make sense down the list, because eventually the leader will forget about these ideas (Maccoby, 2016).
7 Plan your exit strategy. Network with others in order to move to other areas of the organization or to exit the organization. Working with a reactive narcissist can be a challenge and taxing on individuals. Quietly looking for ways to leave the organization is helpful. If you find yourself in the inner circle of the narcissistic leader, you

must be covert in your exit strategy. Any sign of disloyalty toward the leader will backfire and will result in negative consequences. If you are outside of the inner circle, the leader will almost expect that you will leave, but they will no longer have use for you so they will be less concerned. The only time they may be concerned is if your exit reflects negatively on them.

Conclusion

Narcissism is a trait that is found in many of the world's most powerful leaders. There are two forms of narcissism: constructive and reactive. The constructive or proactive narcissist is able to support followers and is able to balance their grandiose ideals with reality. They use charm, personality and communication effectively. In contrast, the reactive narcissist is unable to square their idealized beliefs with reality. They are often destructive, over-estimating their abilities, and are preoccupied with their own need for power and control. They will maintain this power and control at all costs. Characteristics of a reactive narcissist include the following:

1   Unable to empathize with followers, peers, customers or others within the organization.
2   During interpersonal relationships, the focus is primarily on them.
3   Difficulty maintaining lasting relationships.
4   Shows disdain for people who do not show admiration and worship toward them.
5   Position themselves to be extremely important.
6   When working in a team, the focus will be pointed away from the team and toward them.
7   Unable to show gratitude toward others.
8   Uncomfortable with emotional situations.
9   Show high level of distrust toward others.

The reactive narcissist will have varying degrees of impact on both the organization and their followers. From the organizational standpoint, the narcissist leader can do great harm through risky decision making and damaging the culture of the organization, as well as dividing the organization. From a follower standpoint, the narcissist is able to attract followers; however. the leadership of a narcissist is often stressful for the follower, causing them to become disengaged and cynical toward the leader.

The narcissist is one of the most difficult of the dysfunctional leadership behaviors to address. To protect themselves, they will never take responsibility for a situation that has gone wrong and will blame others. It is difficult for them to work through their behavior and they will never see how their behavior negatively impacts the organization or their followers. Ultimately, the façade of the narcissist will begin to crumble and the narcissistic leader will leave the organization or they will self-destruct.

References

Ellis, H. 1927. The concept of narcissism. *Psychoanalytic Review,14*(2), 129–153.
Forni, P. 2008. *The civility solution: What to do when people are rude.* New York: St. Martin's Press.
Foster, J., Shenesey, J., & Goff, J. 2009. Why do narcissists take more risks? Testing the roles of perceived risks and benefits of risky behaviors. *Personality and Individual Differences, 47*(8), 885–889.

Freud, S. 1910. "Wild" psycho-analysis. *Standard Edition, 11*, 219–227.

Glad, B. 2002. Why tyrants go too far: Malignant narcissism and absolute power. *Political Psychology, 23*, 1–37.

Higgs, M. 2009. The good, the bad and the ugly: Leadership and narcissism. *Journal of Change Management, 9*(2), 165–178.

Kets de Vries, M. 2001. Creating authentizotic organizations: Well-functioning individuals in vibrant companies. *Human Relations, 54*(1), 101–112.

Kets de Vries, M., & Miller, D. 1985. Narcissism and leadership: An object relations perspective. *Human Relations, 38*, 583–601.

King, G., Rosenthal, S., & Pittinsky, T. 2007. Narcissism and effective crisis management: A review of potential problems and pitfalls. *Journal of Contingencies and Crisis Management, 15*(4), 183–193.

Kohut, H. 1966. Forms and transformations of narcissism. *Journal of the American Psychoanalytic Association, 14*, 243–272.

Lipman-Blumen, J. 2005. *The allure of toxic leaders: Why we follow destructive bosses and corrupt politicians— and how we can survive them*. New York: Oxford University Press.

Maccoby, M. 2005. Narcissistic leaders: The incredible pros, and inevitable cons. *Harvard Business Review, 82*(1), 92–101.

Maccoby, M. 2016. *Narcissistic leaders: Who succeeds and who fails*. New York: Crown Publishing.

Morin, R. 2013. *The most narcissistic US presidents*. New York: Pew Research Center.

Paulhus, D., & Williams, K. 2002. The Dark Triad of personality: Narcissism, Machiavellianism and psychopathy. *Journal of Research in Personality, 36*, 556–563.

Rosenthal, S., & Pittinsky, T. 2006. Narcissistic leadership. *The Leadership Quarterly, 17*(6), 617–633.

Thomas, D. 2010. *Narcissism: Behind the mask*. Leicester: Book Guild Publishing.

Vaknin, S. 2001. *Malignant self-love: Narcissism revisited*. Rhinebeck, NY: Narcissus Publishing.

Chapter 7

Psychopaths running our organizations

Introduction to corporate psychopaths

When considering psychopaths, our minds wander to their criminal actions, which have been shown on television and in the media. We think about the unstable, destructive criminals who are known to mutilate, murder and inflict physical and psychological harm on others. The psychopaths discussed in this chapter are different. Psychologists have found a type of psychopath who is not prone to the same impulsive, violent or criminal behavior of other psychopaths. As a result, these psychopaths live unnoticed in our societies, comfortably ensconced in professional roles (Boddy, 2005). These psychopaths are found leading organizations, non-profit organizations and governments. Labels for these types of psychopaths include "corporate psychopaths," "industrial psychopaths," "executive psychopaths," and "organizational psychopaths." For the purposes of this chapter, the popular term "corporate psychopaths" will be used. Corporate psychopaths are simply described as psychopaths working in the corporate sector (Boddy, 2014). To date, there has been very little research or literature written on the topic of corporate psychopaths. Researchers have stated that the deviant influence of corporate psychopaths is worthy of further investigation. Research is starting to emerge regarding the topic of corporate psychopaths and is seen as setting a new direction in leadership studies (Gudmundsson & Southey, 2011).

The percentage of corporate psychopaths is relatively small. Researchers have found that they make up between 1 to 3.5 percent of business leadership (Boddy, 2005; Babiak, Hare & Neuman, 2010). Instead of demonstrating the behaviors associated with the typical criminal psychopath, corporate psychopaths are motivated by money, prestige, power, greed, success and admiration. They lead through lying, manipulation, egotism and callousness toward others. These characteristics are similar to the other dysfunctions discussed in this book, but there are subtle differences that will be discussed later in this chapter. They have learned that their deviant behavior can pay off in lucrative ways and they often go unnoticed until it is too late and damage has been inflicted on their targets. In the corporate world their behavior typically plays out in the form of white-collar crime. Corporate psychopaths adopt an existence that is often believed to be parasitic. They live off the generosity, kindness and gullibility of others. They take advantage by abusing other people's trust and their kind nature. They are also more inclined to move from place to place and person to person in order to feed their psychopathy (Babiak & Hare, 2006: 19).

The corporate psychopath will demonstrate traits and behaviors very similar to the reactive narcissist discussed in the previous chapter. They do not care or even understand the feelings of others. They also lack remorse or shame for any harm that they may inflict on others. They are found to be unreliable and have difficulty following through on their promises. Lying is a part of their motivation and is used as a way of getting what they need. For people who are not used to working with psychopaths, they will come across as sincere and genuine, but in reality they are very insincere.

On the surface, corporate psychopaths appear normal, sane, in control, likeable and highly intelligent. They will use flowery language that is full of jargon, but will lack substance. They are extremely polished and dress to impress. Many followers will find them to be non-threatening, reassuring, fun and exciting to work with. They will have a strong need for admiration and attention.

The corporate psychopath can be viewed as a chameleon and they assume whatever persona is required during any particular situation or setting. Their goal is to take advantage of others, usually for monetary gain. They don't care what they say or do. They will assess the person in front of them and determine what that person offers in relation to meeting their own needs and goals. This assessment will include a physical and psychological assessment of the person's needs, strengths and most importantly their weaknesses. Once the psychopath is done assessing their target, they will then manipulate that person with messages that are specifically crafted to meet the psychological needs of the target. For example, Bernie Madoff was an individual who fixated on the psychological needs of his targets. Their needs were focused on the security of their investments. He promised a steady though modest return on their investment. This provided the target with the ability to have less risk while achieving their financial goals. He preyed on his targets and focused on getting what he needed and wanted from them. He was able to steal millions of dollars in life savings from individuals. Some caught on and became suspicious, but others were pulled into the greed of the scheme and ended up losing their life savings. Madoff came across as disarming and sincere, so his targets never guessed that they were part of the largest Ponzi schemes of all time.

The corporate psychopath will use feedback from others as data points in order to change their approach to either maintain their control or to adjust the situation to their advantage. If confronted or challenged, they will maneuver themselves through the situation in order to come out on top. They will associate themselves with all the right people and will align themselves with people who they believe possess both formal and informal power along with control.

Definition of "psychopath"

The word "psychopath" comes from the Greek word "Psyche," which means soul, and "Pathos," meaning disease, providing the definition of suffering of the mind. However, the psychopath is not aware that their behavior is wrong. When asked if they feel any remorse, they will often respond "no." They sincerely believe that there is nothing wrong with their behavior and are often confused by being accused of wrongdoing. Corporate psychopaths are leaders who have absolutely no conscience and will do whatever they need to do to gain the upper hand. This can be accomplished through a charming façade, ruthless manipulation and deception.

Psychopathy focuses on major abnormalities in terms of how people interact with others. The psychopath is unable to relate on an emotional level to how others may feel or what they may be going through. They will display behavior that others view as inappropriate; this may include deceit, aggression, inappropriate thrill seeking, and indifference to the rights and feelings of others. All social, legal and moral norms of conduct are ignored in order to meet their needs at that particular moment. What others may feel is immoral or unethical, the psychopath will see nothing wrong with. Long-term consequences are disregarded in the pursuit of the thrill of instant gains and gratification. They do not think about the moral implications of their actions, merely what is best for their own self-interest. They establish a pattern of behavior that will justify their personal gains and will provide them with the rationale they need in order to continue their pattern of behavior (Shouten & Silver, 2012).

The psychopath does not possess a fear response. For example, when someone does something wrong, they know deep down that what was done was wrong, resulting in a fear consequence. Their conscience is haunted by their actions. Most people wonder what might happen or what will happen when they are caught. This fear will more than likely cause this person to come forward to admit what they have done, make mistakes or correct their behavior. The psychopath does not feel fear or view the negative consequences of their behavior. Fear is clouded by a relentless need to take care of their needs and desires.

Not all psychopaths are created equally. Each psychopath will handle their behavior differently. Some will use violence and aggression, while others will use power, greed, money and success to achieve their goals. The main goal of some is to build wealth and power, while for others, it is to see how far they can go without getting caught. The thrill of getting away with their actions is what will drive the corporate psychopath to continue to push the limits. For them, in order to be successful, their motto is "Whatever needs to be done" in order to achieve their goal. This could be lying, deceitfulness, stealing or whatever else will get them to their goal. This mentality is extremely beneficial when the leader is faced with a pressurized or stressful environment. They will rise to the challenge. Others will view this behavior as an asset in order to get things moving forward, while for the psychopath leader, it is a challenge to get the job done regardless of the consequences they may experience.

The difference between "psychopath" and "sociopath"

Before we move forward in this chapter, we need to understand the terms and differences between "psychopaths" and "sociopaths." Often these terms are used interchangeably as it is believed that they are the same. Some even would argue that there are no differences between the two constructs. However, research shows that there are differences. Let's look first at the similarities. Both are considered antisocial personality disorders and share many of the same traits. These key traits include:

- a disregard for what is right and wrong, not following laws, rules or procedures;
- a disregard for other people's rights;
- an inability to feel guilt or remorse;
- a tendency to display aggressive and at times violent behavior.

The differences between the two are that the sociopath is a result of their environment, while the psychopath is a result of their genetic predisposition. It is believed that sociopathic behavior is something that is learned. If it is learned, it is believed that the sociopath is able to feel emotions. Hiding or diminishing their emotions is used as a coping mechanism in order to deal with other traumas that may have occurred in their earlier life.

The sociopath typically experiences high levels of anxiety and can be irritated or agitated quickly. They tend to have sudden outbursts of rage and anger. Most sociopaths are unable to hold down a job because of their quick temper and are often on the edge of society and socially awkward in their interactions. They struggle to have close relationships with others and typically do not have a strong support system. They are quite disorganized and their actions are spontaneous and scattered.

In contrast, the psychopath is extremely charming. They also struggle with building relationships; however, people are attracted to their charm and their ability to come across as disarming and possessing a magnetic personality. They can easily gain the trust of others through manipulation. They are unable to feel emotions, but they are able to mirror or mimic the emotion suitable for any situation. If the situation calls for them to be social, happy and outgoing, they will transform into this persona. They are extremely intelligent and have the ability to hold on to jobs. Because of their lack of emotions, they are not as likely to have to show their anger quickly; they are able to mask it. The psychopath is the master of disguise. They can have relationships, friendships and be married, yet are not emotionally attached to these relationships. To the outside world, all will seem normal, but their relationships are not normal and are not what they appear to be. They will mimic what they believe is a normal relationship and what they see from others and how others interact. They are highly organized and will plan every detail of their day and actions according to their needs and their goals. Their minds are very strategic, viewing every angle of a maneuver, and they will plan accordingly, even having contingency plans in place for anything that might go wrong. They will be extremely focused and in a crisis will come across as cool, calm and collected. Just like the dysfunctional leadership traits already discussed, they will thrive on the chaos that exists. In the face of chaos and crisis, others will feel high levels of angst and anxiety, but the corporate psychopath will experience feelings of exhilaration, thrills and excitement. A corporate psychopath who is a thrill seeker may intentionally cause chaos and crisis so that they can step in to save the day. In the professional world, the psychopath is talented at white-collar crime and conning others because of their ability to manipulate and mimic what the situation demands. The thrill of getting away with their actions is intoxicating and exciting for them and they will push the limits as far as they can, until they are eventually caught.

The evolution of the corporate psychopath

The corporate psychopath is becoming more pronounced and recognizable in the workplace. To understand this phenomenon, it is important to recognize the evolution of our organizations as well as the evolution of the corporate psychopath leader. The way in which current work systems are set up provides the corporate psychopath with many opportunities to emerge. The following provides insights into the evolution of the workforce and the corporate psychopath.

In the early twentieth century, organizations were relatively stable and slow to change. The status quo was maintained and work continued forward. The majority of individuals began their careers in one organization and from there they retired. Longevity in an organization allowed employees to get to know one another and to build lasting relationships. These relations allowed people to identify strong and poor leaders quickly and organizations to address behavior by terminating the leader or not allowing them to move up within the organization. In these organizational systems there was little tolerance for egos, selfishness or dysfunctional behavior. This is not to say that these behaviors did not exist, but it was much easier to recognize them because of the long-term relationships and employment longevity built up within these organizations.

Later in the twentieth century, organizations began to change through globalization, mergers and acquisitions, and changes in the global economy. In today's modern organizational systems, companies are witnessing mergers and acquisitions, which allow for the acceleration of corporate change. The concept of working for one organization for the lifespan of one's career no longer exists within the modern organizational system. Because of this mentality, the philosophy of employee commitment to organizations is not what it used to be. Job switching or job hopping, which was once considered taboo or career suicide, is now the norm. Organizations believe that people who are in the same position for five to ten years without upward movement are considered complacent. Movement from job to job has resulted in less familiarity with working with others and a lack of building long-term relationships. It has become difficult to identify success in leaders as they are moving back and forth within other organizations and are experiencing rapid career change. Changes within organizations can cause a myriad of issues. An example of an issue that these organizations encounter is inheriting employees when organizations are merged or acquired. If a psychopath leader is part of the mix, it is difficult to determine who they are and where they are until their behaviors emerge. During the period of the acquisition, the leader will mimic the appropriate behaviors to fit into the new organizational system and will be able to adapt quickly. Once ensconced in the new system, they will continue displaying this behavior, but eventually their dysfunction will emerge.

Because organizations lack the formal relationships of the past, it is difficult to recognize corporate psychopaths. Because many psychopath leaders are masters at deceit and act as chameleons, it is challenging to determine what is true behavior and what is the façade. The corporate psychopath will have done their homework and will adjust their style to fit the requirements for the position and build the necessary relationships. Once they are ensconced in the organization, they are able to read the people and will mirror what the organization is looking for.

Corporate psychopaths will use charm and talk their way successfully through meetings, and are highly skilled at social manipulation. They will portray themselves as leaders who like to take charge, can make tough decisions and are able to use their leadership approach to get things done. They will say that they embrace organizational change and enjoy the challenge presented by change. This is appealing to corporate boards and executive leadership as organizations are in need of leaders who are not focused on the status quo and who are not afraid of change. Organizations are looking for leaders who are innovative, are able to rattle cages and are focused on getting things done quickly. The corporate psychopath will be able to portray themselves as the one who fits into the model. They are ideal for leadership positions in today's organizations. Once they have embedded themselves within the organizational system, corporate psychopaths are able to achieve these goals through the use of coercion, domination and manipulation to get what they want. Since long-term relationships that were once established are a thing of the past, they are able to maneuver and position themselves into these roles.

Modern organizational systems have been designed to reward the psychopathic leader's behavior. Because of these systems, it is difficult to address the root cause of the problem. Dysfunctional behavior is often inadvertently rewarded through higher bonuses, pay increases and rewards based on performance. Once a psychopath is discovered, the organization just wants to be rid of the problem and to do it quietly in order to avoid negative press. Ultimately, companies will offer large corporate payouts or severance packages, allowing the leader to move on to another high-profile position while continuing their behavior elsewhere. These systems can manifest a culture of greed, corporate fraud, financial misrepresentation and other forms of misbehavior to advance the psychopathic leader's thrill seeking and need to test the boundaries.

Corporate psychopaths in leadership

Corporate psychopaths often hold many of the high-powered and controlling positions in organizations. Executive leadership is the predominant field for non-criminal psychopaths. They demonstrate very similar personality behaviors to those of a narcissist, but also possess minimal emotions and absolutely no sense of remorse. They are able to effectively climb the corporate ladder to positions of power.

These leaders are masters at conning others, leading to the perception that they have strong skills of persuasion. In the corporate setting the psychopath's behavior is often confused with true leadership. They will be charming and possess high levels of extreme self-confidence. Their inability to feel normal human emotions and their lack of conscience come across as having the ability to make tough decisions or remaining cool under pressure and/or in stressful situations. They are risk takers and like to put themselves and others in harm's way. In the corporate world, risk takers are often perceived as having high levels of energy and being action-oriented and courageous. As organizations experience rapid change, the psychopath leader becomes politically astute and influential. As soon as people begin to question the behavior of the corporate psychopath, either people do not oppose the behavior for fear of retaliation or the leader will move on to the next position.

In the workplace, these leaders put their followers on edge or cause them to feel a level of paranoia. When followers question the behavior of the corporate psychopath leader, they will often use terms such as "You over-think everything" or "You are reading too much into this." The psychopath leader likes to cause followers to question their feelings and values systems in order to throw them off and believe that the leader is not the problem, but maybe they themselves are. The followers walk away from these meetings questioning their abilities, their skills and their intuition.

The corporate psychopath leader thrives on drama. They will either be drawn to the drama and chaos or they will be the ones causing it. They say that they don't like drama and won't tolerate it, but in reality they love the thrill and chaos caused by it. When people come forward to discuss issues, the leader will not want to hear about it and will blame the follower for causing the problem or spreading rumors. This will cause the follower to believe they are the ones at the center or the cause of the drama. The leader will not help to find a solution for the drama and will often work to escalate the drama instead of addressing it. Again, the corporate psychopath finds conflict, chaos and drama exciting.

When a problem comes about and the follower questions the issue, the psychopath leader will often state that the follower has misunderstood the situation, the conversation, the direction, etc. A very familiar tactic used by the corporate psychopath is to deny and then deny again. They will claim that the interaction or the conversation never occurred. This is a tactic that is used to throw the follower off and again to question their own sanity. This type of behavior will continue to occur, causing the follower to question their role and what truly happened.

The narcissist versus the psychopath

As mentioned earlier, we can see similarities between the characteristics and traits of the psychopath and the narcissistic leader, but there are very subtle differences. Table 7.1 compares the similarities and differences in the behaviors of a narcissistic leader and a psychopathic leader.

Not all corporate psychopath leaders will demonstrate the same traits, characteristics or behaviors. There is not one single cookie-cutter way to identify corporate psychopaths. For example, if an individual cons and manipulates, that does not mean that they are a psychopath. What will distinguish a corporate psychopath is an established pattern of behavior that is utilized multiple times and in several different situations. Because the pattern needs to be in multiple different settings, it can be difficult to identify this type of dysfunctional behavior in the workplace. As you will recall, the psychopath takes on the persona of a chameleon and will adjust to the circumstances and situation of the interaction. Based on the situation, they will become the ideal friend, co-worker, team player or whatever and whoever is needed in order to fit the demands of the situation. All the while, they will be sizing up their victims. As they are doing so, they are looking for that person's weaknesses and, once discovered, they will work to fulfill their target's psychological needs. For example, they will focus on the person who has a psychological need to be financially secure and will concentrate on fulfilling the need for that person to feel financially secure. They will give the illusion that they are working on helping that person

Table 7.1 Comparison of the narcissist leader and the psychopath leader

	Narcissist	Psychopath
Lack of empathy or concern for others	x	x
Thrives on chaos	x	x
Questions or distrusts authority figures	x	x
Impulsive		x
Glib yet superficial		x
Emotionally shallow and cold		x
Parasitic lifestyle		x
Immune to stress/stays calm when others cannot		x
Callous		x

fulfill this need, but in reality they may be working to swindle money from that person. In another case, they may help an individual fulfill their psychological need for security. The psychopath leader will tap into that person's need. They will adapt their personality to match what the other person needs and will then lure their target into their trap. The person becomes involved with the corporate psychopath because the latter is able to fulfill that need for the target. The target will feel safe and secure, and a level of trust is established. They cannot believe that this person would do anything to harm them. On the flipside, the corporate psychopath is pursuing whatever angle is necessary in order to make that person feel secure so that they can take advantage of them. Once the target has fulfilled whatever need the psychopath leader has, they will turn on that person quickly and the target is left lost and confused, their psychological need torn and shattered.

The characteristics and traits of a corporate psychopath

The corporate psychopath comes across as the ideal employee and will be identified as a future leader. It is fairly easy for them to move into leadership positions and to position themselves accordingly. They focus on joining organizations that are struggling and will market themselves as the one who can come in and save the organization. The following list demonstrates the characteristics and traits found in psychopath leaders:

- *Lack of emotional connection*: The corporate psychopath has an inability to show interest in other people's welfare or circumstances. They show little care for others and are focused only on their own self-gratification, personal success, greed and monetary rewards. They are driven by their target's vulnerabilities and derive a perverted sense of pleasure from hurting others and abusing their trust. They also lack emotions and are not troubled by their behavior. They are unable to demonstrate remorse or feel sadness toward their actions. The only time they might show remorse is when the situation calls for it. For example, in the courtroom, if they are counseled by their attorney to demonstrate remorse or regret, they will mimic this behavior if they believe it will help their case and ease the sentence that might be handed down. But their remorse is not genuine and at this point people will see through the persona. However, most of the time they will show no emotion or any signs that they recognize that they have done something wrong. They are not troubled by their behavior. They are unable to associate their dysfunctional behavior with anything negative and do not have any sympathy or remorse for any hurt or damage they will cause to the organization or their targets.
- *Deceitfulness*: The corporate psychopath leader is an expert at deceit and pathological lying is a normal behavior for them. Lying and deceit become a way to support their lifestyle. The corporate psychopath likes to flaunt their success through materialistic items. They will demonstrate a life of success and wealth through flashy possessions in order for others to believe that they are successful. They will take on debt to purchase large homes, exclusive country club membership, flashy designer watches and jewelry or luxury vehicles to show others their success, when in reality it is all false – it is merely an illusion for others so that they believe that the psychopath is successful. However, they may achieve this through debt, stealing or other means. This does not mean that they are successful as it is only an attempt to appear that way. These lies are either conscious or unconscious. Another tactic used is aliases

and conning skills for their own personal benefit or pleasure. It is typical for psychopaths to have multiple aliases and different personas in order to hide or to live a new life. In society the psychopath leader will be a chameleon. They do this in order to gain the trust of their target. In a sense, they are never their true self, since they have no sense of self. At some point their lies become their reality and they begin to lose touch with who they really are. These tactics are used to their advantage and to move forward. As they gain their own personal wealth, they will continue to accumulate more and more in order to continue the social climb and fuel their pathology.

- *Manipulation*: Along with deceit and lying, the psychopath leader is a master at manipulation and is the ultimate con artist. Corporate psychopath leaders are very adept at manipulation, especially when they are alone with their target and it is a one-on-one situation. They are able to con others easily through their brilliance at playing psychological games, with the focus on winning. In addition, they are drawn to the vulnerabilities of their targets. These vulnerabilities are used to hurt and abuse their targets. They are very open to exploiting the kindness of others.

- *Organizational skills*: The psychopath leader is very good at planning their next move and calculating how they will move forward. They will have thought through every situation and possible scenario, and are prepared with contingency plans in case there are problems. Their focus is only on themselves and the immediate situation to gain an advantage. They are known for their lack of following through and are viewed as being unreliable. This may be caused by their constant calculation and maneuvering; as they progress further into their pathology, they forget all that is going on and lose sight of their direction and promises.

- *Aggression*: There are several ways to categorize aggression. The first is instrumental aggression, which focuses on being planned, controlled and purposeful in order to assert dominance. This aggression is focused on a desired outcome. It does not come from emotions, but instead from a calculated agenda focused on the use of aggression as a tool or instrument to get what the psychopath wants. The second form of aggression is called reactive aggression. As the term "reactive" implies, this form of aggression is impulsive, driven by emotion and displayed when there is a perceived threat. The next form of aggression is called relational aggression and focuses on social norms and relational components. This type of aggression can take the form of different types of abuse, including gossiping, excluding others, malicious rumors and verbal humiliation. All of these levels of aggression are subtly different, but ultimately are used to take advantage of an individual or situation. Typically the corporate psychopath will utilize instrumental aggression and relational aggression, but that is not to say that they won't use reactive aggression as well. Since this form of aggression is based on emotions, it is the least common form used by a corporate psychopath. This would be linked more to a sociopath than a psychopath. Aggression will be used as a tactic for the corporate psychopath and it will be based on what they feel best suits them in a particular situation.

- *Inability to take responsibility*: As with most dysfunctional leadership behaviors, the psychopath leader fails to take responsibility for any of their actions. This is because of their lack of emotions – they do not feel or recognize that they are doing anything wrong. They view others as being at fault and take no responsibility for their actions.

- *Financially irresponsible and impulsive*: As mentioned earlier, finances are normally used as part of the psychopath's persona. The corporate psychopath is typically not fiscally responsible and will experience extravagant spending or reckless behavior related to money. They feel they deserve the best and will spend the money that they have gained, whether through ethical or unethical means. Impulsive buys are very common with psychopath leaders and they have no problem spending money belonging to others or the organization. They feel a sense of entitlement, especially in relation to money. By being extravagant, they are able to demonstrate to others their wealth and success, even if it is just smoke and mirrors. As their persona escalates, so does the need to fuel the persona of wealth and success, resulting in excessive behavior.
- *Thrill seekers*: The psychopath leader loves thrills and excitement. They are constantly looking for the next thrill. This is considered a form of stimulation for them. As a result, they may engage in reckless and unsafe behaviors. Focused on the thrill of the game or the chase, they are looking for that next big thing to keep them stimulated and motivated. Once a thrill is achieved, they will become bored quickly and will look for the next big win. Problems with self-control and self-regulation become an issue for them. They are viewed as willing to take risks at any cost. At times they may put themselves as well as others into harm's way. They have little regard for other people's safety or well-being. In the corporate setting, they will look for areas that are ripe with conflict. Instances of change, turmoil, conflict or other forms of distress will breed uncertainty in others, but the corporate psychopath leader finds these types of situations and environments full of excitement and this helps to fuel their energy levels.
- *Intelligence*: Corporate psychopaths are highly educated, holding PhDs, MDs and law degrees. Many believe they are highly intelligent and will look down upon others, including anyone who cannot assist them in reaching their goals. They are well read and well versed in any topic that is being discussed. They love to use corporate jargon and will fill conversations with fluff in order to impress others. To others they come across as knowledgeable about topics. In other cases they may not have completed higher levels of education, but they will come across as extremely intelligent. Because of their use of jargon-filled language, people believe they are educated and well versed on the topic being discussed. However, upon closer examination of the content of the discussion, people may find there is little substance to their conversation. When criticized for something, they will become quite defensive and aggressive as they feel their intelligence as well as the persona that they have created are being threatened. Because of their high regard for their own intelligence, they are able to circumvent processes and create loopholes to get away with white-collar crimes.
- *Callousness*: Psychopath leaders are extremely insensitive to others. People and situations exist solely for the purpose of meeting their own needs and wants. They do not view people with an emotional attachment, but instead as a means for achieving their success. They can come across as detached, cold and aloof. They are unable to share emotions, but can mimic emotions, although these emotions are cold and shallow.
- *Immunity to stress*: The corporate psychopath appears to be immune under stress and will remain calm under pressure. When pressure intensifies, it seems that the corporate psychopath is able to thrive. While others are struggling with the pressure and stress of the situation, they appear cool, calm and collected. People envy their ability to effectively navigate through the situation and to remain unaffected. The corporate

psychopath leader will create chaos in order to throw others off. In one case, a CEO came in to create change for the sake of change; there was no need for the change to happen as the organization was working effectively, but the leader felt that the environment was boring and that they needed to change everything. He purposely created scenarios of change followed by chaos, which made him excited. By doing so, he was able to show his strength under pressure while others were falling apart under the constant stress that was caused. In this case the chaos that he created was something that he could control and he perceived himself as a successful leader who was able to think outside the box. The problem was that he chose to implement the same changes that he used with another organization and to create a system that he was most familiar with. Because of these changes, others failed within the system and the organization struggled under the weight of constant change. Those in upper leadership started to question him and they were called obstructionists and were terminated to be replaced by yes people.

- *Parasitic*: The corporate psychopath's parasitic personality creates relationships which focus on attaching themselves to people who will help them to move forward. They will latch on to a person, get what they can from them and then move on to someone else. There is no personal attachment to the person who they are connected with.

- *Charming yet superficial*: The corporate psychopath is extremely charming. As a result of this charming presence, they are viewed by others as extremely likeable, intelligent and fascinating. This is a person who people want to get to know. They will use storytelling that is captivating and enticing. Through these stories, they will build a rapport with others. They come across as entertaining. When talking to a corporate psychopath leader, they will have an answer for everything and will come across as intelligent and wise. They will use their charm to ingratiate themselves with others, especially at a leadership level. This charm will be used on people who can help them to further their career. In these cases they will come across as engaging, gracious, kind and patient. The charm is superficial and while on the surface it seems impressive, there is little to no substance to their actions. In addition to coming across as charming, they will also appear to be very polished. They are extremely professional and self-assured, yet when their actions are confronted, they will come across as frightening, terrorizing and intimidating.

- *Ruthless and calculating*: As stated earlier, psychopath leaders enjoy considerable power. In order to promote themselves, they will surround themselves with people who will support their mindset. Usually, when a new psychopath leader takes on a new team, they will size up the players, building their trust and confidence so that they will share information. This is done in a calculating way in order to weed out people who they feel are threats. The leader will then surround themselves with "yes" people in order to implement their goals. These people will be hand selected by the leader and will be chosen based on what they can offer to them. Once they are no longer needed or suit their purpose, they are discarded.

- *Extroverted*: The psychopath leader will possess strong communication skills and will have no social inhibitions whatsoever. They are extremely outgoing and, coupled with their charm, they can come across as being too good to be true. They demonstrate high levels of extroversion and will insert themselves easily within any social setting or situation.

- *Politically astute*: The psychopath leader will be a master at navigating the political environment of the organization. They align themselves with the right people who provide them with the most benefits. They know all the key players and individuals who can help them to succeed. They identify people who can benefit them the most: individuals who control resources, decision makers, gatekeepers or people with some form of formal or informal power and status. They understand and recognize the political landscape. While others may struggle with the internal politics of the organization, the psychopath leader is fully aware and excels at these dynamics.
- *Strong influencing skills*: Because of their ability to influence others, the corporate psychopath seems to be the ideal leader. They possess many of the characteristics we look for in leaders. They come across as extremely confident, charming and intelligent. They are well liked by their followers, who they can influence to follow them and to implement their visions. They will come across as very normal and well functioning. They are extremely capable of getting people to buy into their vision, strategy and direction.

Hiring a corporate psychopath leader

Earlier we touched upon how organizational systems are designed to assist the corporate psychopath. Many wonder how a psychopath leader can be hired by an organization and go unnoticed. However, it is very easy to be impressed by their credentials and the portrayed success of the psychopath leader, whether this success is true or false. The psychopath will use impression management, including charisma and creative verbal skills, to win over interviewers. Corporate psychopaths have been known to provide fake résumés with false credentials, degrees that do not exist and exaggerated work experience. An excellent example of an individual who was able to effectively exaggerate and lie about his credentials was Frank Abagnale, Jr. We know him best from the movie *Catch Me if You Can*. In real life he was able to successfully draw paychecks from Pan Am as a pilot and later portrayed himself as a doctor and as a prosecutor without ever having the training or skillsets required for these positions. Corporate psychopaths manipulate people who do not have work experience with them to provide glowing references. Their résumés are embellished to fit whatever position they are applying for. During interviews, they are perceived as the perfect fit both on paper as well as in person. They will have completed their homework on the organization and the key leaders, as well as the position they are applying for. As a chameleon, they will change to fit the hiring needs of the organization.

As stated earlier, corporate psychopaths enjoy working for organizations that are in chaos and turmoil, and will play this to their advantage during the interview process. They are drawn to these types of positions, which offer high rewards, salaries and positions that draw bonuses based on performance. When applying for positions, they will deliberately look for organizations that may be struggling or ones that have loose organizational systems in place. These are prime targets that can be easily manipulated and the corporate psychopath will use these loose systems to benefit their agenda and to feed their need for greed. Once they have been hired, they will meet the goals set forth by the organization, or at least will appear to. In some cases, this is done in an ethical manner and in other cases they will create fictitious accounts, over-inflate numbers and use clever manipulation in

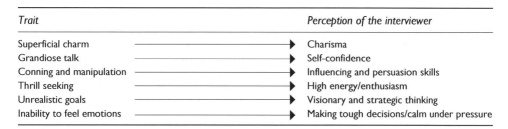

Figure 7.1 Perceptions of the corporate psychopath leadership candidate

order to make their business units look successful. Once they recognize little attention is being paid to them, they will quickly maneuver themselves into leadership positions in order to have greater access to finances, status or whatever they are looking for.

The perception that the corporate psychopath demonstrates during the interview process can often be perceived differently through the lens of a business leader. During the interview process, the following traits of a psychopath leader can often be misconstrued. Figure 7.1 demonstrates the traits demonstrated and how they can be perceived by the interviewer.

Why people follow the psychopath leader

The psychopath leader is one who is viewed by their followers as being creative and innovative. On the surface, their ideas will come across as being revolutionary and communicated in such a way that most people want to buy into the idea. Because the psychopathic leader is a strong verbal communicator, they are able to communicate ideas and innovations effectively. However, while the communication comes across as full of flowery business jargon on the surface, it is very superficial and the communication has little to no substance. Nonetheless, followers will regard the corporate psychopath as someone they want to get to know, to be associated with and to follow. They are enthralled by their persona.

Once followers recognize that something about the behavior of the psychopath leader is off, they become fearful of that leader. The psychopath leader will begin to develop or create a culture of fear. Employees will fear a climate of aggressive retaliation. In some cases the corporate psychopath leader will become aggressive in their behavior, using verbal abuse or public humiliation, and they will single out and isolate their targets. In other cases they will use charm and persuasion, causing the follower to fall under their spell, only to be exploited and abused to meet the needs of the leader. How the leader perceives the situation is how they will act. Depending on the psychopath leader's behavior, followers will either be charmed or will dread working for them. Those who dread working with the leader will eventually leave the unit of the organization for another job. Those who are charmed will be left confused and dazed once these behaviors come to the surface and they realize they have been used.

Upper leadership and key clients will find the psychopath leader very charming and pleasurable to work with, because corporate psychopaths adjust their persona to charm key clients and upper leadership so the latter they become enamored with them. These key constituents play a major factor in increasing the psychopath's need to be accepted into the inner circle and they will adjust their behavior according to the situation. They will focus their attention on building their relationships with people who are known to hold positions of power and who can help them.

Addressing the psychopathic leader

When working with a psychopath leader, people are often caught off-guard, realizing too late the type of leader they are dealing with. People do not recognize the corporate psychopathic leader's behavior until it is too late and usually after they have left the organization. Due to no fault of their own, individuals lack the understanding and awareness of these behaviors. In addition, it can be difficult to understand this type of behavior and we are unable to think like a psychopath or to comprehend the extremes that they will go to in order to achieve their goals. When exposed to a psychopath leader, targets will not see the behavior immediately. Since people do not encounter corporate psychopaths on a daily basis, many are not skilled at addressing this type of behavior. Having the skills to deal with someone who is manipulating, conniving and deceitful can be a challenge. We are not aware of these behaviors until it is too late and we are entangled within the web that has been spun. The behavior will manifest slowly and in time the behaviors and traits will start to show through, but only after the damage is done. The corporate psychopath will have embezzled or stolen millions of dollars, implemented false reporting of numbers or created elaborate schemes that are difficult to unravel.

When addressing a psychopath leader, the target may be faced with several different behaviors. The first is that the psychopath may become defensive and continue to lie. They may become charming and try to take on the psychological persona that they believe will appease the target's needs. For example, if the target has a psychological need to be liked, the psychopath leader will change their persona to address this need, which will shift the focus away from the issue. They might befriend this person, focusing on building a false relationship with them. In other cases the psychopath leader will try to minimize the situation or shift the focus toward someone or something else. This tactic is designed to catch the target off-guard and then go in for the strike. The strike might not happen right away; the leader will divert the topic or focus and then may strike later when the target does not expect it. When the strike takes place, it will be swift and unexpected. The follower will begin to fear the leader and will not address the behavior again. The target may be blamed or in the middle of an unethical situation that the corporate psychopath has created and will then find the need to report the events in order to protect themselves from further damage.

What is important to recognize is that this type of personality (much like that of the narcissist) is difficult to change. It is also hard to oust corporate psychopaths from the organization and they will leave on their own terms, often with a hefty severance package in hand. If someone is willing to try to oust the psychopath leader, they should prepare for a battle, since such leaders will not leave willingly or without some sort of payout. In addition, the corporate psychopath leader will have the upper leadership charmed and it will be difficult to get the latter to see what is happening. Only if there is malicious disreputable behavior will the upper leadership pay attention. However, because of the depth and breadth of this behavior, the organization may not want the outside world to find out what has happened and may quietly pay the corporate psychopath to leave the organization, allowing them to move on to another organization.

Building the skills to recognize the behavior of the corporate psychopath

As mentioned above, the dysfunctional psychopathic behaviors of the corporate psychopath will manifest slowly and over time. When individuals start to recognize the behavior and stop to reflect on this person's actions, clarity starts to set in. In hindsight, individuals will recognize that this is not the first time they have experienced this type of abnormal behavior – there was the time that they were blaming someone else or taking the credit for other people's work. When dealing with a psychopath leader, it is imperative for the person involved to listen to their inner voice and their feelings. In this case, intuition is a follower's best friend. We put leaders on a pedestal that many believe makes them infallible. This is what the psychopath leader is hoping for – they are hoping to be worshiped and to be looked upon as incapable of doing wrong. By listening to their inner voice and feelings, individuals will become aware of understated clues. After working with the leader, an individual may feel anxious, confused and like something just isn't right. More than often, the person is left questioning the situation and in many cases questioning themselves. They feel ashamed, naïve, humiliated and angry, often not reporting what has happened to them. However, they must recognize that they are not at fault. The psychopath leader has spent years fine-tuning their skills of deception and lying. This may be the first time that an individual has been exposed to this type of behavior and it does not seem natural because it isn't.

Conclusion

The corporate psychopath has the skill and ability to manipulate, con and lie to others. Understanding their dysfunction is often difficult until it is too late. We are frequently pulled into their web as a result of their charm, intelligence and persona. They fulfill something in us that we are looking for or need. They are masters at this type of manipulation. Loose systems and constant change help to fuel the corporate psychopath's pathology. They are able to come across as successful individuals who are able to handle pressure, chaos and change effectively. They will position themselves as saviors to the organization or to the target. They take on whatever persona is needed at that time and they enjoy fitting into the scenario that is best for the organization or the situation, adjusting their behavior accordingly.

For many, the behavior of a psychopath will be foreign. We may be enamored by their behavior and enthralled by who they are and how they portray themselves. We may have little experience with these types of individuals. Identifying their actions is often only achieved long after they are gone. They are masters of deception and at building strong relationships. They will ensconce themselves within an organization and embed themselves into leadership quickly. These individuals meet the psychological and physical needs of their followers and will fit into the persona that is needed.

References

Babiak, P., & Hare, R. 2006. *Snakes in suits: When psychopaths go to work*. New York: HarperCollins.

Babiak, P., Neumann, C. S., & Hare, R. D. 2010. Corporate psychopathy: Talking the walk. *Behavioral Sciences & the Law, 28*(2), 174–193.

Boddy, C. 2005. The implications of corporate psychopaths for business and society: An initial examination and a call to arms. *Australian Journal of Business and Behavioral Sciences, 1*(2), 30–40.

Boddy, C. 2014. Corporate psychopaths, conflict, employee affective wellbeing and counterproductive work behavior. *Journal of Business Ethics, 121*(1), 107–121.

Gudmundsson, A., & Southey, G. 2011. Leadership and the rise of the corporate psychopath: What can business schools do about the "snakes inside"? *Journal of Social and Behavioral Research in Business, 2*(2), 18–27.

Shouten, R., & Silver, J. 2012. *Almost a psychopath: Do I (or does someone I know) have a problem with manipulation and lack of empathy?* Cambridge, MA: Harvard University Press.

Chapter 8

Machiavellian leadership
The story of a prince

> A man who wishes to make a profession of goodness in everything must necessarily come to grief among so many who are not good. Therefore, it is necessary to learn how not to be good and to use this knowledge and not use it, according to the necessity of the case.
>
> Machiavelli (1532)

Introduction

Machiavellianism is named after the sixteenth-century politician and philosopher Niccolò Machiavelli, who is known as one of the greatest theorists on the subject of power and most notably for his book, *The Prince*. The book focuses on the political and moral perspectives of leadership. Machiavelli explains that in the sixteenth century, in order for political leaders and nobility to be influential, powerful and successful, it was crucial to utilize any tactics necessary. These tactics included lying and deception, as well as manipulation. These suggested tactics were methods to be used in order to excel as a leader.

Machiavelli is credited for the phrase "the end justifies the means" (Machiavelli, 1950). In 1532, his compelling and popular narrative, *The Prince*, was published. This narrative provided advice to leaders of that time in terms of how to go about acquiring and main-taining power over others during times of uncertainty and change. His approach to power focused on ways to achieve and maintain it, and to prevent others from taking it away. The focus was devoid of trust, honor or democracy. He believed that followers could be easily manipulated to follow the leader's agenda and goals.

Many researchers have analyzed the writings of Machiavelli and *The Prince*, labeling him as the Anti-Christ and a tortured soul, and *The Prince* as a handbook for tyrants. Yet it is still one of the world's most influential leadership books, even in today's modern leadership studies. During an interview with Jared Diamond, a Pulitzer Prize-winning author, he was asked which book would he require President Barack Obama to read and he replied "*The Prince*." Diamond went on to say that all US presidents and leaders should read the book as a guide on how to be strategic, to prepare for what can go wrong and to plan accordingly for it (Shorey, 2013). Some call the works of Machiavelli a guide to amoral behavior, while others believe that his work focused on encouraging leaders not to feel helpless, regardless of the situation they found themselves in. Some view his works as having negative constructs, while others view this type of leadership approach as being positive for organizations. The writings of Machiavelli at the time were fitting based on the societal norms and constructs. The perceptions today fluctuate between positive and negative depending on the interpretations of the reader.

The Prince remains one of the most controversial yet influential books ever written; almost 500 years after its publication, it remains one of the most debated and discussed leadership titles. Some argue that while the book was written during a time when nobles used whatever means they could to conquer and maintain empires, it is not suited to today's leadership. The perception is that this type of leadership approach in today's world is one that is tied to tyrants and other dysfunctional leadership traits. Others argue that Machiavellian concepts have been misunderstood. Some believe that *The Prince* is a handbook for leaders to restore and fix problems within organizations and governments. Each view has its merits. From the dysfunctional leadership aspect, Machiavellian leadership is the third component of the Dark Triad. It is similar to narcissism and psychopathy, yet there are subtle differences with this dysfunctional leadership style. For the purposes of this book, we will explore the dysfunctional components surrounding Machiavellian leadership.

Niccolò Machiavelli

To understand Machiavellian leadership and how it applies to the twenty-first-century leader, it is important to understand just who Niccolò Machiavelli was, along with his insights into leadership; understanding his approaches and beliefs is important in order to understand his philosophies and how they were applied during this time.

Niccolò Machiavelli was born in Florence in 1469 to a Tuscan family (Harris, 2010). The Machiavellis owned properties in Santo Spirito, located near Santa Felicita and the Ponte Vecchio in Florence, where the family was well established, were notable members of society and served as leading civic figures. Some have hinted that Machiavelli's father was illegitimate (Jensen, 1960). Because of this thinking, it is believed that he was precluded from being a candidate for any political positions, but this did not exclude him from service as a public servant to the city. As such, he spent most of his career serving powerful political figures.

At a young age, Niccolò received his first lesson in leadership when a coup failed which was focused on the Medici family. Supporters of the coup included the Pope and the Archbishop of Florence. During this time, Lorenzo de Medici was nicknamed Lorenzo the Magnificent. The aim of the coup was to kill Lorenzo and his brother. During prayers, the coup was put into action and Lorenzo's brother was killed, but Lorenzo was able to escape. The government rallied behind the Medici family and those supporting the coup were arrested, including the Archbishop who was hanged in public by his robes. Others were severely tortured and executed; the forms of execution included being torn limb from limb and being roasted over an open flame. The executions were documented by paintings on the wall depicting the execution along with a description of the moral shortcomings of the person and a descriptive account of the execution. The mastermind behind the coup was executed as well. After being buried, it was believed that his body and flesh would pollute the land. His body was exhumed and burned, and his ashes were tossed into the river.

Young Machiavelli was well educated. He was taught Latin, had access to history and was exposed to many of the leading scholars of the time. At the age of 29, he was recognized for his administrative talents and was elected to the post of Chancellor of the Second Chancellery. This was a well-respected position and he was given duties in the Council of Ten of Liberty and Peace, which focused on foreign affairs (Jensen, 1960; Harris, 2010). He went on to serve as a special diplomat and advisor to the Head of the Republic of Florence, Piero Soderini, from 1502 to 1512. Machiavelli served him in several capacities and different interests. He was associated with Da Vinci, Galileo, Raphael and Michelangelo, along with administering funding for their projects. He also managed government regulations and policy. As his career continued to evolve, he was associated with missions to Louis XII and to the Holy Roman Emperor Maximillian in Austria. He associated with the Borgia family, along with Cesare, who was the illegitimate son of Pope Alexander VI. After watching over the papal elections of 1503, he accompanied the newly elected Pope Julius II on his first campaign to conquer Perugia and Bologna. In 1507 he was instrumental in organizing a military force which fought to capture Pisa in 1509. Later this militia force was defeated by the Holy League at Prato and the Medici family returned to power. Following this, Machiavelli found himself excluded from public affairs. As can be imagined, during this time he was able to make both friends and enemies. Many of his powerful enemies were determined that he should not retain any position of power (Harris, McGrath & Harris, 2008).

It was suspected that Machiavelli was involved in the plot against the Medici family. He was imprisoned and falsely accused of involvement in the plot. However, during his imprisonment, he was repeatedly tortured using a hoist and drop device, which fractured his collarbone. He repeatedly maintained his innocence and under the direction of the new Medici Pope, Leo X, he was granted amnesty. He returned to his home, retired and lived with his wife and children. He desperately wanted to return to government service, but because of his past associations, he was restricted and never regained a position in public service. At the age of 43, his public service career was over. It was during this time that he focused on the studies and writings for which he is best remembered for today. Several decades later, his principles resonated with many. It is the emphasis on the acquisition of power that allows these concepts to thrive in today's world of leadership.

Machiavelli on leadership

Machiavelli's stance on leadership has always been viewed as controversial. He does make it quite clear that his view was not always based on virtuous principles, but focused on effective leadership at any means possible. He did not wrestle with the concept of leadership. He judged mankind as having two constructs: good and evil. He had a keen understanding of human nature and was focused on ways in which leaders could control followers. At that time, his advice to leaders was to be ruthless and cunning. He believed that there was only one type of bad leader and that was a leader who was weak. He believed the role of a leader was to keep subordinates in line, even if it meant using cruelty (Kellerman, 2004). It is crucial to note that during this time, individuals were ruthless when it came to power and control. Assassinations, attempts to overthrow opposition, and executions to eliminate threats were common practice.

Machiavelli believed that liberty is dependent upon internal stability and the state being free of any type of external domination (Machiavelli, 1950). The first priority of the state or government was to secure liberty and freedom for all. Having said that, he believed that the state should do whatever needed to be done to secure liberty and freedom. This meant tactics of kindness or cruelty, justice or injustice, grace or disgrace. His focus was an honorable one in today's world of the pursuit of liberty and freedom. It could be argued that in today's world, many have died to ensure that these rights have been and will be maintained in many countries.

Machiavelli goes on to share that he believed that mankind is never truly content with what it has. It is mankind's ambition that will ultimately cause corruption, and corruption will spread, causing a cycle (Machiavelli, 1950). He suggested that the state was constantly undergoing changes because of corruption. He also believed that leaders needed to take bold action and leadership to seize the moment and to move the state forward, even during times where corruption was rife (Viroli, 2008).

Machiavelli's stance on leadership is quite pessimistic. He dispelled the notion that a leader should be virtuous. He believed that if a leader acts in a principled and moral way, they are being naïve in a world where others may not act in that way. Furthermore, he believed that leadership is not measured by the character of the leader, but instead by the acquisition of power through the gaining of land and wealth, as well as influence and power. How the leader goes about obtaining these items is not important as long as the ultimate goal of achieving power and success is achieved while maintaining liberty and freedom.

Machiavelli believed that at the root of mankind was evil. Because evil was inherent in all, it was important to be on one's guard at all times: "Men have less hesitation to offend oneself who makes himself loved than one who makes himself feared; for life is held by a chain of obligation, which, because man is wicked, is broken at every opportunity for their own utility, but fear is held by dread of punishment that never forsakes you" (Machiavelli, 1950: 67). The translation of this quote is that it is more beneficial for a leader to be feared than to be loved. When a leader is feared, this will ensure loyalty from followers. Machiavelli believed that because mankind is prone to "evil," eventually people will turn on the leader if there is an element of love. Essentially, if the leader is feared, then there is an element of control that the leader possesses over the follower and the follower is less likely to turn on the leader.

Leadership in the eyes of Machiavelli was something that could be achieved by anyone; he believed that leadership was not issued through "divine birthright," which was primarily the case in his time. In *The Prince*, he does not use the term "Prince" as it relates to nobility or royalty; instead, any person who is able to acquire land, wealth, success and prestige was considered a "Prince."

Machiavelli also believed that most leaders start off fighting for a cause and following a belief that what they are doing is right. Eventually, as the leader tastes power, status and prestige, their motive changes and focuses on their own personal advancement and acquisition of power and wealth. For many, power is considered to be a very addictive drug that stimulates the need for more. In order to achieve and maintain power, Machiavelli believed that a leader needed to be ready at all times and to have the ability to change quickly. This change might be a change in methods, strategy or direction. The leader should be ready for the next political maneuver and those leaders who are not ready will ultimately fail. This means that the leader needs to be constantly analyzing and strategizing the next move of their opponents and must never let their guard down. Machiavelli's philosophies are a product of his time, during which these principles may have been successful. He did not advocate that brutal and devious actions should be adopted as the norm; he believed that leaders should act in accordance with the times.

Machiavellianism defined

Through the years, as the principles of Machiavelli and *The Prince* have been adopted, a type of leadership philosophy has emerged called Machiavellian leadership or Machiavellianism. There are many different definitions of Machiavellianism. The *Oxford English Dictionary* defines it as "the employment of cunning and duplicity in statecraft of general conduct." Christie and Geis (1970b) defined the Machiavellian leader as one who uses manipulation and individuals to achieve their goals. They found that in today's world, Machiavellian principles focus on self-love, never needing to apologize for one's actions and twisting the truth to one's own advantage.

Machiavellian research

Based on the works of Machiavelli, Christie and Geis (1970a) explored the concept of Machiavellianism from a personality standpoint. They went on to investigate whether or not the concepts presented by Machiavelli were practiced in modern times. Their research found that Machiavellianism was a personality trait focused on the willingness and ability to manipulate and deceive others in order to achieve personal gain. They found that individuals possessing this type of dysfunctional style were low in terms of personality trait agreeableness. Typically, these individuals come across as cynical, rude, suspicious and manipulating. Through their research, they developed an instrument called the MACH-IV scale, which measures levels of Machiavellianism. Often referred to as MACH scores, individuals rate either high or low. Individuals scoring high on the MACH-IV scale were found to have low emotional involvement with individuals and/or situations. It was also discovered that high MACHs were successful at manipulation, effective at task orientation and had a high tendency to control (Christie & Geis, 1970b). There are three sets of values that are measured through the instrument:

1. A belief in the effectiveness and manipulative tactics in dealing with others. Ultimately the leader should never tell anyone the real reason behind their motives unless sharing this information is beneficial for them.
2. A cynical view of human nature. It is best to believe that all people have an evil streak and that eventually it will display itself at some point. For the leader, it is best to be on guard and prepared. Having this viewpoint will not result in the leader being surprised by the motives and actions of others.
3. Moral outlook can put expediency above principle. It is hard to get ahead without cutting corners and ultimately the leader should take whatever steps they can to achieve their goal, regardless of how they get there. Individuals are reminded in this case that "The end justifies the means" (Machiavelli, 1950).

Further research from Christie and Geis (1970b) focused on four components associated with manipulation:

1   Lack of affect in interpersonal relationships. People are viewed as objects or as pawns used as a means to an end. Once used, they are quickly disposed of and others are identified to help identify needs that should be met.
2   Lack of concern with conventional morality. People who manipulate others do not have a moral view, but rather a single view of themselves and their goals
3   Lack of gross psychopathology. These are individuals who manipulate and do not hold a rational view in relation to others. Their reality of people and situations is distorted to justify their actions.
4   Low ethical commitment. Manipulators are focused on accomplishing tasks in the present and give little regard to the long-term ramifications of their actions. They are not interested in the ethical or moral implications of their actions.

Machiavellianism is "a strategy of social conduct that involves manipulating others for personal gain, often against the others' interest" (Wilson, Near & Miller, 1996: 285). Machiavellian leaders are known for their political and strategic thinking in leadership roles. They are masters at effectively navigating complex power dynamics, as well as looking for opportunities to abuse power without guilt or shame (Judge, Piccolo & Kosalka, 2009). The positive construct of this leadership approach demonstrates leaders who have high motivation and who are very effective in leading. Their motivation is the achievement of their own goals along with the goals of the organization. These leaders are motivated by extrinsic factors such as financial gain. They have similarities to the narcissist and the psychopath, as they are very politically astute and understand the importance of navigating the political landscape of the organization (Becker & O'Hair, 2007).

Ethics and Machiavellianism

In the 1970s, researchers (Christie & Geis, 1970a) focused on the concepts of Machiavellianism. They examined this construct through the lens of Machiavelli's *The Prince*. Concepts in *The Prince* were used as the best way to rule subjects or, in today's world, followers. Machiavelli advocated using manipulative, harsh and deceitful behaviors, but he also said that such behaviors should only be used when necessary. Today's scholars argue that Machiavelli's approach was unethical. Others argue that his approach was too simplistic. It is important to point out that Machiavelli advocated these approaches only when the freedom of the state or justice was threatened. In today's world, this would be considered a state of emergency. In Machiavelli's time, there was a time and a place for this type of leadership – a time of corruption, amoral activity and instability. Others argue that Machiavelli's leadership approach is one that is best suited for today's world of leadership.

Accordingly, Machiavellian leadership endorses a negative view of people, resulting in tendencies to act in an unethical manner (Kish-Gephart, Harrison & Trevino, 2010). This type of dysfunctional leader believes that they are highly skilled at the art of manipulation, while circumventing rules and regulations established by organizations. They try to bend the rules without breaking them and to walk a thin line between ethical and unethical behavior. The Machiavellian leader finds rules and structures to be a restriction on their behavior. They are usually fairly successful in their careers, especially in environments that lack structure. As the organizational structure begins to tighten and more control is established, the success of the Machiavellian leader will begin to decrease. They are typically disliked by others and, as a result, they may struggle with politicking and positioning in the workplace. They are not as charismatic as the narcissistic leader or the psychopath. Instead, they rely on the tactics of manipulation, lying, cheating and betraying others.

The principles of Machiavellianism

In order to understand Machiavellian leadership, it is important to understand the principles surrounding the construct. It is through each individual's viewpoint that the principles derived from Machiavellianism may be interpreted. Leaders who are considered to be Machiavellian leaders are seen as being politically astute and attuned to the politics of the organization. They are able to effectively navigate the power dynamics within the organization and possess strong strategic skills, recognizing and anticipating their opponent's next move. For the Machiavellian leader, it is up to their own interpretation of the following as to whether they will use the principles in a positive or negative way:

- *It is better to be feared than loved*: The Machiavellian leader is likely do whatever it takes to achieve their goals. Building relationships that are based on fear is the foundation of the Machiavellian leader's behavior. Through fear, it is believed that the leader will be respected. The Machiavellian leader will have a low level of emotional involvement with others. They do not care about other people's feelings, rights, personal needs or goals. They will come across as cold, rude, suspicious of others, cynical, manipulative and detached. Their focus is on their own needs and not the needs of others. They are predisposed to take revenge on others.
- *Avoid being hated except during war*: In non-competitive situations and low-stakes environments, the Machiavellian leader can be quite tolerable. It is during times of stress, competition and chaos that their personality will change. When there is something to be gained, they will view this as an opportunity for competition and their focus is on winning. During this time, they become difficult to work with, competitive and aggressive. They believe everything is part of one big game that they are playing – the workplace, their careers and every interaction with every individual are all part of this game. It is part of a master plan to either gain power or influence, or position themselves in an advantageous spot. They are not focused on the feelings of others, let alone the feelings of members of a team or group. They invest little time and energy in maintaining relationships within a group.
- *A capable leader must be cunning*: The Machiavellian leader believes that they were born to lead and that this is their destiny. As a result, they feel that they need to be in charge, in positions of authority, and will do whatever it takes to get there. The tactics they use to achieve these goals include being underhanded, deceitful, two-faced or stepping on people to get to the top. Some view this as a negative trait, while others view the leader as being driven and determined to win. They will never reveal their true motives and intentions. They will control all situations and individuals, sharing information only on a need-to-know basis. They can be extremely controlling and can be persuasive when necessary.
- *People will inevitability lie to you, so it is OK to lie to them*: As mentioned above, there is little trust felt by the Machiavellian leader. They do not trust others and are highly suspicious of the actions and motives of others. They are likely to take revenge on

others and they lie regularly to their friends, co-workers and superiors. They are a chameleon who is able to adapt to different situations and will subtly manipulate the situation with their behavior (Rauthmann & Kolar, 2013).

- *The ends justify the means*: Many Machiavellian leaders believe that the end justifies the means – that any actions or steps taken to allow them to achieve their end result are justified, even if these acts involved are unethical. They are constantly analyzing their next move and strategizing how to win and who their opponent is. They are very politically astute and will know all the power players along with the power dynamics within the organization.

From these principles Machiavellian leadership derives its negative connotation. However, it is also easy to see how others believe that these principles are necessary in the highly competitive, global and diverse organizations that exist today. There are the components of Machiavellian leadership that were best suited for Machiavelli's time, while other concepts can be modified to fit leadership today.

The positive lens of Machiavellian leadership

The works of Machiavelli have been gaining more attention in today's organizational systems that are politically charged and ripe with complexity and ambiguity. There are some who believe that Machiavelli's approach to leadership is best suited for today's organizations. Even in the twenty-first century, his work is studied by many scholars and can be found as part of the curriculum of business schools. There is merit to this line of thinking. It can be argued that there are positive constructs related to Machiavellian leadership. Machiavellian leaders tend to be highly motivated to lead and are very effective at running organizations. It is their philosophy to invest in their own goals and, as a result, they achieve the goals of the organization. Their motivation is extrinsically and financially rewarded. When organizations tie compensation to productivity and profitability, these leaders thrive. With extrinsic rewards tied to performance, it is the goal of the Machiavellian leader to produce the results needed to achieve this goal. In a sense, it is a win/win for both the Machiavellian leader and the organization. The leader will be highly motivated in achieving results to attain their extrinsic motivating factors. They are able to effectively use various leadership styles such as influencing, impression management and charisma to achieve these goals.

The characteristics and traits of a Machiavellian leader

There are four constructs of Machiavellianism as outlined by Dahling, Whitaker and Levy (2009): (1) distrust in others; (2) desire for status; (3) desire for control; and (4) willingness to engage in the amoral manipulation of others (as cited by Zettler and Solga, 2013). Leaders demonstrating high levels of Machiavellian tendencies are focused on quick gains and wins rather than principles and morality. In many cases, they will tell people what they want to hear, even if it is a lie. They believe that no one should be completely trusted and will withhold the truth from others. They believe that trusting others will only result in negative consequences. Organizational Machiavellianism is the belief that manipulation is necessary to achieve one's desired ends in the context of the work environment.

The Machiavellian leader can be manipulative and deceitful, yet can be accommodating and respectful if necessary in order to get what they want.

The Machiavellian leader believes in people's gullibility and, with their lack of concern for individual's rights, they will lead with manipulation. The following list will detail the four constructs of Machiavellianism in the corporate context in further detail:

- *Distrust of others*: The Machiavellian leader is highly distrustful of others. As a result, they will not openly share information with others and will withhold vital information in order to protect themselves. In the corporate setting, they come across as quite dishonest and deceitful. Their actions will be very contradictory. They are masters at the art of being cunning and politically maneuvering for their own benefit and gain. They will tell followers and other leaders what they want to hear in order to achieve their goal, even if what they are telling them is a lie. They believe that one should not completely trust others and doing so results in nothing but negative outcomes.
- *Desire for status*: The Machiavellian leader can demonstrate other traits of the Dark Triad, such as narcissism or psychopathy. They will demonstrate excessive or exaggerated feelings of self-importance, though these feelings often masquerade as something noble. Self-interest is a characteristic associated with a narcissist. The Machiavellian leader is highly intelligent and is motivated by extrinsic factors related to with financial success, status, perks associated with levels of status and prestige, and monetary benefits.
- *Desire for control*: These types of leaders are highly task-focused, with a high tendency to control and give orders. In a sense, they are micro-managers, ensuring that all tasks are monitored and controlled. They will shift their commitments based on what is best for their personal strategy. Leaders demonstrating high levels of Machiavellian tendencies are focused on expediency as opposed to principles.
- *Willingness to engage in amoral manipulation of others*: The Machiavellian leader is less likely to follow rules, procedures and processes or obey ethical and moral standards.

Machiavellian leadership in modern times

In modern times, there are some who believe that Machiavelli's ideas are fundamental principles in today's international laws and the basis of good governance and business practices. There are leaders who have taken the words of Machiavelli quite literally. The Machiavellian leader in today's modern society looks to manipulate and use methods of deceit as a means to justify their behavior. Both formal and informal power is used to control and/or manipulate others in order to gain an advantage over these others. The leader's ultimate aim is to achieve their goals rather than care for the well-being of others.

Conclusion

Machiavellian leadership is quite controversial and a source of much debate in leadership research. The principle of Machiavellian leadership was well suited at one time and the debate continues as to whether this approach is still applicable in today's organization. While the concepts of Machiavellian leadership can be applied today, it is the dysfunctional components of the theory that are detrimental to organizations and followers. Negative Machiavellian leaders are dangerous in their approach to leading and maneuvering for their own personal gain. Through deception, manipulation and unethical behavior, the negative Machiavellian leader is able to excel. The concepts of strategic thinking and navigating politically charged environments can be an advantage for leaders today. So, while some of the concepts and beliefs of Machiavellian leadership have a place in organizations today, other negative features of this type of leadership do not.

In Part II we have examined each of the elements of the Dark Triad: narcissism, psychopathy and Machiavellian leadership. As has been demonstrated, there are similarities in these leadership constructs, but there are also subtle differences. The Dark Triad continues to attract attention in scholarly research as there is more to understand in relation to organizational and follower impact, as well as addressing these behaviors. Next we will examine the impact of dysfunctional leadership on followers as well as organizations.

References

Becker, J., & O'Hair, H. 2007. Machiavellian's motives in organizational citizenship behavior. *Journal of Applied Communication Research, 35*(3), 246–267.

Christie R., & Geis, F. 1970a. *Studies in Machiavellianism.* San Diego, CA: Academic Press.

Christie, R., & Geis F. 1970b. Relationships between Machiavellianism. In *Studies in Machiavellianism.* San Diego, CA: Academic Press.

Dahling, J., Whitaker, B., & Levy, P. 2009. The development and validation of a new Machiavellianism scale. *Journal of Management, 35,* 219–257.

Harris, P. 2010. Machiavelli and the global compass: Ends and means in ethics and leadership. *Journal of Business Ethics, 93,* 131–138.

Harris, P., McGrath, C., & Harris, I. 2008. Machiavellian marketing: Justifying the ends and means in modern politics. In D.W. Johnson (ed.), *Handbook of political management* (pp. 537–555). London: Routledge.

Jensen, D. 1960. *Machiavelli: Cynic, patriot, or political scientist?* Lexington, MD: D.D. Heath and Co.

Judge, T., Piccolo, R., & Kosalka, T. 2009. The bright and dark sides of leader traits. A review and theoretical extension of the leader trait paradigm. *Leadership Quarterly, 20,* 855–875.

Kellerman, B. 2004. *Bad leadership: What it is, how it happens, why it matters.* Boston, MA: Harvard Business School Press.

Kish-Gephart, D., Harrison, D., & Trevino, L. 2010. Bad apples, bad cases, and bad barrels: Meta-analytic evidence about sources of unethical decisions at work. *Journal of Applied Psychology, 95*(1), 1–31.

Machiavelli, N. 1950. *The Prince.* New York: Modern Library (original work published in 1532).

Rauthmann, J., & Kolar, G. 2013. Positioning the Dark Triad in the interpersonal circumplex: The friendly-dominant narcissist, hostile-submissive Machiavellian, and hostile-dominant psychopath? *Personality and Individual Differences, 54*(5), 622–627.

Shorey, P. 2013. Interview with Jared Diamond. *New York Times Book Review.*

Viroli, M. 2008. *Machiavelli.* London: Granta.

Wilson, D., Near, D., & Miller, R. 1996. Machiavellianism: A synthesis of the evolutionary and psychological literature. *Psychological Bulletin, 119*(2), 285–299.

Zettler, I., & Solga, M. 2013. Not enough of a dark trait? Linking Machiavellianism to job performance. *European Journal of Personality, 27,* 545–554.

Part III

Addressing dysfunctional leadership from an organizational and individual standpoint

Chapter 9

The role played by organizations and followers in dysfunctional leadership

> The culture of an organization is like a river. It can be fluid, strong and consistent, serving as a lubricant while guiding its members in the right direction. In contrast a river can become stale and toxic, silently killing those who drink at its shores.
>
> Ron Kaufman (2002)

Introduction

At this point in the book, we will shift gears and examine the context of how the organization helps to support the behavior of dysfunctional leadership. We will also explore how dysfunctional leadership impacts the organization, including how it works against the organizational culture, norms and behaviors. In some of the chapters, we have touched upon this impact to organizations, but have only done so in relation to that specific dysfunction. Organizations may face one or several different types of dysfunctions. In most cases it will experience several different types. This chapter explores the overall impact of dysfunctional leaders and the costs associated with these behaviors.

Impact on the organization

Leadership plays a critical role in relation to the organization that they lead. Positive leaders have paved the way to creating exciting, innovative, creative, healthy and successful organizations. In contrast, dysfunctional leaders have led to the downfall of once-successful organizations. These types of leaders ultimately abuse their position, status and power, and will leave their organizations worse than when they arrived (Ashforth, 1997; Aubrey, 2012).

A study conducted by Moore and Lynch (2007) found that organizations exposed to dysfunctional leadership experienced work cultures that were autocratic, bureaucratic and hands-off. Of course, organizations that were not exposed to dysfunctional leadership found work environments to be friendly, supportive and productive. Dysfunctional leadership impacts many different levels within the organization. From the front line of leadership to the executive office, dysfunctional leaders are embedded. Their behavior affects morale, motivation, teamwork, the organizational culture and productivity, as well as the overall health of the organization and followers. The cost of dysfunctional leadership impacts many other areas. Table 9.1 illustrates further insights into other types of impacts on the organization.

124 Enabling dysfunctional leaders

Table 9.1 The impact of dysfunctional behavior

Avoidance	Ostracizing	Increase in gossip or rumors
Withholding important information needed to complete work	Elimination of proactive behaviors Behaviors become more reactive	Lost time/lost productivity
Employees become less committed to the organization and/or work	Decreased time in the workplace and increase in absenteeism	Higher turnover rates

The following list will examine in further detail the impact of dysfunctional leadership on the organization from many different viewpoints:

- *Poorer financial results*: A tangible result of dysfunctional leadership is the impact on the organization in terms of poor financial performance and lack of goal achievement. These factors are demonstrated in a negative impact on the bottom line. Dysfunctional leaders, regardless of their type of dysfunction, are unable to inspire their employees to perform at their best. Instead, they lead by fear, intimidation and manipulation, resulting in employees who become disengaged, are less productive, experience lost time, waste and inefficiency. All of this impacts the organization, resulting in negative financial results.
- *Lack of team synergy*: One of the main points of discussion throughout this book is that the dysfunctional leader thrives in chaotic and tense situations. At times, they will create tension and turmoil in order to further their agendas and goals. Organizational disorder within a team setting is usually focused on dividing the team and pitting team members against one another. Team performance is stalled and employees begin to work in their own personal silos, as they feel that they can't trust others. The synergy of the team is negated. Idea sharing and open discussions are silenced. The leader may choose people who are "yes" people and will agree with them. Other employees recognize that in order to get ahead or to survive, they must agree with the leader. Competitive teamwork becomes the norm as team members compete for the favor of the dysfunctional leader. Departments become fragmented and work roles become less defined. Employees begin to question their importance in the department or the organization as a whole. As a result of the lack of team synergy, there is a natural decline in innovation and creativity, causing teams to become stagnant and stale in their thinking.
- *Healthy conflict is impeded*: Dysfunctional leadership interferes with and blocks healthy conflict. Healthy conflict is needed in organizations in order to drive creativity, innovation and diverse thinking, and to help with decision making. When unhealthy conflict is paramount, individuals tend to want to avoid these types of situations and interactions. Instead, they will go with the flow and focus on not rocking the boat or causing the dysfunctional leader to react. In order to boost the ego of the dysfunctional leader, followers tend to go with whatever decision, agenda or motive is important to that leader. The team or group eventually agrees and in some cases they move into groupthink mode. During healthy conflict, organizations are able to engage in innovation and creative thinking. During unhealthy conflict, innovation and creative thinking become halted and will not move the organization forward. Change becomes difficult, if not impossible, to implement and resistance increases.

- *Low morale*: When employees feel mistreated either by the dysfunctional leader or the organization's lack of addressing the problem, they begin to feel uncertain about the stability of the organization and their careers as a whole. Their focus is no longer on their work, but waiting on the actions of the leader and wondering what the next move from the leader will be. Morale and organizational commitment decline significantly. Employees become angry and mourn the organization that once was. They lose faith in leadership, allowing these types of behaviors to continue.
- *Lost time*: The amount of time and lost productivity related to dysfunctional leadership is extremely high. The following list outlines examples of where time is lost when dealing with dysfunctional leadership:

  (i) the time lost because of employee absenteeism;
  (ii) employees discussing the situation with others, including gossip, rumors and closed-door discussions;
  (iii) lost time for the organization addressing or investigating the situation;
  (iv) lost time and opportunity costs increase.

Increase in turnover. When employees have had enough of the negative behavior, they will look elsewhere. They will either look at other departments within the organization or outside the organization. The dysfunctional leader may block any movement of employees, especially within the organization. They don't want to get rid of their target and will do what they can to prevent this from happening. The dysfunctional leader usually derives a perverse sense of pleasure in keeping employees in their unit so that they can continue to target them. If an employee feels as though they are being blocked or cannot move within the organization, then they will look to leave the organization. Often, the employee will not care where they are going as long as they are out of the clutches of the dysfunctional leader. Leaving is not always easy for the employee. During the interview process for a new position, the employee feels exposed and vulnerable, and their confidence is negatively affected. As a result, they may not interview well. In other cases, they might be going to another dysfunctional leader who picks up on their vulnerable state and identifies them as their next target. If the employee is not careful, they may not recognize the signs as they are excited to leave one predator, only to find themselves back in a negative situation. Eventually other employees will begin to leave the organization and the turnover costs begin to increase. Turnover includes several hidden costs, such as increased overtime, recruitment costs, orientation of a new employee, decreased morale and lost opportunity costs. The following provides an example of a real case that took place, which reflects the costs and impact on the organization.

> Bob ran the GI lab at an inner-city hospital. The GI lab was a profit center for the organization and was the only unit making money in a hospital that was running in the red. Bob liked to hire young nurses to work in his unit. The hospital had a 30-day probationary period. The nurses would be hired, excited to start working at their first job and for the opportunity to make an impression. Bob was very charming and always pleasant during interviews. Nurses were excited to work for Bob. They would start their job with an enthusiastic mindset. Usually on day 28 or 29 of the probationary period, Bob was in the Human Resources department saying that the new nurse or tech was not working out for his unit. Without explanation, the employee

was terminated. The only reason the employee was given was that they were not a good fit for the organization or were not successful during the orientation program. The organization knew about the high turnover rate of the department, which ran at 65 percent. Instead of finding out the root cause of the problem, which was Bob, the organization hired a recruiter whose sole responsibility was to hire for the GI lab. Because of the results within the department, Bob was labelled as a high-potential employee, was put into the cue line for succession planning, and within two years was appointed as director of several departments. In one such department, the turnover rate prior to Bob coming in as director was five percent. Less than a year later, under the direction of Bob, the turnover rate increased to 45 percent. Today Bob is an administrator at this hospital, but they are finding it very hard to recruit for his units since the word is out about the high turnover rate and former employees advise applicants not to work under Bob's direction. In addition, the organization is viewed negatively for allowing this behavior to continue.

Organizational culture and dysfunction

Organizational culture in its most simplistic form can be defined as the roles, norms and values of the organization. Through these norms, roles and values, the organization is able to define and recognize appropriate behaviors as well as encourage healthy behaviors between leaders and employees and also between employees and employees. Employees are indoctrinated into the culture of the organization from their first day with the organization. During their early days of employment, they are exposed to the culture of the organization and begin to internalize these components. Lease (2006) stated that: "Control through cultures is so powerful because once these values are internalized, they become part of the individual's values and the individual follows organizational values without thinking about them."

Researchers have provided many different definitions of organizational culture. The father of organizational culture, Dr. Edgar Schein, provides the following definition: "A pattern of shared basic assumptions learned by a group as it solves its problems of external adaptation and internal integration . . . a product of joint learning" (Schein, 1996: 41). He further identified four categories related to culture: macro-cultures such as nations and global organizations; organizational cultures; sub-cultures (groups within organizations) and micro-cultures (microsystems within an organization). From the basic definition of an organization, he identified three levels of organization cultures, including artifacts (visible), beliefs and values, and basic underlying assumptions (unconscious taken-for-granted beliefs and values).

The most important component of Schein's definition relating to organizational culture is that the "Human mind needs cognitive stability and any challenge of a basic assumption will release anxiety and defensiveness" (Schein, 1996: 44). The research points to one common understanding of organizational culture, which is the strategic element of behaviors and the interactions of individuals within the organization. Schein's belief focuses on the core concept that leadership is the source of the beliefs and values of employees and the organization, and the most central issue for leaders is to understand the deeper levels of a culture within an organization. It is critical that leaders deal with the anxiety that is unleashed when assumptions along with values and norms are challenged.

When employees see that their beliefs of what a leader should or shouldn't be are challenged by the actions of a dysfunctional leader, these assumptions are changed forever. Either anxiety will set in for the followers or they will change their assumptions to fit into the new reality or new culture. In order to further understand the role of organizational culture, let's explore each of its components.

Organizational values

Values are the basis for normalizing behaviors within the organization. "Organizational values reflect the basic beliefs and understandings of individuals about the means and the ends of the organization" (Reino & Vadi, 2010; see also Aubrey, 2012). The values of the organization help to define what the organization believes in and provide insights into how employees should interact with others. Leadership plays a role in defining how people will interact with key stakeholders connected to the organization, while the organizational systems emulate the values and behaviors of their leaders, especially at the senior levels of leadership. When a dysfunctional leader is in place, behaviors will begin to mimic the same dysfunction displayed by that leader. Organizational systems may become a breeding ground that fosters dysfunctional leadership behaviors, while promoting this behavior at all levels of the organization, whether directly or indirectly.

Within an organization, leadership embeds its interpersonal characteristics and personal attributes into the organization. Leaders tend to attract similar individuals to the organization. For example, if the leader is positive and focused on innovation and creativity, then they will attract individuals that encompass these characteristics. If a leader is dysfunctional and promotes a dysfunctional environment, they will likely attract similar individuals into the organization. Just as a positive leader has the ability to influence a positive organizational culture, a dysfunctional leader has the ability to completely morph a culture into a dysfunctional one lasting for many years, long after they have left the organization.

Organizational norms

Norms are embedded into the organizational culture and reflect the actions of the employees within the organization. Typically, they are developed within groups and they may be more susceptible to the positive or negative influences of leadership and other members of the group. Stamper, Liu, Hafkamp and Ades stated "Behavior which is not governed by any kind of norms is by definition, intrinsically chaotic or random" (2000: 110). The norms within a group provide structure and guidance on acceptable behavior within the organization. As a new team or group forms, they will identify the behavior that is acceptable in order to interact and work together. When exposed to a dysfunctional leader, the group may witness their dysfunctional behavior. In turn, the organization may excuse negative behavior and establish these behaviors as the appropriate behavior for the organization. This is especially true if followers see the leader being rewarded for their dysfunctional behavior and view this as the leadership approach that the organization abides by.

Norms provide insights into how employees should interact within the organization, but also provide a guideline in relation to equity, equality and responsibility of how resources and rewards are distributed within the organization. In healthy organizational cultures, employees are rewarded and respected for the work they do and are treated as individuals and people who have value within the organization. In a dysfunctional environment, employees are rewarded for supporting and promoting the leader's agenda, and conforming to the dysfunctional behavior and norms of the leader, along with not challenging the leader.

Individuals, who embody the positive norms once established by the organization, may challenge the leader or challenge the new negative norms that are being displayed. In turn, these employees may be viewed as obstructionists and may be ostracized and cut off from resources such as information or work-related resources, resulting in them being unable to perform their work. Others within the group recognize which behavior is rewarded and which is punished. In contrast, individuals who view themselves as not being valued by the dysfunctional leader are more likely to withhold information, resist change and demonstrate a decline in organizational commitment.

Behaviors

Behaviors within the organization are the tangible actions relating to the norms and values of the organization. Tepper, Hoobler, Duffy and Ensley (2004) found that "employees who perceive that their supervisors are dysfunctional are less satisfied with their jobs . . . and are less willing to perform pro-social organizational behaviors" (as cited in Aubrey, 2012: 11). Pro-social behaviors are identified as behaviors including initiative, helping and loyalty, which are also examples of organizational citizenship. In reverse, anti-social behaviors include obstruction, resistance, non-compliance and lack of teamwork.

Typically, behavior such as initiative is inspired by leadership. As we have already discussed, dysfunctional leaders lack the ability to inspire others. If they are able to inspire, more than likely they will inspire the wrong kind of behavior. Dysfunctional leaders tend to micro-manage, discourage initiative and encourage an environment that is destructive toward others. Behaviors are acted out in a negative ways, including ostracizing, humiliation, harassment, belittling and threats, and these tangible and visible actions become the normal and accepted behavior within the organization.

Organizational influence on dysfunction and impact

As we have touched upon earlier, organizations may directly or indirectly influence dysfunctional leadership behavior. Upper-level leadership is responsible for cultivating and developing the organizational culture. This can be enhanced by the direct and indirect behavior of leadership. For dysfunctional leadership, behaviors may be instilled through acts that are considered unethical, bullying or abusive behaviors. As dysfunctional leaders are rewarded for their achievements, provided incentives and promotions, other leaders and followers are incentivized to embrace these same dysfunctional behaviors as a means to obtaining power, status and promotion. In other cases, leaders may promote tasks and results (profits by any means) that are self-serving and align with the goals of the leader rather than the organizational goals. Other acts may include that the organization embraces task-related duties versus people-focused relationships. Organizations may overlook dysfunctional behavior either by ignoring the behavior or by reassigning work that will accommodate the dysfunctional leader, thereby retaining that individual. Organizations that consist of loose systems, along with a lack of rules, policies or governance to address dysfunctional behavior, cause these behaviors to flourish.

Organizational commitment

Organizational commitment relates the psychological relationship between employees and the organization. Mowday, Steers and Porter (1979: 226) defined organizational commitment as "the relative strength of an individual's identification with and involvement in a particular organization . . . can be characterized by three factors: 1) A strong belief and acceptance of the organization's goals and values; 2) A willingness to exert effort on behalf of the organization; and 3) A strong desire to maintain membership and affiliation to the organization." These three factors allow the employee to give their all to the organization and build an emotional attachment to its identity and goals.

Organizational commitment develops over time based on the relationship between the employee and the organization. There are two thoughts related to organizational commitment: attitudinal and behavioral. Meyer and Allen (1984) describe attitudinal commitment as the emotional attachment of employees toward the organization. When employees feel an emotional attachment to the organization, they are able to identity and feel as though they are involved and belong in the organization. Behavior commitment is defined as the employee's commitment to the organization based on wages, commission and perks. Employees will weigh the cost of their work back to the benefits they receive. This weight is usually a factor in determining whether to stay or leave the organization – for example: "I don't get paid enough to put up with this type of behavior." Normative commitment is the third component. This refers to the employee's feelings of obligation to stay with the organization.

Employees who are committed to the organization experience different types of rewards. The first reward is aligned with monetary rewards, such as promotion, increased salary and bonuses. The second is psychological rewards, such as increased job satisfaction, engagement in their work and strong interpersonal relationships between co-workers and leadership. Organizations with employees who are committed to the organization also benefit. They experience lower turnover rates and increased employee engagement, along with an extension of work responsibilities and innovativeness coupled with creativity, which provide an increased competitive advantage for the organization.

Organizations that have dysfunctional leadership provide an environment where commitment is lacking. Those who experience dysfunction in their workplace either directly or indirectly become less committed from a psychological perspective. They do not feel that the organization is committed to their well-being, resulting in their lack of commitment back to the organization. Employees are less engaged, innovation and creativity are stifled by the leader, or the employees begin to shut down emotionally, becoming unwilling to engage in the operations of the organizational system. Decision making and idea generation becomes one-sided and there is a lack of interest in the well-being of the organization and the organizational culture, values and behaviors.

Social justice

Social justice within an organization is defined as how employees perceive the level of fairness and equal treatment they receive from others within the team, leadership or the organization as a whole. Lind and Tyler (1988) suggest that employees value fairness from leaders and peers as an indication of acceptance within the group. Employees exposed to dysfunctional leadership experience higher levels of unjust treatment, along with perceived injustice through rewards and punishments. When employees perceive that there is unfair justice or treatment in the workplace, they often act out through, anger, resentment, outrage, reduced commitment, vandalism, resistance, sabotage and withdrawal or isolation from social norms within the organization. If employees feel that there is injustice within the team or group, they may be less engaged or feel ostracized by the team as well as the organization. When injustice or unfairness is experienced, employees have a lower level of trust toward the leader. Lencioni (2002: 195) defined trust as "the confidence among team members that their peers' (including leadership) intentions are good and that there is a no reason to be protective or carful around people." As has been demonstrated in previous chapters, dysfunctional leadership exhibits behaviors that test and challenge trust, demonstrate a disregard for followers and lead through control. These behaviors are detrimental in terms of building trust within groups, teams and organizations. Employees begin to distrust others and fear for their positions as well as their standing within the team. If there is distrust amongst the employee and the leader, the employee will become less willing to engage with the work, the team and the leader.

The culture of any organization is a key strategic factor that separates one organization from its competitors. Organization culture is also an essential factor in defining what are the acceptable behaviors, norms and practices of an organization. Leaders within an organization leave their mark on the organizational culture through their own personal values and norms. If a positive leader is at the helm of an organization, it will attract like-minded positive individuals who in turn create positive norms and values within the organization. If a dysfunctional leader is part of the institution, their behavior encourages dysfunctional norms and values. These same dysfunctional behaviors embed themselves into the organizational culture and become the lasting blueprint of the organization. It is believed that elements of the organization are thought to influence whether or not a leader will engage in dysfunction. Ways in which the organization may promote dysfunction include:

1   how power is distributed throughout the organization;
2   competition levels;
3   loose systems and structure (usually implemented through constant restructuring);
4   stressful environments subject to frequent and unexplained change;
5   organizations that struggle with conflict resolution.

Dysfunctional leaders impact the organization's culture by engaging in self-destructive behaviors, which negatively impact the organization and followers. These behaviors have been discussed earlier in this book. Such behaviors compromise the leader's reputation along with the values and the reputation of the organization. When personal and organizational values no longer align, the results reflect negatively on work attitudes and outcomes. Little regard is paid to the good of the organization or the followers.

In many cases, the environment allows or creates a situation where these behaviors thrive. Goldman (2006) explained that in some cases where dysfunctional leadership behaviors are dominant, organizations have been known to alter their policies and cultures to indirectly support the dysfunction. If the leader is dysfunctional, they drive the environment and create a culture that encourages the dysfunction to thrive and multiply.

When the organization does not address the problem, others believe that these behaviors are the norm. Members of the organizations become convinced that this type of behavior is permitted. In other cases it demonstrates that the organization may lack the skill to address the situation. By ignoring these behaviors, it sends the message to others inside and outside the organization that this type of behavior is recognized and rewarded. Once a dysfunctional leader applies their dysfunctional values instead of the core values of the organization, then dysfunction will dominate the values and will become the new norm.

When dysfunction comes from the top, it flows down throughout the organization. Aquino and Thau (2009) found that most powerful predictors of workplace mistreatment were failures at higher levels of management, including the actual behavior of leaders. The quality of interactions between leadership and followers set the foundation and tone for the organizational culture. Leaders who are dysfunctional have learned their dysfunction from previous leaders. This is the same for followers within the organization – they are taught the same dysfunction and begin to emulate these behaviors as they are groomed for the next level of leadership. Followers may view this behavior as acceptable and as a strategy to use in order to be promoted within the organization. When this occurs, it allows for the behavior to infiltrate all layers of the organization. Organizations that encourage competition create an environment that is competitive, as tactics are used to achieve numbers, meet goals and compete for resources or recognition. This can create a breeding ground for dysfunctional behavior to occur, as this type of environment may encourage unhealthy competition. In some cases, employees who are mistreated by leadership are viewed by others as part of the out-group, while those who are friends with or are accepted by the dysfunctional leader are viewed as part of the in-group.

Organizational stress

Complexity within organizations is associated with increased stress for leaders and followers. When the environment becomes stressful, organizations encounter an increase in dysfunctional behaviors. Organizations facing a shortage of skilled workers, limited resources and experiencing demands for more work with fewer resources all cause additional stress for leaders. When this occurs, leaders may reach their tipping point, allowing for dysfunctional behaviors to emerge. In today's workforce, organizations are asked to be leaner and constantly competing for resources, creating additional stress for the leader and allowing dysfunction to thrive.

Organizational structure

Research studies have indicated that participants believed that the organization contributes to dysfunctional leadership. Deciphering dysfunctional leadership attributes can be difficult for any organization to do. Determining dysfunctional behavior may take months of data collection, interviews and observation of behaviors. Many organizations do not have the mechanisms in place to address dysfunctional behavior. In addition, they may lack the structure to formally go through the process of terminating a leader. They may struggle through potential legal issues, protocols and procedures to properly address the problem.

Kusy and Holloway (2010) stated that one way in which organizations may address dysfunctional leadership is through restructuring the organization. They stated that restructuring may be a code word for something being wrong with a unit or division and by restructuring it, it may be possible to fix the problem. The goal of restructuring is that the leader will be pressured and will eventually leave the organization on their own initiative. In other cases, we see many dysfunctional leaders moving up within an organization in order to provide additional responsibility for the dysfunctional leader in the hope that they will leave the organization. Another tactic for reassigning a dysfunctional leader is to provide relief from the immediate problem, causing time for the organization to regroup. In other cases, the organization may hope that by providing coaching, training or counseling, it will be able to help the leader change, that the leader will see what the problem is and what they can do to change, but that is not the case. The problem does not go away; it will still exist. All of these are just short-term solutions to address the problem and eventually the behavior will resurface.

Restructuring or reassigning a dysfunctional leader causes more problems within the organization. Followers within the organization see that the organization recognizes that there is a problem, yet doesn't know or want to address the problem. It also sends the message that while the organization knows that the problem exists, it is willing to allow it to continue. Kellerman (2004: 45) explained that this type of leadership is often viewed as being very insular and suggests that upper leadership "is willing to minimize or disregard the health and welfare of others and the organization for which they are directly responsible." Insular leaders tend to operate on the basis of a need to preserve the integrity of their organization at any cost – even at the cost of the employees working in the organization as well as the culture of the organization. This type of leadership results in employees feeling as though they do not matter or that their welfare is of no concern to the organization. They do not feel valued and as a result of not feeling valued, they in turn do not reciprocate any loyalty back to the organization.

Results and dysfunction

Many of the dysfunctional leaders who have been discussed in this book thrive on chaos and instability within organizations. An organization with strong structures and governance in place is not somewhere that the toxic leader will survive in. Having a chaotic system or work environment is typically conducive of this type of behavior and of followers who will support this behavior. These components make for fertile ground for a dysfunctional leader to be successful in an organization. By enabling this type of behavior to happen within it, the organization is enabling harm to happen to its employees.

Many people ask how it is possible that a dysfunctional leader can stay in place and still be in a leadership position. The answer to that question is that the leader produces results and that they are productive within the organization; simply stated, they are getting results. Typically senior leadership sees the results, but nothing else. They do not look at how the results are achieved or are offset by the consequences of having a dysfunctional leader. More than likely, results will be short-lived. Dysfunctional leaders strive for quick wins in order to draw focus away from their behavior. By producing results, it makes it extremely difficult for the organization to address the dysfunctional behavior. After all, the leader is performing, producing results and meeting the expectations of the position. Visible results in terms of metrics related to productivity, costs and revenue is something that leadership can view and often cause them to overlook the negative behavior that exists.

Followership and enabling

Enabling dysfunctional leadership cannot be blamed on the organization alone. Followers play a role in enabling this type of behavior. In order for a dysfunctional leader to be successful, they need followers to help them to maintain their persona and to allow for their dysfunction to develop. They will use their followers to promote their agenda and to achieve results. The methods used may include focusing on fear and intimidation, but the leader will take credit for the results that are achieved. If followers are not willing to help the leader, then the leader becomes powerless.

Followers may also receive something from the dysfunctional relationship. This may mean they are connecting with the leader, receiving recognition, or another basic need is being met. For example, the dysfunctional leader finds a person who wants to move up within the organization or has goals that they want to achieve. The dysfunctional leader may focus on supporting that person as a way to get what they want from them. The relationship then becomes a co-dependent relationship and they rely on each other to promote each other's agenda. The follower learns leadership methods through their dysfunctional leader. Individuals typically mirror the behavior of people who are in authority positions, thereby leading them to learn and adopt dysfunctional behaviors from their leaders. Other followers may not want to engage with the dysfunctional leader and they become the brunt of negative interactions or are targeted. While the followers who are supporting the agenda of the leader are rewarded through promotions, monetary rewards or perks, others are being punished and targeted in order for the leader to retain their position of power. Followers who enable the dysfunctional behavior do so due to a survival instinct. In other cases, the organization does not have the structure for followers to report dysfunctional behavior. Often the follower is intimidated into not reporting the leader to individuals higher up in the leadership hierarchy and will just say nothing about what they experience or witness.

It is also difficult for followers to report dysfunctional behavior when the dysfunction is found at higher levels within the organization. Padilla, Hogan and Kaiser (2007) explain that dysfunctional leadership is most likely found in senior jobs where there is little supervision. When a follower or junior leader experiences dysfunctional leadership at the upper levels of the organization, they may find it difficult to report these behaviors and may just suffer in silence. If employees are suffering in silence, upper leadership may not even be aware that the behavior is happening. They see the dysfunctional leader producing results, but they are not hearing or seeing anything that would indicate that dysfunctional actions are taking place. Remember, the dysfunctional leader will often come across to senior leadership as charming, competent and capable. When they are out of sight of senior leadership, the situation may be very different and the dysfunction can thrive in other areas and go unreported. As organizations become leaner and flatter, they find that there are fewer structures in place to identify dysfunctional behavior or mechanisms for followers to report this type of behavior.

Organizational conflict and dysfunction

Through the analysis of each of the dysfunctions examined in the previous chapters, we find that the dysfunctional leader loves to create and thrives on conflict and turmoil. Conflict is often referred to as counterproductive behavior impacting the normal functioning of productivity and efficiency (Boddy, 2014; Dunlop & Lee, 2004). Unhealthy conflict may cause dysfunction at all levels of the organization. For many, when negative conflict occurs, there is a need for revenge, sabotage and counterproductive behavior to take place. When an organization does nothing to address these behaviors, employees act out by fixing what is wrong and working against the leader, as well as the organization that they feel has wronged them. It does not mean that they will lash out at the dysfunctional leader, but they may instead lash out at the entire organization. This behavior can be subtle in terms of abusing sick time or work hours to outright sabotage within the organization and, in rare cases, can include acts of physical violence.

How dysfunctional leadership impacts followers

Kellerman (2004) suggests that followers need safety, security, group affiliation and some predictability. Traditionally, people are taught to respect people in positions of authority. Just as organizations are impacted negatively through dysfunctional leadership, the follower or the target experiences the brunt of the dysfunction. There are many ways that the target suffers, including job-related issues, physical distress and emotional distress. The following explores these concepts in further detail.

Dysfunctional leadership behavior and job satisfaction

Job satisfaction is a well-researched area within organizational studies; however, definitions pertaining to job satisfaction have been elusive. They include the range of employee feelings, emotional, mental and physical demands. Others have defined job satisfaction as being connected to highest earnings with the least amount of effort, while others define it as "an attitude toward one's job" (Brief, 1998: 10). Others have defined job satisfaction as an individual's general attitude as it relates to their work environment (Robbins, 2003). Griffin and Ebert (2002) stated that satisfied employees experienced higher levels of morale and more commitment to their organizations. Research has found that there is a relationship between performance and job satisfaction. Ostroff (1992) explained that satisfied workers are productive and are more likely to engage in activities that are focused on collaboration and increased productivity. In contrast, unsatisfied employees fail to meet organizational goals and move away from efforts to achieve these goals. Ultimately, dissatisfied, unmotivated workers who struggle to reach organizational goals are detrimental to the life of the organization.

Research conducted by Aryee, Sun, Chen, and Deborah (2008) found that dysfunctional leadership affects personal and job satisfaction, including turnover intentions, health problems, psychological distress and lack of belonging within an organization. Research has found that the levels of commitment demonstrated by employees are critical components linked to performance, satisfaction and intention to leave. Tepper, Duffy, Henle and Lambert (2006) explained that followers who perceive that their supervisors are abusive are less satisfied with their jobs and are less willing to perform pro-social organizational behaviors. Pro-social behaviors include initiative, assisting and loyalty in relation to the organization. When employees demonstrate anti-social behavior, this is manifested as obstruction, sabotage, resistance and non-compliance with the rules and organizational goals of the organization.

Emotional impact

All of the examples of dysfunctional leadership elicit some type of emotional response from their target. This could manifest itself in the form of fear, anxiety, anger, sadness or depression. The most common emotion experienced by targets relates to the stress caused by the dysfunction. Stress may manifest itself in emotional symptoms, physical symptoms or both. In this section, emotional impact related to stress will be explored.

Work and family conflict

Targets exposed to dysfunctional leadership experience an increase in work and family conflicts. Relationships with peers suffer as targets are either isolated from them or begin to socially withdraw. Conversely, the target may seek out peers to talk about the experience and the peers may begin to withdraw from the target as a way to protect themselves. The target may choose to share experiences with family members who are unable to understand or relate to the situation, and slowly the relationship with family members may begin to suffer. Targets may go home and take their anger and frustrations out on their family members. In other cases, the target may talk obsessively about nothing but the experience and the dysfunctional leader. As the target continues to suffer from emotional distress, they begin to withdraw from social and family obligations. Friends start to distance themselves from the target and the target feels abandoned by friends and family, who by now are tired of discussing the issue repeatedly.

Depression

Targets typically experience depression along with feelings of hopelessness and darkness. They feel as though they are alone in their suffering. They feel stuck in a situation. A job that they once enjoyed and loved now becomes something that they dread. They start to apply for other positions or look for ways to leave the abusive situation, only to find that there may not be any opportunities for them. They feel as though they deserve what is happening to them. As in battered wife syndrome, the target believes that they deserve or have asked for this abuse to happen. Their world darkens and the lack of joy begins to seep into their personal lives as well. If the depression goes untreated, then the target may begin to contemplate methods to escape the situation. In some cases, the escape is contemplation of suicide. For some, the thought of death is better than living in this type of situation. In rare cases there are reported incidents of suicide related to interactions with a dysfunctional leader.

Anxiety

Another form of emotional distress is anxiety in relation to the situation. The target is always afraid of when the next explosive episode will take place. They become anxious about their work and they start to question themselves and decisions they may make. Some have described the anxiety as waiting for the next shoe to drop. If nothing happens, they may let their guard down. They become anxious when they see the dysfunctional leader or anticipate an interaction with that leader. This anxiety may creep into their personal lives, interrupting their sleep as the anxiety keeps them awake, worrying about the next work day and what awaits them. Or they may replay interactions with the dysfunctional leader repeatedly and wonder how they could have handled the situation differently.

Humiliation

Targets describe that they feel humiliation from events involving the dysfunctional leader, whether this is humiliation from being diminished or from repeated criticism, belittling or gossiping. In other cases the humiliation occurs when the target is let go from the organization or blocked from moving up within the organization as the dysfunctional leader holds them back. Humiliation occurs from having peers, other leaders and bystanders witnessing the behavior directed by the dysfunctional leader toward the target. False accusations regarding incompetence, blame, weaknesses and being unprepared are other examples of how the target may experience humiliation.

Isolation

Many targets will experience some form of isolation. This may be self-imposed isolation, where the target will intentionally distance themselves from others. They will first try to distance themselves from the person inflicting the pain. They will try to avoid them. Targets have stated: "When the leader is gone, it is usually a good day. When they return, I spend most of my day planning techniques to avoid them and finding ways where I don't have to interact with that person" (research study conducted by Roter in 2016), Targets will also begin to isolate themselves from others within the organization. In some cases, they may experience humiliation and feel embarrassed or ashamed to interact with others, resulting in further isolation. In addition, they begin to distrust co-workers and other leaders. They start to question who they can and cannot trust. Barriers are built and trust is now replaced with mistrust, suspicion and barriers, which becomes their normal behavior.

Lack of personal control

Targets begin to suffer from a lack of control in their lives. Ultimately the dysfunctional leader is the one who is in control at all times. Their main agenda is focused on controlling others, situations and events. The target on the other hand feels as though they have lost all control. The first loss of control is in their work life. Emotionally they feel as though they are unable to control anything in the workplace. The dysfunctional leader controls the target through their work. They begin to either overload them with work and demands or they start to remove responsibilities from them. The target does not dare challenge the control as they are afraid of how this will impact them further. Then the target begins to feel as though they are losing control over their professional lives. Opportunities do not exist for the target as their careers begin to derail. The dysfunctional leader will remove opportunities for development or they will prevent the target from moving up within the organization. Eventually, the without pay or apply for unpaid family medical leave. Alternatively, they may just take time off in order to avoid the dysfunctional leader. They may be faced with either termination, quitting or accepting a position with lower pay. In extreme cases employees will leave the organization without a job to go to. Personal savings, retirement savings and funds from house sales are used to supplement lost wages and unpaid doctors' bills until another job is found. Depending on their levels of PSTD and their physical and emotional issues, they may not return to work as quickly as is financially necessary. In cases of unemployment, it is not uncommon for the dysfunctional leader to dispute unemployment claims as the final insult to the target. In some cases the target may file harassment and discrimination suits against the organization and/or the dysfunctional leader, resulting in costly legal fees and dragged-out legal disputes.

Bystanders

The target is not the only one who is impacted by the dysfunctional leader. Bystanders who witness the dysfunction often experience negative fallout from the dysfunctional leader. Though their experience may not be the same as that of the target, they do see the pain inflicted on one of their co-workers as well as others in the unit. They may experience feelings of regret, helplessness at not being able to help and guilt. They may also experience anxiety, wondering whether they will be identified as a target. Many bystanders often say that they keep their heads down and try to stay out of the line of fire. Often they are just as much a target as the target because they feel as though they are unable to report it and are helpless. They fear retribution or retaliation if they act out. They also fear becoming a target.

Stages of understanding

Ultimately employees are faced with a myriad of emotions when dealing with a dysfunctional leader. While feeling controlled, manipulated and used, employees look to find a place to discuss these feelings. However, in the majority of cases, employees feel that they have no place to go to report dysfunctional leadership behavior. Often, they suffer in silence for long periods of time. Suffering can last longer than a year as the employee goes through different stages of understanding. The first stage is questioning the behavior. Questions asked by the target include "Is it me or is it them?" and "How can a person act this way?" During the second phase, the person starts questioning themselves. They see that the leader continues to get away with their behavior, in many cases being praised by upper leadership. Then the employee starts to ask questions like "Maybe they are right – they are being recognized by some of the smartest people in the organization – maybe I am incompetent." Next they move into a phase of wanting to fix the problem by changing their work performance so that perhaps the leader will leave them alone. They start to work harder and second-guess their every step, resulting in more mistakes or being called out again for being indecisive. This only increases the focus of the dysfunctional leader on the target even further and the cycle escalates. Eventually, the target surrenders and gives up. They move into a phase of realizing there is nothing that can be done. They start to look for ways to leave the organization or to give in to the continued abuse from the dysfunctional leader, hoping that in time it will stop or maybe the leader will go somewhere else.

Conclusion

Dysfunctional leadership damages the organization's culture by violating the interests of the organization and diminishing the commitment and motivation of members within that organization. The behavior of dysfunctional leaders causes lasting harm to the organization's culture, values and norms. This damage impacts how members are guided through the navigation of proper protocols within the organization. Culture influences the way employees feel about the organization and how they interact with one another. The way in which the organization addresses issues of dysfunctional leadership has a lasting impact on the culture of the organization, whether in the short term or the long term.

The impact of dysfunctional leadership as it relates to members of the organization also has a damaging impact in relation to the physical and psychological toll on followers. Whether directly or indirectly impacted by dysfunctional leaders, all of them suffer as a result of the behavior of a dysfunctional leader. The cost is high in terms of a person's mental and physical well-being. In some cases, the cost can be a life, when an employee feels as though they can no longer cope with dysfunctional leadership and feel that the only escape or relief is by taking their own life.

References

Aquino, K., & and Thau, S. 2009. Workplace victimization: Aggression from the target's perspective. *Annual Reviews Psychology, 60*, 717–741.

Aryee, S., Sun, L., Chen, Z., & Deborah, Y. 2008. Abusive supervision and contextual Performance: The mediating role of emotional exhaustion and the moderating role of work unit structure. *Management and Organizational Review, 4*(3), 393–411

Ashforth, B. 1997. Petty tyranny in organizations: A preliminary examination of antecedents and consequences. *Canadian Journal of Administrative Services, 14*(2), 126–140.

Aubrey, D. 2012. *The effect of toxic leadership.* Carlisle, PA: United States Army War College.

Boddy, C. 2014. Corporate psychopaths, conflict, employee affective well-being and counterproductive work behavior. *Journal of Business Ethics, 121*(1), 107–121.

Brief, A. 1998. Prosocial organizational behaviors. *Academy of Management Review, 11*, 710–725

Dunlop, P., & Lee, K. 2004. Workplace deviance, organizational citizenship behavior, and business unit performance: The bad apples do spoil the whole barrel. *Journal of Organizational Behavior, 25*(1), 67–80

Goldman, A. 2006. High toxicity leadership: Borderline personality disorder and the dysfunctional organization. *Journal of Managerial Psychology, 21*(8), 733–746.

Griffin, R., & Ebert, R. 2002. *Business* (6th ed.). Upper Saddle River, NJ: Prentice Hall.

Kaufman, R. 2002. *Promethean builds a company culture that serves, sizzles, and succeeds.* New York: Houghton Mifflin.

Kellerman, B. 2004. *Bad leadership: What it is, how it happens, why it matters.* Boston, MA: Harvard Business School Press.

Kusy, M., & Holloway E. 2010. Disruptive and toxic behaviors in health care: Zero tolerance, the bottom line, and what to do about it. *Journal of Medical Practice Management, 25*(6), 335–340.

Lease, D. 2006. From great to ghastly: How toxic organizational cultures poison companies. The rise and fall of Enron, Worldcom, Healthsound, and Tyco International. *Academy of Business Education, April, 6*(7).

Lencioni, P. 2002. *The five dysfunctions of a team: A leadership fable.* San Francisco: Jossey-Bass.

Leymann H. 1990. Mobbing and psychological terror at workplace. *Violence and Victims, 5*, 119–126.

Lind, A., & Tyler, T. 1988. *The social psychology of procedural justices: Critical issues in social justice.* New York: Plenum Press.

Meyer, J., & Allen, N. 1984. Testing the "side-bet theory" of organizational commitment: Some methodological considerations. *Journal of Applied Psychology, 69*, 372–378.

Moore, M., & Lynch, J. 2007. Leadership, working environment and workplace bullying. *International Journal of Organization Theory and Behavior, 10*(1), 95–118.

Mowday, R., Steers, R., & Porter, L. 1979. The measurement of organizational commitment. *Journal of Organizational Behavior, 14*, 224–247.

Ostroff, C. 1992. The relationship between satisfaction, attitudes, and performance: An organizational level analysis. *Journal of Applied Psychology, 77*(6), 963–974.

Padilla, A., Hogan, R., & Kaiser, R. (2007). The toxic triangle: Destructive leaders, susceptible followers, and conducive environments. *Leadership Quarterly, 18*(3), 176–194.

Reino, A., & Vadi, M. 2010. What factors predict the values of an organization and how? University of Tartu-Faculty of Economics & Business Admiration Working Paper Series no 7:5.

Robbins, S. 2003. *Organizational behavior.* Upper Saddle River, NJ: Prentice Hall.

Schein, E. 1996. Culture: The missing concept of organization studies. *Administrative Science Quarterly, 41*(2), 229–240.

Stamper, R., Liu, K., Hafkamp, M., & Ades, Y. 2000. Understanding the roles of signs and norms in organizations: A semiotic approach to information systems design. *Behaviour & Information Technology, 19*(1), 15–27.

Tepper, B., Duffy, M., Henle, C., & Lambert, L. 2006. Procedural injustice, victim precipitation, and abusive supervision. *Personnel Psychology, 59*(1) 101–124.

Tepper, B., Hoobler, J., Duffy, M., & Ensley, M. 2004. Moderators of the relationships between co-workers' organizational citizenship behavior and fellow employees' attitudes. *Journal of Applied Psychology, 89*(4), 455–465.

Chapter 10

Addressing dysfunctional leadership

Introduction

Addressing dysfunctional leadership is important both from an individual and an organizational standpoint. Everyone has the responsibility to expose these behaviors along with leaders who are involved in this type of destruction. Often these behaviors are ignored in the hope that they will go away or that the problem will resolve itself. Organizations and others hope that their assessment of the situation is false. In any case, addressing the topic of dysfunction is critical. This chapter addresses what organizations can do to tackle the phenomenon of dysfunction in leadership and what individuals can do, as well as exploring what countries are doing from a legal standpoint as more of them are beginning to address the topic of dysfunction in the workplace.

Dysfunctional behavior does not always manifest itself quickly. However, when left unchecked, the problem continues and can destroy the organization slowly, along with the people associated with the dysfunction. It is essential to note that addressing these behaviors is never easy and creates challenges for all involved.

There are many components that link back to why these dysfunctional behaviors are not addressed. One is that most people look for the good in other people. It is typical human nature to want to find the positive in others, especially when the person is in a position of leadership or authority. The first time a leader lashes out, it is viewed that maybe that person is having a bad day or is under stress. We usually give them the benefit of the doubt, in the hope that they are truly good and that their behavior that day is just a one-off. The natural inclination is to stay quiet and not say anything; after all, it is a one-time event. Yet, we tend to be suspicious about the behavior and the hope is that the leader will prove us wrong. As time goes by, the behavior continues. By this time, the leader has instilled a level of fear into their followers and/or the person they are focused on. Their targets possess fear of retaliation and retribution. They fear being wrong, having their careers ruined and what the person will do to them next. As the behavior increases, the level of fear rises and addressing the situation becomes even more challenging. The following discussion addresses these challenges in more detail.

Fear of retaliation

Retaliation is an issue that is often a concern for individuals who are targets of or bystanders witnessing dysfunctional leadership. When these behaviors are recognized, it is usually not reported. There is the fear of the behavior escalating, being accused of

Addressing dysfunctional leadership 143

being too sensitive, over-reacting or, in rare cases, being labeled as emotionally unstable (Martin, 2010). There is also the fear of losing credibility with other managers or other leaders who view this dysfunctional leader as highly respected and competent. There is also the worry of not being promoted or being labeled as a person who likes to cause trouble, is difficult to work with or is not a team player. There is the chance that the tables can be turned and the target may be the one who is accused of dysfunctional behavior or poor performance.

Lack of training (individuals)

As employees, we are not trained to recognize these behaviors, let alone what to do about them. At some point in our careers, we will experience a dysfunctional leader at some level, yet having the ability to define and recognize the behavior is rare. Organizations train employees on how to address sexual harassment in the workplace, but few countries actually have employment laws in place relating to dysfunctional leadership or behavior in the workplace.

Making sense of the situation

The typical reaction when dealing with a dysfunctional leader is to try to understand the behavior. Questions are asked: "How can a decent person act this way?" "Why are they doing this?" "How can they be so evil?" "Why does this person get away with this?" "Why is this happening to me?" This behavior does not make sense to the average person. Many try to understand this behavior, but there really is no making sense of the situation. Ultimately it is a waste of energy and time fixating on trying to make sense of or excuses for the actions of this person. There is no rhyme or reason to their action or why they have picked a certain individual as their target. It is difficult to understand why they behave this way. The key focus should be on surviving and working through the situation.

Suffering in silence

When a target or victim faces a dysfunctional leader, they tend to suffer alone. The target feels as though others will not understand what they are going through. They think that others will side with the dysfunctional leader's actions. That is what the dysfunctional leader wants – for the target to suffer in isolation. If the person can suffer in isolation, they will begin to believe what has been said about them and this will only demoralize them further. They will become more vulnerable and weaker in the eyes of the leader.

Suffering in isolation is the worst thing to do. It is important to share feelings and events with people who are trusted or to seek professional help. It is also crucial to seek help quickly. These events can be easy to handle or extremely difficult, even traumatizing for the target. At times, when the target needs to talk to medical professionals, it is critical to discuss the situation with someone who the target feels comfortable with and who has experience with this type of behavior. Seeking professional attention or therapy does not make the target weak; it shows the person regaining control over the situation and seeking help to address the behavior in order to protect themselves.

Speaking up

When a person is made a target, they usually don't speak up right away. Research finds that less than seven percent of individuals who are targeted will file any form of complaint (Namie & Namie, 2009). Typically, they will suffer in silence for a long period of time before they finally bring it up. Most dysfunctional relationships in the workplace can last more than 12 months before being addressed. The target suffers in silence until someone comes to them and mentions that they have witnessed the behavior or that they have been a target as well, or the target seeks out help. It is important for the target to recognize that they are not the first person to experience this dysfunctional behavior from this leader and more than likely, they will not be the last. It is critical to recognize people who can help and if they are trusted, to approach them to discuss the situation. There are many people who have experienced dysfunctional leaders and there are tactics that can be learned to address these behaviors.

Coping mechanisms

Addressing dysfunctional leadership is not easy. Once defined, finding strategies and ways to approach the topic is a challenge. Employees struggle with ways to find help with coping with this type of behavior in organizations. Employees will try to reach out to others in the organization. They might talk to a trusted co-worker, only to find out that they have also endured the same type of punishment or ridicule, or that they have witnessed others who have experienced the behavior. In this phase the employee becomes angry: "How is it that no one in the upper leadership has noticed this behavior?" "How does this person get away with what they are doing?" The employee starts to question the organization's ability to hire and promote the right people. They start to question what is wrong with the leadership of the organization that allows this to happen. Engagement and loyalty decline as the employee does not feel the organization or leadership deserves their best efforts. Their focus is on survival and they do what they can to survive and to lie low.

When the target feels as though they may be losing control, they will turn to coping mechanisms, of which there are two forms: negative and positive. For the target, a coping mechanism is a way to deal with the problem or the issue at hand. Negative coping mechanisms may relieve some of the distress, but ultimately impacts other areas negatively. The following compares and contrasts each of the coping mechanisms in further detail.

Negative coping mechanisms

Negative coping is considered a form of passive coping which causes additional stress for the target. Passive coping is normally used when the individual believes that there is nothing that can be done about the situation. The organization knows about what is happening and is not acting upon the situation, or the person feels as though they have lost all control of the situation and other aspects of their life. They find themselves having to cope with the situation alone and not having someone to reach out to. Suffering in silence and alone is a dangerous area for the target. Silence allows them to dwell on the negatives of the situation, which only perpetuates the situation further. Negative coping mechanisms may provide short-term relief for the target, but the negative feelings will continue to escalate the need to find more relief.

Trying to appease the dysfunctional leader

The first coping mechanism is one of the most common for targets to utilize – trying to appease the dysfunctional leader. The target believes that if they just bend to the demands of the dysfunctional leader, the leader will eventually let up and the behavior will stop. This never happens. It might keep the leader at a distance for a short period of time, but eventually they will demand more and more from the target. Once the dysfunctional leader sees that their target is bending and appeasing them, they know that the person is vulnerable and they will continue to intensify the behavior to see how far the person will go in bending to their demands. The dysfunctional leader will continue to control the situation and the person. By appeasing the leader, the target has given in to the demands, but they are not being true to their beliefs and values. They begin to resent the leader and themselves even more, and the leader will pick up on this. An example of bending to a leader may include falsifying financial records, participating in illegal practices, targeting another co-worker by bullying or abusing that person, or going against organizational values and norms. The target may try to befriend the dysfunctional leader to get close to them. This is never helpful. First, the leader has singled out the target for a reason, whatever that may be. The leader may view the target as more competent or having something that they want. Befriending the dysfunctional leader might help, but it will become negative eventually. Many of the dysfunctional leadership behaviors we have discussed in the previous chapters demonstrate that these types of individuals are unable to build lasting relationships. They will use relationships as a means to get what they need and will discard people quickly. This coping mechanism will not cause the leader to give up and the threat still remains. The dysfunctional leader does not want to be a friend to the target. They may come across as a friendly to get information or to get them to drop their guard, but in the end they will continue this behavior. They will turn on the target eventually. It is very common for targets to believe that the dysfunctional leader is a friend, but in reality they are not.

Denial and avoidance

Another passive coping method is denial and avoidance. If the problem is ignored, it does not exist. Excuses are made for the behavior of the leader. But the problem continues and it is real. Denial does not make the problem go away and eventually leads to other negative coping mechanisms. Isolation is also utilized as a form of avoidance. Isolation, whether self-imposed or imposed by the leader, is very common. Targets may intentionally isolate themselves from the dysfunction or others in the workplace. Through isolation or avoidance, they believe that the actions will stop: "Out of sight is out of mind." If they do not face the dysfunction, then the leader may forget about the target. This is not true; ignoring the leader or avoiding them will result in them finding the target and escalating their behavior. Dysfunctional leaders achieve power from belittling and gaining control over their target. When a person isolates themselves, they are vulnerable and there are no witnesses. They can be viewed as an animal that has separated itself from the herd. The target has separated the individual from their social group and they are vulnerable and exposed. Targets may avoid social events and begin to close themselves off as a form of passive coping. In many cases they are exhausted by the constant barrage of insults, humiliation and other causes of stress from the dysfunctional leader. The target will lack

146   Addressing dysfunctional leadership

the energy to interact with others and will separate from them in order to rest. They find themselves alone and lack the support network that they need in order to cope with the situation. Suffering in silence and alone is a dangerous area for the target. They will relive the events, analyze the situation in a negative light and may move into more negative coping mechanisms.

Self-medicating

Many targets will self-medicate and focus on ways that will ease their pain. These self-medicating mechanisms are short-term fixes. Self-medicating options include the abuse of alcohol, prescription or recreational drug use, retail therapy, gambling and over-eating. A combination of two or more forms of self-medicating may be used. Others move into self-harm, such as cutting, hair pulling, nail biting and other self-destructive acts against themselves. These methods are used as a way to numb or mask the pain that they are experiencing. It provides for a temporary escape, but does not remove the cause of the stress. Individuals experience a short-term release, but look for more in order to continue to mask the pain further. All of these behaviors also eventually have a negative impact on the individual's health, such as heart disease, depression or psychosis. In extreme circumstances targets contemplate or attempt suicide as a way to escape the situation permanently. For these individuals, the pain is just too great.

All of these negative coping mechanisms will result in the target suffering from physical or psychological issues. They will suffer feelings of self-defeat, abandonment and that they are not being their authentic self; they are someone they don't want to be. When coping is negative or passive, it is critical that the individual finds help and positive coping mechanisms in order to manage the situation.

Example of negative coping

Susan was a top performer with an organization for 10 years. Everyone loved her in the community and as well as the organization – that is, until a new leader, Woodrow, came in. He was your typical bully, ostracizing, belittling and humiliating people who stood in his way. It was obvious to many that Susan was more competent than Woodrow. Woodrow went after Susan with a vengeance. Finally, she felt as though all she could do was try to survive, to make it through the day and then the week and through each month. Every day she was scared. When Woodrow was out of the office, Susan felt as though she could finally breathe. When he was in the office, it felt like the walls were closing in on her. She did everything she could to avoid him. She isolated herself from others in the organization because she did not know who she could trust and who was a part of his inner circle. The more she isolated herself, the more Woodrow isolated her from her work projects. Not having anything to do during the day, she found herself online purchasing clothing, things for her home and racking up thousands of dollars of credit card debt. During the 10 years that she was employed with the organization, she was the first to come to the office. No matter how sick she was, she was in the office. She did everything for the customers she served. All this ended when Woodrow became the leader. She focused heavily on ensuring that she did only the minimum and started to use up her sick time and vacation days. She avoided Woodrow as much as possible and became less engaged in the organization along with the community. She was no longer focused on the work; she was focused on how to get out of the organization.

Positive coping mechanisms

Positive or active coping mechanisms are used when the person believes that the situation can be changed. Active coping helps stimulate health as well as positive control over the situation. Social support and adopting an active, positive attitude can influence physical and mental health. It can help to neutralize the cause of the stress, lessen negative reactions and contribute to a faster recovery from events associated with the situation. It is very common that this active strategy is used first; however, if the situation or problem is not addressed or resolved, the targeted individual may move into employing passive coping mechanisms.

Problem solving

The aim of positive coping mechanisms is to address the problem and have a constructive conversation about the situation in order to find ways to identify and address it. The individual needs to recognize that this is not a quick fix and that it may take time and several attempts to resolve the situation. The goal is to keep the conversation focused. There is a good chance that the leader will become argumentative, attacking, denying the behavior or becoming passive. After the conversation, progress should be monitored. Does the behavior change after the conversation? There might be a change in the behavior for a brief time, only for the dysfunctional behavior to return. Once the behavior continues, address it again to find a solution to the problem. If progress is not made, then there might be a need to escalate the situation.

Addressing the situation

Whether dealing with a bully or a psychopath, it is important to address the situation. The key to doing this is to focus on the problem and not the person. This can be extremely difficult since emotions are usually running high. These emotions include feelings of hurt, being slighted, anger or humiliation. Emotions will kick in and the first action is to hurt the person. Addressing negative behavior with negative behavior will only lead to negative results. Address the situation by focusing on the situation and keep personal feelings out of it. This is a challenge, but it can be done with practice and coaching.

Checking emotions

When a situation occurs, the first thing to do is to check emotions. If emotions are running high, the best thing is to walk away until your emotions calm down. It is important to think carefully about how to address the situation. Any sign of weakness or vulnerability will allow the person to get more aggressive and to go in for the kill. Making the decision to confront someone is never easy. One has to weigh the pros and cons. What will happen if the situation goes unresolved? What happens if the issue is resolved? How the person will react and how to address that behavior should be explored.

148 Addressing dysfunctional leadership

The first step is to analyze the situation to determine what the risk is to yourself, others or your position. Once it is clear that there are minimal risks, be sure to confront the situation. Be gentle, yet also be direct and very specific. Talk to the person about what was observed and what occurred. It is important to be clear about the concerns and what needs to be done to correct the situation. Focus on language that is assertive and not timid. Ensure that the message is delivered in a confident manner.

Here is an example of a negative way of addressing a conversation. This example statement demonstrates many "ins" for the aggressor to come back in for an attack:

> Hi Karen, I would like to talk to you about something. I don't know, maybe it's just me, but I noticed that you can be, I don't know, somewhat rude when I speak up in a meeting. Again, I could be wrong, but it makes me uncomfortable and well, sometimes it hurts my feelings.

There are several areas in this statement where the conversation can go in the wrong direction. The tone is hesitant. The person making the statement is almost blaming themselves. Finally, the person is telling the aggressor that their feelings are hurt and they are uncomfortable, providing insights and validation to the dysfunctional leader that they have been able to succeed in their mission and that they now know how to continue to gain control. Notice the change in tone in the following statement:

> Karen, in yesterday's meeting you cut me off when I was talking about the product numbers. I want to talk to you about how we can work better together in the future.

In this statement, what happened is specific. It does not share emotions with the aggressor. It helps to establish strength in the comment and stress that the behavior was noticed and that it will be addressed. The behavior is noticed and it needs to be addressed. Focus specifically on solving the problem and not fixing the person. As was discussed in earlier chapters, it is extremely difficult to change the behavior of a leader who is dysfunctional. The only behavior that can be changed is that of the person receiving the attacks. How they handle the situation will establish the events that happen in the future. It is important to focus specifically on the situation and the problem. Once the statement has been made, the target needs to be prepared for the comeback. Listen to the person and hear what they have to say, but also assert yourself and provide boundaries and expectations of acceptable and unacceptable behavior. Followers may believe that this can't be done with a leader because of their levels of authority. Keep in mind that for the dysfunctional leader, it is difficult to admit that they have done anything wrong. Don't expect an apology. Listen for the response. The response will probably be filled with denial that there is a problem, shifting the blame toward others and possibly you, or filled with excuses. Keep the conversation focused and don't get tied up in the blame game. The goal is to put the person on notice and to demonstrate that this behavior will not be tolerated.

Timing is everything

Timing in relation to these types of conversations is extremely important. It is OK to cool off and let emotions settle, but don't let too much time go by. The dysfunctional leader is planning the next attack and usually the attacks are close together; they will look for the next opportunity to move in. Once a pattern is established, it is difficult to address, especially if it has happened multiple times. Address the situation quickly and specifically, and keep it focused.

Document, document, document

After the conversation or the interaction occurs, it is important to document the events. It is extremely important to support statements with documentation. Inevitably, when confronting a dysfunctional leader, they will have built strong alliances with key stakeholders, including senior leadership. These alliances are built on charm and their ability to lie and deceive. It is important to counteract lies and blaming with facts and documentation. Having solid evidence and data in the form of documentation will help to support your statements. Documentation also helps to move the discussion away from feelings and specifically focus on facts which can be hard to dispute. It also provides a record of the pattern of behavior that is demonstrated over time. Also, it is important to identify witnesses to the interaction that is being documented, along with times, dates and specifics. No detail is unimportant when documenting.

Getting out of the situation

Removing oneself from the situation is sometimes the only option in some cases. The goal of the target should be to get out of the situation on their terms in order to regain control. This means finding a way out by transferring to another department in the organization of finding another position outside the organization. Gaining back one's power over the situation is critical. Note that even after leaving the situation, the dysfunctional leader may continue to cause harm. After all, they have lost their target and they don't like to lose. The dysfunctional leader will view the target leaving the organization and regaining control as the ultimate act of betrayal. Some will continue the attacks after the target has left the department or the organization. Typically, once the target has left, anything that happens will be blamed on them. The dysfunctional leader will continue to slander the person, use them as a scapegoat or spread rumors and gossip about them. However, eventually the novelty will wear thin, since the dysfunctional leader cannot gain power from the reaction of the target. Other ways in which the dysfunctional leader will continue the behavior is through slanderous job references, contacting the target's new leadership and poisoning others against them. There are ways to address this. Utilizing reference checking groups to follow up on what is being said is a strong tactic, as is explaining the situation to a new leader and, if all else fails, contacting a lawyer for a defamation lawsuit or letter to stop the behavior.

Other ways to address the behavior

- Address the behavior right from the beginning. Doing so will put the dysfunctional leader on guard, realizing that they have a worthy adversary who will stand up to them. More than likely, the dysfunctional leader will back off and move on to someone else.

150 Addressing dysfunctional leadership

- Realizing that you as the target have done nothing wrong. The problem is the dysfunction of the other person. This is not about weakness or being incompetent; actually, it is the direct opposite. It is about the leader seeing something in that individual that they feel threatened by.
- Talk to others who are trusted. Build a support network. Draw from past experiences and the experiences from others in similar situations.
- Recognize strengths, focus on these strengths and relive past wins. Go back to former performance reviews. Talk to other individuals who respect your work. Constantly reaffirming your strengths and abilities can help to provide some counterbalance to the negatives.
- Find others who are experiencing or have experienced this leader's behavior. Reporting multiple instances of the behavior is better than one complaint. Focus on the power of numbers.
- Discuss the situation with senior leadership and document that discussion as well. Document all events. Present information and data as factual and not emotional.
- Find positive ways to cope with the situation. Working out, going back to school, picking up a new hobby and volunteering are all tactics that can be used to rebuild your positive focus as well as your self-confidence. Focusing on the positive versus the negative is crucial during this time. Surround yourself with positive people and recognize that there is life outside of work and that you are not defined by this one person.

Organizational mechanisms for individual coping

Within the organization, there are mechanisms that can assist the target with coping with dysfunction in the workplace. The following discussion outlines typical organizational mechanisms that are in place to help individuals with addressing dysfunction in the workplace.

Human Resources

Human Resources (HR) is a source of assistance in these cases. However, the amount of support provided may be limited. If a complaint is filed with the HR department, employees should not expect the complaint to be confidential. It is the responsibility and duty of the HR department to investigate these complaints. This means that they will have to take these complaints to the person who is being accused of the dysfunctional behavior in order to hear their side of the story. It is important to be prepared that the dysfunctional leader will find out about the complaint filed. The role of the HR department is to be objective. They need to hear both sides of the complaint. A response to the situation may not come as quickly as one would expect.

When you file a complaint, you should be prepared with facts, data and names of witnesses when talking to the HR department. You should attend the meeting with specifics and strong documentation. Ideally, if possible, find others who are willing to come forward as well, as, more than likely, there will be others who have experienced problems with this particular leader. If an investigation occurs, keep in mind that people who have had a negative experience with the dysfunctional leader may not come forward. This is very common and often they will say that they have not had a negative experience with the leader or that they have not witnessed anything. They will do this to protect themselves because of the fear of retaliation from the dysfunctional leader if nothing is done to address the problem. Don't get angry with them, as this is a means of survival for them. Focus on your documentation along with focusing on the facts that you have.

Along with documentation, also discuss how this leader's behavior is impacting productivity, morale, turnover and others in the department. Remember to focus on the issue and on the business impact. Even if the person is causing stress, there is a business-related component that needs to be addressed, such as lost time due to leave, reduction in productivity and increased sick time. Focus on the business impact and leave personal issues out of the discussion.

Targets get discouraged if results do not happen right away. It will take time for the situation to resolve itself. When filing the complaint, establish a pattern of behavior that demonstrates impact to the business. The dysfunctional leader has taken years to perfect their dysfunction and it will take time to unravel. It is critical to create a record and draw attention to the issues. Address the situation, keep it focused and it will eventually resolve itself, but it will take time. Be patient as any investigation needs time to be investigated. If the situation is not resolved and the behavior continues, it is possible that the dysfunction is occurring on a larger scale. One important note to followers is to recognize that the role of HR is to protect the organization as a whole. The HR team is a part of the management team and typically will side with management or leadership. If the dysfunction is at the leadership level, most likely the HR team is already aware of the situation through other complaints or exit interviews. In some cases the HR department may have been told by senior leadership to ignore the situation or may have tried to address the problem with little success. HR is focused on protecting the organization as a whole. Being asked to ignore the behavior may be to specifically protect this leader, especially if they are higher up in senior leadership. If that is the case, it is best to explore options to exit the department, unit or organization. This a decision that is difficult to make, but weigh up your options and determine how the behavior of this dysfunctional leader is impacting your work and, most importantly, your health and well-being. HR may be willing to assist in making this transition happen if the organization is large enough to accommodate a move.

Employee Assistance Programs

Individuals may seek support through counseling. In the US, several organizations provide Employee Assistance Programs (EAPs). These programs are paid for by the employer and are confidential. The employer does not know what is discussed or who specifically is utilizing the services. The EAP is provided as a mental health service and a referral can be made by the employer on behalf of the employee. The employer will typically use this service for employees who may be displaying negative behaviors that need to be addressed. In other situations, employees are encouraged to use the services for their own needs. In cases of dysfunctional leadership, employees who are targeted may turn to EAPs for counseling. The counseling is a neutral program. The providers can provide advice that is active or passive. In one qualitative study conducted by Roter (2011), several employees contacted their EAP and found that providers were employees of the organization. When they contacted the program for help, they were told that their organization

152 Addressing dysfunctional leadership

was aware of the dysfunctional leader, the situation and what the leader was doing. The best advice that could be offered to them was to lie low and wait out the situation. One individual was told to steer clear of the leader and not to cause any problems that would allow the leader to terminate the employee. Most of the participants of the study stated that the program did not offer much help and did not provide a solution to the problem. However, the program may also provide insights into how to address the situation or just to act as a sounding board for the employee. Sometimes, the employee merely needs to talk to someone and counseling services can provide a different perspective from someone who is not involved in the situation.

Going higher up

One technique used to report dysfunctional leadership is going to those higher up in the organization. This can be extremely challenging. As you will recall from previous chapters, the dysfunctional leader wears a mask, giving the impression to others that they are charming, competent and talented. More than likely, their leader hired them. These leaders won't want to admit that they made a mistake by hiring or promoting this individual. In addition, the dysfunctional leader is extremely cunning. They may have already poisoned their boss against their target. If the dysfunctional leader senses that there may be a report against them, they will lay the foundation of blame, which is usually focused on the target. This can be done by sharing that the target is difficult to work with, is not open to change, is not a team player, is a complainer, can't be trusted, shows incompetence in their work, is a problem employee, etc. They will have shared with their leader the problems that they are having with the target and all that they are doing to help the target to be successful. The target will report a different story to the dysfunctional leader's leader and typically this will not sit well with either one of them. Also, remember that the dysfunctional leader is very good at blaming others for mistakes. It is very possible that you as the target have been someone they have blamed for past mistakes. Upper leadership may have a negative view of you as an employee, so tread carefully in this area.

If the target believes that the best recourse is to go higher up, then they need to focus on data and events and to try not to make it personal. When sharing documentation, the target needs to be careful as to whom they share this information with so that it is not used against them. Again, it is vital to focus on the behavior and how it impacts the business. This diverts the focus away from the individual to the business, which is easier to investigate versus personal behaviors that are more than likely masked by the dysfunctional leader. If mistakes have happened before, demonstrate how the responsibility belongs to the leader and establish a pattern to the behavior. This should not be a one-time event or situation; focus on the pattern of behavior to demonstrate what is happening.

Seeking legal advice

If you decide to take legal action or seek legal advice, look for an attorney who will take the case on a contingency basis versus coming up with expensive retainers. These cases can be dragged out for long periods of time and, depending on the resources of the organization, can be costly and filled with red tape. Choose an attorney who is well versed in employment law, especially relating to harassment and/or discrimination.

Filing complaints with your country's legal bodies is also suggested. It may be discovered that others have made the same type of claims in the past. Continue to find others who can support your claims. Look for current employees as well as past employees who may be willing to share experiences or join the complaint.

Filing a complaint against a dysfunctional leader will create an adversarial relationship with both the employer and the leader. Other employees will pick sides and for safety reasons they are likely to side with the employer, even if they have witnessed and/or experienced the dysfunction. This is not personal against the target; this will be due to a fear that they may be targeted or they may experience retaliation from the company and/or leader. The dysfunctional leader does not want to be exposed. Once exposed, they will move into self-preservation mode, which for them is usually a retaliation focusing on inflicting harm in order to push the complainant out or to retract the complaint. Filing a complaint should be done as soon as possible. Waiting too long may result in responses that the reported abuse was not a major concern and that the employee reporting it has a different agenda.

Organizational coping

Just as individuals are not equipped to handle dysfunctional leadership, organizations typically are not skilled in assessing this type of behavior, let alone how to effectively handle these situations. Organizations recognize and identify that there is a problem, but they don't know how to address it or fix it. Eventually it seems easier to just ignore the situation or person and hope that it goes away. It is not uncommon to ask people if they have reported the situation to the organization. Most responses are yes they have and that nothing was done to address the problem.

Understanding organizational processes

Most organizations have a process or procedure for filing workplace complaints relating to discrimination, harassment or unethical behaviors. Understanding organizational policies related to reporting these incidents is critical for both the organization and its employees. While there are processes and procedures in place to address harassment, organizations typically do not have specific policies in place regarding harassment as it relates to a dysfunctional leadership. The closest process or policy in place will be sexual harassment policies. Look into the organizational policies related to these topics and specifically harassment and hostile work environments.

It is important for the follower to be politically astute in understanding the network and relationships of others within the organization. Understanding who the dysfunctional leader is closely linked to is important. For example, if the company policy states that complaints should be filed with the direct manager and the dysfunctional leader is connected to that direct manager, it is unwise to talk to that direct manager about the problem. More than likely the complaint will be ignored or reported back to the dysfunctional leader. When being discussed, the dysfunctional leader will twist the truth and before long the person making the complaint rather than the leader will be the problem. After all, the dysfunctional leader will have established themselves as being highly credible to this manager through their connection. If that is the case, go to others in leadership

Helping the target

Bystanders are witnesses to the behavior of the dysfunctional leader, yet they are afraid to address the situation for fear of retaliation or being targeted as well. They may keep quiet and feel as though they cannot do anything to help. If a bystander is afraid to address or report the behavior, the next best alternative is to provide support to the target. The following list gives insights into how the bystander can actively support the target:

- *Active listening*: When listening, do just that and listen to that person. It might be the first time that they have spoken about the situation. Don't try to analyze or evaluate the situation. At this point, the person just wants to be listened to. Solving the problem is not needed at this point; it is about providing support to the person
- *Confirm and validate the situation by what has been witnessed or experienced*: Targets they feel as though they are crazy. They may have shared this information with others in the past and may have been told they are being overly sensitive to the situation. Help the target understand what is happening is real and provide insight on what has been observed. Share experiences or behaviors that have been witnessed.
- *Focus on the reality of the situation*: The target usually does not recognize the reality of the situation and starts to believe the insults and humiliation that are being inflicted on them by the dysfunctional leader – for example, when the target states "Maybe they are right, maybe I am incompetent." Spell out the reality of the situation. This is not about them being incompetent – this is about the dysfunctional leader tearing them down and trying to destroy their self-esteem. Refocus them on what the truth is. Have them focus on how competent they are and projects or work that demonstrates this reality.
- *Provide education and options for the target to follow up on*: Understand organizational processes relating to harassment and reporting. Provide any insights in order to educate and inform the target in this respect.
- *Suggest that the target seek help.* This help might be in the form of professional assistance either within or outside the organization. Options for professional help may include professional therapy, talking to a counselor, a physician, legal advice or someone within the organization who can help. It is important to understand that bystanders should not be in the position to provide counseling for the target. If the target needs help, then providing avenues is helpful for them. Encourage them to seek out professional counseling if necessary and provide avenues of support.

Healing from dysfunction

Once out of the situation, the target needs to heal. Take time to focus on healing and pulling yourself back together. If you are starting a new job, take some time off beforehand, if at all possible. When starting the new job, it can be a challenge to rebuild one's self-esteem. Many targets will have suffered months or even years of abuse that has chipped away at their self-confidence. They will continue to question their abilities and competence, and will question themselves. It is important to rebuild your self-esteem in order to recognize the patterns of behavior related to the dysfunctional behavior and to avoid finding yourself in the same situation again.

It is important to address physical and emotional issues. Notice the cues that something is physically or emotionally wrong. Address what is causing the symptoms by seeking out help from a professional. It is important to recognize and deal with any physical or emotion distress and to get healthy.

Legal rights

Finally, it is important for employees to understand their legal rights. In the US, recognizing and understanding state laws relating to workers' compensation, unemployment and disability benefits is important. By exploring state and federal employment laws and understanding workplace policies related to the reporting of harassment and discrimination suits is important. Other countries provide other forms of legal relief relating to dysfunctional behaviors. Most countries focus on harassment and bullying as the dysfunction, however these can be applied. Table 10.1 provides a list of countries and states and the types of action that are in place to address these behaviors, as well as a summary of actions that can be pursued.

Unfortunately, the US is one of the last countries to introduce laws tackling bullying in the workplace. A number of countries have recognized that dysfunctional behavior in the workplace is detrimental to employees, the organization and society as a whole. Many European countries provide employees with protection against bullying or dysfunctional behaviors, which requires employers to address these types of behaviors. Each country addresses these types of behaviors differently.

To date, the US does not have any type of anti-bullying legislation or laws to protect employees from bullying. The US Equal Employment Opportunity Commission (EEOC) (2003) recognizes that US laws pertaining to hostile work environments need to be changed and expanded upon to include bullying actions in the workplace. Currently, the EEOC defines "hostile work environment" as "behaviors which occur when unwelcome comments or conduct based on sex, race, or other legally protected characteristics unreasonably interferes with an employee's work performance or creates an intimidating, hostile or offensive work environment" (Federal Communications Commission, 2012: 1). Yet specifics related to dysfunction in leadership or the workplace have not been addressed.

The organizational role in dysfunction

Leadership has the power to influence and motivate employees by demonstrating appropriate and inappropriate behavior for the workplace. Encouraging a positive work environment and communication regarding what is appropriate and inappropriate behavior is essential for the organization. Up until this point in the book, we have examined the different dysfunctional leadership styles and traits along with the ability to recognize these dysfunctional leaders. While this information is helpful in terms of identifying and coping with dysfunctional leaders, we need to discuss how the culture of the organization may attempt to address some of the dysfunctional attributes that have been discussed in this book.

Table 10.1 Laws related to harassment by country/state

Country or region	Date(s) established	Type of action
Australia	2005	Adopted a workplace harassment code that provides practical advice about ways to prevent or control exposure to the risk of death, injury or illness create by workplace harassment. In 2005 it was amended to include bullying among workplace behaviors covered by an employer's duty of care for their employees; failure to meet this responsibility can result in prosecution and/or fines. (Beyond Bullying Association)

Australia	2008, 2010	First criminal law prohibiting workplace bullying (2008). Police can be called instead of health and safety investigators. The law was prompted after the suicide of a 19-year-old waitress who was bullied by three co-workers. Bullying acts included pouring beer and oil on her, taunting her, and calling her fat, ugly and a whore; she was physically restrained so that one person could pour fish oil on her and spit on her, and provided her with rat poison after an earlier suicide attempt failed. The three co-workers were convicted in February 2010 under occupational health and safety laws and were fined $85,000. The owner of the establishment and his company were fined $250,000. Her parents lobbied for stronger sanctions against workplace bullying. Because of the laws existing at that time, no one was jailed. In April 2011 a law was introduced entitled "Brodie's Law." It became law in June 2011. The law amends three criminal laws, including stalking crimes, stalking intervention and personal safety intervention. The existing law carries a penalty of up to ten years in prison if convicted of the crime. Under the new law, it is unlawful to make "threats to the victim" and to use, perform or direct toward the victim "abusive or offending" words or acts. Also punishable is acting "in any other way that could be reasonably be expected to cause physical or mental harm to the victim, including self-harm." "Mental harm" is defined as psychological harm and suicidal thoughts:
		
		• Development of an employer's guide to workplace bullying.
		• Defined bullying as "repeated less favorable treatment of a person by another or others in the workplace which may be considered unreasonable and inappropriate workplace practices. These behaviors include:
		
		  ○ Intimidation.
		  ○ Offending, humiliating or degrading another person.
		  ○ Under law the employer is responsible for protecting their employees from workplace bullying. If the employer does not protect employees, they can be found liable for physical and psychological harm" (www.workplacebullying.org/docs/Brodies-law.pdf).

| France | 2001 | Definition: Mobbing (bullying) is "The perverse implementation of power … a means of subjugation and persecution of the other questioning his fundamental rights as the respect which is due him or her." |

Protection of private workers: national anti-bullying law

- May request external mediation with a one-month time limit for both parties to appear.
- Retaliation is prohibited against testifying, recording or relating bullying behavior (whether direct or indirect), whether it concerns remunerations, training, redeployment or appointment.
- Evidence of harassment is first provided by the victim.
- Onus of proof is on the accused harasser to show: (a) that there is not bullying; or (b) that the decision was objectively justified.
- The perpetrator has the opportunity show their good faith because "false accusations of harassment can themselves constitute an effective form of harassment."
- Unions may go to court on behalf of an employee, providing support (financial or otherwise).
- Employers are responsible for bullying and they are to "take all necessary steps in view to prevent mobbing behavior."
- Executives can possibly be perpetrators or their accomplices or be victims themselves. It is thus essential that they should be fully informed by training of staff in the field of harassment and general HR management.

Civil servants

- Remunerator retaliation permitted when annual bonuses (up to 50 percent of income) can be arbitrarily reduced when the accuser's superior claims "the way it is" and used by administrative judges in cases heard, despite not being defined by law.
- No mediation option.
- Unions are prohibited from court involvement on behalf of the worker.
- No time limit for procedures.
- No manager or minister is held responsible.
- Case matters are not to be discussed; thus, bullied workers effectively risk termination for participating in the process if their superior chooses to invoke this principle whose interpretation is left up the administrative judges on a case-by-case basis.

(France's Law for Social Modernization, January 2002. Compiled by the Workplace Bullying Institute)

(continued)

Table 10.1 (continued)

Country or region	Date(s) established	Type of action
Sweden	1994	Employer should plan and organize work to prevent victimization of employees, which includes activities for early detection of signs and rectification of unsatisfactory working conditions. Special investigation shall be taken and followed up. Victims shall be given help or support quickly. Employers must have processes in place to provide support. Victimization includes recurrent reprehensible or distinctly negative actions which are directed against individual employees in an offensive manner and can result in those employees being placed outside the workplace community. The phenomenon includes: sexual harassment, adult bullying, mental violence, social rejection and harassment:

- Plan and organize works so as to prevent victimization.
- Make clear that these behaviors are not acceptable in the workplace and will not be tolerated.
- Provide methods for early detection and elimination of unsatisfactory working conditions.
- Implement measures that act on victimization early on and address the way in which work is organized.
- Provide support to employees who are targets.

(Complied by the Workplace Bullying Institute, *Victimization at Work: Sweden*, 1994)

Country or region	Date(s) established	Type of action
Britain	1997 (enacted in 2001)	**Workplace bullying**: Unfair dismissal of claimants might be compensated at tribunal for injury to feelings, including compensation for distress, humiliation and damage to their reputation in the community or to family life. Claimant's injury must constitute a clinically diagnosed psychiatric illness (therefore, catch-all conditions such as "stress," anxiety" and "depression" will not suffice) and an employer will only owe a duty of care to an employee if it is reasonably foreseeable (to an ordinary bystander) that a psychiatric disorder will arise. "Circumstances of danger" applied to any danger include that of harassment by a fellow worker, not just physical danger relating to work premises.

Examples of favorable bullying rulings

- A period of constant criticism, excessive monitoring and a tirade of unsubstantiated allegations (no substantive or quantifiable evidence) of underperformance which brought to an unexpected end a successful 25-year career.
- Unfair dismissal by new supervisor causing high workloads and malicious allegations.
- Injury to health caused by the bullying behavior of a female head teacher led to a stress breakdown following a yearlong series of confrontations with the headmistress whose methods he questioned.
- An employee bullied from her job because she asked to change shifts in order to share childcare with her husband when on return from maternity leave; she became a scapegoat for the section's ills, had her sickness record exaggerated and became the subject of unduly punitive attitudes. She was subjected to constructive dismissal following a spate of

false allegations by her supervisor who regularly criticized her performance, constantly undermined her position and speciously claimed that others were dissatisfied with her performance, lost her temper and reduced the plaintiff to tears, and the appointed mediator made matters worse. HR was notified but no appropriate action was taken.

- Constructive unfair dismissal when a manager was motivated by "spite" and senior managers were "vindictive," "refusing or failing to recognize he was the target of bullying." Tribunal found a breach of the implied term of mutual trust and confidence.
- British Health and Safety Executive (HSE) guidelines are provided to employers focused on preventing stress at work regarding bullying that can cause stress as well as preventative measures that should be in place to address bullying.
- Employers are responsible for the general care of employees. The target can make a claim for damages if the target incurs injury.
- Contractual agreement as in a labor agreement or implied "mutual trust and confidence" to provide a safe system of work for employees.

(*Review of International Laws Related to Workplace Bullying*. Compiled by the Workplace Bullying Institute: Great Britain: Protection from Harassment Act 1997)

Ireland	2007	In 2004 the Expert Advisory Group on Workplace Bullying compiled recommendations to address the phenomenon. In 2005 an amendment was passed by the National Safety, Health and Welfare Act recognizing bullying in the workplace as a societal issue. The Code of Practice falls under the Safety, Health and Welfare Act of 2005 and is aimed at preventing and addressing bullying in the Irish workplace. Bullying is a cost for both employers and employees. The cost can be in both financial and human terms. If not sorted out internally, a serious case could bring an employer before a tribunal, the Labour Court and/or the civil courts. If destructive behavior is tolerated and continues, it affects the performance and general health and well-being of individuals and/or groups. The negative effects can last a long time. Bullying can be carried out by supervisors, managers, subordinates, fellow employees, customers, business contacts or members of the public. The Code recommends dealing with cases internally through informal resolution by a responsible person and/or a formal complaints procedure. Only if internal processes fail should it be necessary to get outside support. The employer has a duty to manage and conduct work activities in such a way as to prevent any improper conduct or behavior likely to put the employee's safety, health or welfare at work at risk. The prevention of bullying must therefore be part of the management system. Risk is the likelihood of a hazard causing harm and the extent of that harm. (Health and Safety Authority, *Code of Practice for Employers and Employees on the Prevention and Resolution of Bullying at Work*, www.hsa.ie)

(continued)

Table 10.1 (continued)

Country or region	Date(s) established	Type of action
Italy		PRIMA, a non-profit organization founded in 1996, is the first Italian association against mobbing and psychological stress in the workplace. It works to address mobbing and providing assistance and support to victims. It also works to inform the population on mobbing by providing supporting studies, publications and meetings on this phenomenon. It also provides training and behavior counseling with courses and experiences to help individuals protect themselves against mobbing and to effectively handle conflict (http://www.mobbing-prima.it/chi_siamo-associazione_en.html).
Germany		KLIMA, a German organization, is focused on providing services related to mobbing, providing counseling and to help prevent mobbing in the workplace. This association is independent of employers. In addition, the General Equal Treatment Act has been enforced, which provides clear guidelines regarding anti-discrimination. The guidelines also provide information that every employer must have complaint mechanisms in place to which employees can turn if they feel they have been discriminated against by their employer, supervisor, other employees or third parties. Currently there are no statutory legal definitions related to workplace bullying.
Canada	2008	Federal workers: "Workplace violence" constitutes any action, conduct, threat or gesture of a person toward an employee in their workplace that can reasonably be expected to cause harm, injury and illness to that employee. The employer shall develop and post at a place accessible to all employees a workplace violence prevention policy that outlines the following:

* to provide a safe, healthy and violence-free workplace;
* to dedicate sufficient attention, resources and time to address factors that contribute to workplace violence, including but not limited to bullying, teasing and abusive and other aggressive behavior, and to prevent and protect against it;
* to communicate to its employees information in its possession about factors contributing to workplace violence; and
* to assist employees who have been exposed to workplace violence.

The bill addresses areas such as:

* Identification of factors that contribute to workplace violence.
* Assessment.
* Controls.
* Workplace violence prevention measures review.
* Procedures in response to workplace violence.
* Notification and investigation.
* Training.

(Canada Labour Code: Regulations Amending the Canada Occupational Health and Safety Regulations)

| Quebec | 2004 | Psychological harassment is defined in the form of misconduct, verbal comments, action or gestures. It can be characterized further by the following four criteria: |

- The behavior is repetitive or a single serious incident of behavior. It may also constitute psychological harassment if it undermines the person's psychological or physical integrity and if it has a lasting harmful effect.
- They are hostile or unwanted.
- They affect the person's dignity or psychological integrity.
- They result in a harmful work environment.

Psychological harassment may come from a superior, a colleague, a group of colleagues, a customer, a supplier, etc. Common ways in which harassment is expressed:

- Making rude, degrading or offensive remarks.
- Making gestures that seek to intimidate, engaging in reprisals.
- Discrediting the person: spreading rumors, ridiculing him, humiliating him, calling into question his convictions or personal life, shouting abuse at him or sexually harassing him.
- Belittling the person: forcing him to perform tasks that are belittling or below his skills, simulating professional misconduct.
- Preventing the person from expressing himself: yelling at him, threatening him, constantly interrupting him, prohibiting him from speaking to others.
- Isolating the person: no longer talking to him at all, denying his presence, distancing him from others.
- Destabilizing the person: making fun of his convictions, his tastes and his political choices.

Management practices:

- Promote respectful interpersonal communication.
- Manage the members of staff fairly.
- Take quick and appropriate action to manage conflicts; do not allow the situation to deteriorate.
- Clearly define the responsibilities and tasks of each employee.
- Put in place in their undertaking a procedure that is known, efficient, credible and adapted to reality in order to allow persons to report cases of harassment confidentially.
- Resort, in certain cases, to specialized resources to help put a stop to psychological harassment situation and to prevent such situations from arising.

(continued)

Table 10.1 (continued)

Country or region	Date(s) established	Type of action

Preventing psychological harassment in the workplace:

- Talk about the problem you are experiencing with someone that you are close to, a person who you trust. Do not remain isolated.
- Express clearly to the person who is the source of the unwanted behavior your wish to see such behavior cease immediately.
- Check inside the undertaking if there is a procedure making it possible to report the unwanted behavior confidentially.
- Bring the matter to the attention of your employer who must put a stop to this behavior by taking appropriate steps.

(Quebec Provincial Government Labour Standards, Sec. 81.18, effective June 1, 2004)

Saskatchewan 2007 Amendment to the Occupational Health and Safety Act, 1993. Harassment is defined as any inappropriate conduct, comment, display, action or gesture by a person that either:

- is based on race, creed, religion, color, sex, sexual orientation, marital status, family status, disability, physical size, or weight, age, nationality, ancestry or place of origin; or
- subject to adverse effects to the worker's psychological or physical well-being and that the person knows or ought to reasonably know would cause a worker to be humiliated or intimidated; and
- that constitutes to a threat to the health or safety of the worker.

The following was added in relationship to harassment:

- repeated conduct, comments displays, actions or gestures must be established; or
- a single serious occurrence of conduct, or a single, serious comment, display, action or gesture, which has a lasting, harmful effect on the worker is established;
- harassment does not include any reasonable action that is taken by an employer or a manager or supervisor employed or engaged by an employer, relating to the management and direct of the employer's workers or the place of employment.

(Bill No. 66: An Act to Amend the Occupational Health and Safety Act, 1993)

Ontario   2010   The Occupational Health and Safety Act defines workplace harassment as engaging in a course of vexatious comment or conduct against a worker in a workplace that is known or ought reasonably to be known to be unwelcome. The definition of workplace harassment also includes what is often called "psychological harassment" or "personal harassment." The comments or conduct typically happen more than once. They could occur over a relatively short period of time (for example, during the course of one day) or over a longer period of time (weeks, months or years). However, there may be situations where the conduct happens only once. Workplace harassment can involve unwelcome words or actions that are known of would be known to be offensive, embarrassing, humiliating or demeaning to a worker or group of workers in a workplace. It can also include behaviors that intimidate, isolate or even discriminate against the targeted individual(s). This may include:

- making remarks, jokes or innuendos that demean, ridicule, intimidate or offend;
- displaying or circulating offensive pictures or materials in print or electronic form;
- bullying;
- repeated offensive or intimidating phone calls or emails; or
- workplace sexual harassment.

Workplace harassment policies should:

- show an employer's commitment to addressing workplace harassment;
- consider workplace harassment from all sources such as customers, clients, employers, supervisors, workers, strangers and domestic/intimate partners;
- outline the roles and responsibilities of the workplace parties in supporting the policy and program; and
- be dated and signed by the highest level of management of the employer or at the workplace as appropriate.

Workplace harassment programs must include:

- measures and procedures for workers to report incidents of workplace harassment to the employer or supervisor;
- measures and procedures for workers to report incidents of workplace harassment to a person other than the employer or supervisor, if the employer or supervisor is the alleged harasser;
- how incidents and complaints of workplace harassment will be investigated; and dealt with
- how information obtained about an incident or complaint of workplace harassment, including information about individual involved, will not be disclosed, unless the disclosure is necessary for the purposes of investigating the incident or complaint, or for taking corrective action, or is otherwise required by law;
- how the worker who alleged harassment and the alleged harasser (if he or she works for the employer) will be informed of the results of the investigation and of any corrective action; and
- any prescribed elements that may be included in regulations made under the act.

(Health and Safety Guidelines, Ontario)

(continued)

Table 10.1 (continued)

Country or region	Date(s) established	Type of action
Manitoba	2011	Under the Manitoba Workplace Safety and Health Regulation, harassment is defined as: • an objectionable conduct that creates a risk to the health of a worker. If it is based on race, creed, relation, color, sex, sexual orientation, gender-determined characteristics, marital status, family status, source of income, political belief, political association, political activity, disability, physical size or weight, age, nationality, ancestry or place of origin; or • severe if it could reasonably cause a worker to be humiliated or intimidated and is repeated, or in the case of a single occurrence, has a lasting harmful effect on a worker; • reasonable conduct of an employer or supervisor in respect of the management and direction of workers or the workplace is not harassment. (Workplace Safety and Health Act)
US	2003 (has not been enacted)	The Healthy Workplace Bill was introduced in 2003 in 17 states. It has not been enacted to date. In January 2015, California mandated training in abusive conduct for supervisors in workplaces of 50 or more employees. Also, in 2015 Utah mandated training, but only to state employees.

Addressing the work environment

Characteristics of the work environment have an impact on feelings of frustration and stress. Scholars have found a link between aggressive behavior in the workplace and poor working conditions (Lawrence & Leather, 1999). These feelings lead to unhealthy and unresolved conflict, resulting in a work environment that is ripe for dysfunction. As leaders continue to experience stress and increased demands, they are faced with feelings of frustration which may manifest as dysfunction. Such feelings are often at the core of dysfunctional environments. When organizations are filled with stress and frustration, positive coping mechanisms are hampered. If leaders do not have an outlet for their stress, there is no place for these emotions to evolve except into negative and dysfunctional ways.

Dysfunctional leaders are quite astute in terms of disguising their dysfunctional behaviors through results and productivity. This can be apparent for a while, but eventually the dysfunctional behavior is recognized and, by that stage, the behavior has significantly impacted the organization in a negative way. Typical signs of a negative impact on the organization include non-compliance issues and not following proper procedures and policies within the organization.

Internal organizational interventions

There are a number of interventions that can be made within an organization to address dysfunctional leadership behaviors. The following list gives some of the interventions that can be employed within the organization to provide proper channels for preventing and/or addressing this type of behavior:

- *Organizations can set zero-tolerance expectations*: By properly defining what behavior will and will not be tolerated is critical for the organization. "Zero tolerance" means that any type of dysfunctional behavior, such as harassment, bullying, disruptive behaviors, discrimination or abusive behavior, will not be tolerated. Setting a base line to correct and address behaviors is central to communicating to employees what will and will not be accepted in the workplace. Many organizations set limits of basic respect in the workplace. These types of policies must be supported from the top down and need to be demonstrated by executive leadership. Anyone breaking these expectations should be coached regarding these behaviors or removed from the organization. It is important that while having these policies as part of the culture, whenever the policy is broken, it needs to be addressed quickly in order to demonstrate that the policy is not just words on paper. It is also vital to address issues of retaliation and that individuals who come forward to report dysfunctional behavior will be protected during and after an investigation.
- *Building a strong organizational culture*: Building a culture that has structure and provides the ability for employees and leaders to be held accountable for their behavior is important. We discussed earlier the role that organizational culture plays in dysfunction. The impact of this on the organizational culture can be damaging. However, building an organizational culture that promotes a healthy environment along with ensuring that the organization provides support to its employees is key to reducing these behaviors. Successful organizations require a culture where employees feel safe both physically and mentally.

- *Psychological safety*: Organizational cultures should strive to build an environment where employees feel safe to express their ideas, to learn for the betterment of themselves and the organization. Psychological safety is defined by Kahn (1990: 705) as the employee's "sense of being able to show and employ one's self without fear of negative consequences to self-image, status or career." Psychological safety positively correlates back to employee engagement, one's interpretation to work, availability and safety. Later research by Amy Edmondson (1999) focused on psychological safety in the construct of work teams and linking safety to learning and outcomes. There is a positive connection related to psychological safety and an employee's willingness to take risks and express themselves without fear. Increased psychological safety benefits the organization by generating new ideas while encouraging innovation and creativity. When employees feel free to express themselves and openly engage with the organization, innovation and creativity are allowed to flourish and thrive. Employees who feel psychologically safe in the workplace tend to be more engaged and satisfied with their work. Leaders who are supportive, democratic, concerned with the needs and feelings of employees, encourage questioning, listen to opinions and solve work-related problems create an environment of psychological safety. These leaders encourage employees to step past the constraints of their job description in order to try something new and to challenge themselves to grow and expand in their work. Psychological safety is hindered in a work environment where the leader motivates through fear and retaliation.

  Kahn (1990) stated that there are four factors that have a direct influence on psychological safety. The first factor explores interpersonal relationships as relating to trusting and supportive relationships. An environment that encourages trust is non-threatening, and supportive. Employees are more confident in taking risks, in being proactive and in openly sharing ideas, as well as feeling comfortable asking for help without fear of criticism. Employees who feel safe are more willing to collaborate with others as well as solve problems that may arise. When employees feel disconnected from their co-workers or leaders as a result of ostracizing and isolation, they often refrain from speaking up or sharing ideas and collaboration. The next feature of psychological safety relates back to team and group dynamics. Each group or team adopts roles and characteristics that are usually influenced by the action of the leaders. Other factors such as authority, competition and respect help to influence levels of psychological safety. Members of groups that feel less powerful and more controlled by a leader express lower levels of psychological safety than groups that experience higher levels of power and influence within the organization. The third factor relates to leadership. Leaders who are supportive, provide clear expectations, and are trusting, foster a work environment that is safe for employees. Those who are open and trusting of their employees encourage employees to come forward to share their ideas and to express themselves without fear or repercussions. Edmondson (2004) stated that leaders who promote an environment of psychological safety invite input and feedback, and tend to be approachable to employees. Leader inclusiveness fosters words and actions that demonstrate appreciation for employee contributions, encouraging learning and constructive feedback. The final factor relates back to organizational norms that are shared expectations among employees and leadership. These norms are linked back to the behaviors and expectations of the organization. Employees who work and behave according to these norms feel safer within an organization than employees who have less structure or less control within an organization.

Throughout this book we have explored dysfunctional leadership that does not provide psychological safety. While this may happen in an organization, it is critical that the environment embeds psychologically safe practices into the work environment and culture. Mechanisms and protocols to address issues where psychological safety is hindered may be used as a means of addressing this type of behavior. Creating outlets for employees to speak up without fear of retaliation is also critical to the success of the organization, along with its leadership and followers.

Keep in mind that dysfunctional leadership thrives in environments that are chaotic, full of change, have loose systems and struggle with accountability. Providing a solid foundation where employees are able to openly discuss these issues allows employees to openly address these behaviors and to squash the platform that is trying to be established by the dysfunctional leader. This is one of the best ways of preventing this type of behavior from entering the organization.

- *Performance management system*: Implementing management systems is another way to address as well as identify dysfunctional behavior. Employee surveys that are anonymous, 360-degree feedback instruments, and exit interviews are examples of how organizations can collect data on dysfunctional leadership in the workplace. This can be used to hold up a mirror for the leader to see the problem, as well as providing executive leadership with insights into what the issues are and where they exist in the organization. Data should be collected at all levels of the organization, from the CEO down. As mentioned in several earlier chapters, dysfunctional leaders will take on different personas with different groups of employees, peers, customers and leadership, so relying only on the insights of leadership is not enough. These behaviors need to be explored with direct reports, peers, and even internal and external customers. Pay attention to comments that are being made about the leader. Employees may be afraid to share direct comments, but examining the data for qualitative responses or themes can provide insights into the behavior of the leader. Listening to complaints as well as listening to the grapevine is another way to gather information. Whether through word of mouth, exit interviews or employee surveys, it is important to listen to what is being said. Don't ignore the comments as idle gossip; explore and see if there is truth behind the comments. Usually there is an element of truth behind these comments and, if so, it needs to be addressed. Too often, comments are written off as complaints by disgruntled employees. This might be true, but the organization needs to investigate these behaviors to see if there is an element of truth behind them. If it is from a disgruntled employee, then the organization also needs to protect the leader from these comments.

- *Address problems*: Weed out and address the problem. Ignoring the situation will not make the problem go away; it will only allow the behavior to continue to fester and to grow, spreading to other levels of the organization. If behavior is ignored, it sends the message that this type of behavior is acceptable, reinforced and tolerated. Employees will pick up on this message and will feel as though they are not valued by the organization. In addition to recognizing that the behavior is acceptable, employees may imitate the behavior of the leader, since it seems to work for that leader. Witnesses and bystanders will also notice the behavior and will begin to talk to others, adding to the gossip and rumor mill. People will be discouraged from applying for positions within the organization as the gossip and rumors permeate outside of the organization. Organizations have been known to simply remove the dysfunctional leader from one particular unit to another area of the organization, but this only passes the problem on to another area and spreads the dysfunction. It does not fix the problem and is only a temporary solution. Dysfunctional behaviors should not be tolerated by leadership, employees, customers, contractors or vendors. The organization needs to demonstrate a culture that focuses on respectful behavior from all who come into contact with the organization.

- *Addressing the hiring process*: Following a tight hiring process is another mechanism that can be used to address the problem. Look at references and screen thoroughly. While references today are focused on ensuring that they do not share too much information for fear of lawsuits, it is important to pick up subtle cues from the person giving the references. If phone calls are being made about references and are not being returned, this might mean something. When hiring from within, seek references from people who have worked directly or indirectly with the leader. Review employee surveys or exit interviews and explore turnover rates for that leader. If the person is moving into a leadership position for the first time, focus on interactions with fellow employees and other leaders, as well as employees outside of the work unit to get insights into any behaviors the employee may have demonstrated. Examine how that person handles stressful situations. Utilize behavior-based questions that ask for both positive and negative examples. For example, "tell me about a time you had conflict in the workplace: how did you handle it?" "Also, tell me about a time you had conflict in the workplace that did not go well. What did you learn from the experience and what would you have done differently?" If the response is "I don't have conflict with others," that is a red flag. Listen for patterns in the answers that are given and how they can demonstrate the situation, but remember that the person may be well versed in interviewing, so look for patterns and match these up with other data sources. Questions should include how the person handles stressful situations, interactions with others, and perceptions of the person and their leadership style. In addition, assessing the candidates regarding emotional intelligence or personality assessments may shed light on potential dysfunctional behavior. Remember that dysfunctional leaders like working in environments that are loose as well as full of chaos. The hiring process can be a signal to the dysfunctional leader of the type of system they are entering. If the hiring process is loose, then the leader will continue to pursue the opportunity. If the system appears tight, then the dysfunctional leader may eliminate themselves from the process, which is a way for the organization to inadvertently prevent the dysfunction from entering the workplace.
- *Education and training*: Educate and train employees and other leaders to recognize dysfunctional behaviors both within and outside the unit. Dysfunctional leaders are masters at disguising their behavior. Their goal is to go undetected and unreported. In order to accomplish this goal, they will use coercion, causing fear and intimidation. Organizations should provide communication along with education on the process of how to report dysfunctional behavior. It is also important to stress that the environment is one in which employees are safe from retaliation. This needs to

be linked to a zero-tolerance policy along with building an organizational culture of trust and safety. In order to open the doors of communication, employees need to feel that they will not be retaliated against. Focus on building a culture of psychological safety where employees feel safe to report situations and observations, without fear of such retaliation.

- *Behavioral observations*: Observe how others in the organization are acting within and outside of the unit. Are they engaged and are they feeling as though they are part of the organization? Do they share thoughts and ideas openly? Is the unit innovative or lacking creative ideas? What is the absenteeism rate within that unit? What is the body language of the people within the unit? Other signs may include reduction in productivity, lower employee satisfaction results, increase in waste, more overtime that was not planned or scheduled, customer complaints, etc. Explore the many signs that employees send out and explore the issues that may arise. Don't just look at the unit; look across the organization.

- *Address conducive environments*: Dysfunctional leaders need a system and a culture that will support and sustain their dysfunction, either directly or indirectly (we have addressed this in earlier chapters). Environments in which upper leadership encourages unhealthy competition and conflict are often those where dysfunctional leadership resides. As a result, complaints are filed and the organization will ignore these complaints. In some cases the target will find that the organization may address the problem, but will only make matters worse since most organizations are not equipped to handle these behaviors. When this occurs, it results in making the problem worse through retaliation or other forms of punishment. Address these types of environments as well as addressing sub-cultures within the organization that may promote this type of behavior.

Conclusion

The behavior of the dysfunctional leader is not within anyone's control. The only control the target has is in how they react to the situation and handle the problems that arise. The target cannot control when the dysfunctional leader will act out. The leader controls the situation, including when and where the next strike will take place. It is central for the target to anticipate that there will be an attack and to be prepared for the next instance; however, it is important that they do not obsess over when the next attack will be or what could have been done differently during the last attack. Once the target realizes that they cannot control the situation, they can begin to focus on healing and taking control of their lives. Utilizing positive coping mechanisms will help the target to identify healthy ways to address the problem. Equally important for the target to understand is that they are not alone; they are not the first target of this dysfunctional leader. There are probably many, many more who have or are currently experiencing this leader's dysfunctional behavior. Talking to others will uncover those who have experienced this same situation and the target will be able to learn from these experiences.

The organization has a role to play in addressing dysfunctional behavior. Building a strong culture that focuses on building psychological safety, trust and zero-tolerance policies is a start. Leadership must effectively demonstrate how to promote positive and healthy leadership behaviors and to make clear behaviors that will and will not be tolerated. If an organization is struggling with building this type of culture, it will be necessary to reach out to organizational consultants who can assist with helping to build a strong culture that is healthy for all. The lifeline of the organization and the employees depends on a healthy environment.

References

Edmondson, A. 1999. Psychological safety and learning behavior in work teams. *Administrative Science Quarterly, 44*(2), 350–383.

Edmondson, A. 2004. Psychological safety, trust and learning in organizations. A group level lens. In R.M. Kramer and K.S. Cook (eds.), *Trust and distrust in organizations: Dilemmas and approaches* (pp. 239–272). New York: Russell Sage Foundation.

Kahn, W. 1990. Psychological conditions of personal engagement and disengagement at work. *Academy of Management Journal, 33*(4), 692–724.

Lawrence, C., & Leather, P. 1999. *The social psychology of violence and aggression. Work-related violence: Assessment and intervention.* New York: Routledge.

Martin, R. 2010. *The psychology of humor: An integrative approach.* New York: Elsevier Academic Press.

Namie, G., & Namie, T. 2009. US workplace bullying: Some basic considerations and consultation interventions. *Consulting Psychology Journal: Practice and Research, 61*(3), 202–219.

Roter, A. 2011. *The lived experiences of registered nurses exposed to toxic leadership behaviors.* Dissertation. ProQuest.

Index

Aasland, M. 10
Abagnale, Frank Jr. 106
absenteeism 13, 37, 124, 125, 169
abuse of power 4, 11, 14, 57, 58, 116
abusive leadership 10–11, 46
accountability: bullying 20, 33, 38; ethical conduct 62, 63; organizational culture 73, 165
accusations 35
acquisitions 60, 99
active listening 154
Adams, Andrea 20
Ades, Y. 127
admiration: narcissists 76, 82, 86–87, 88, 90, 92, 93; psychopaths 95, 96; toxic leaders 9
Adorno, T. 46
affairs 68–69
age 34
aggression 8, 68; bullying 20, 21, 32; Dark Triad 73; Machiavellianism 117; narcissists 79, 87, 91; psychopaths 97, 103, 107; tyrants 45; *see also* violence
agreeableness, low 73, 74, 115
al-Assad, Bashar 51–52, 55
alcohol use 13, 137, 146
aliases 102–103
alienation 13, 46, 50
Allen, N. 129
ambition 6, 12, 29, 45, 76
Andersson, L. 36
anger 135, 138, 147; narcissists 84–85, 89, 91; sociopaths 98
anti-social behavior 73, 74, 86, 128, 134
anxiety 37, 73, 98, 126–127, 135–136, 139
appeasement 145
Aquino, K. 131
arrogance 6, 12; narcissists 73, 74, 75, 76, 87; psychopaths 73; tyrants 46
Arthur Andersen 4

Aryee, S. 134
Ashforth, B. 8, 46, 57
attention seeking 73, 75, 76, 86
Aung San Suu Kyi 15
Australia 156
avoidance 145–146
Avolio, B. 15

bad leadership 4, 8
Baron, R. 8, 10
Barrow, L. 20
behavioral observations 169
behaviors 128
Bin Laden, Osama 53
Bing, S. 5
blame 148, 152; bullying 25, 33; false accusations 136; narcissists 78, 82, 84, 91, 92, 93; passive-aggressive leadership 12; tyrants 45, 46, 47, 57
boasting 45, 46, 57
body language 25, 40
Bonaparte, Napoleon 16
Bond Institute 10
Bond, S. 20–21
bonuses 14, 15, 67, 68, 100, 106, 157
boundaries 41, 42, 86–87, 100
bribery 65
Brouer, R. 8
Brown, M. 62, 64
Buckley, R. M. 8
bullying 5, 7, 8, 16, 19–44, 145, 146; abusive leadership 11; characteristics of 21; choice of target 39–40; critical bullies 25–26; dealing with 40–42; definitions of 20–21; destructive leadership 10; friendly bullies 26–28; gender 31–32; hoarder bullies 28–29; impact of 36–37; incivility versus 36; laws against 155, 156–157, 158–159, 160; mobbing 20, 30–31, 42, 157, 160; opportunistic bullies 29–30; organizational

172 Index

role 37–38; public or direct bullies 22–24; recognizing 38–39; silent or indirect bullies 24–25; tactics 32–35; zero tolerance 165
Burns, J. M. 6–7, 62
Bush, George W. 53
bystanders 89, 139, 154, 168

Caligula 5
callousness 73, 95, 101, 104
Canada 160–164
Castro, Fidel 16
Chandler, D. 64
change 15, 130; Machiavellianism 111, 114; psychopaths 99, 104, 105, 109; resistance to 124, 128
chaos 8, 15, 124, 132, 168; bullying 38; Machiavellianism 117; narcissists 90; psychopaths 98, 100–101, 104–105, 106, 109
charisma 10, 15; Machiavellianism 118; narcissists 77, 80, 88; negative 15–16; psychopaths 106, 107
charm 149; narcissists 77, 87, 93; psychopaths 73, 98, 99, 100, 105, 107–108, 109; toxic leaders 9
cheating 64, 65, 117
Chen, Z. 134
chief executive officers (CEOs) 59–60, 67–69
Christie, R. 115–116
Churchill, Winston 15, 16
coercion: abusive leadership 11; coercive power 14, 15; psychopaths 100; tyrants 45, 57; unethical behavior 64
coldness 73, 74, 117
commitment 3, 9, 99; impact of bullying on 37; impact of dysfunctional leadership on 11, 124, 125, 128, 129; job satisfaction related to 134
communication: narcissists 77, 80, 93; psychopaths 105, 107
competitiveness 7, 60, 74; bullying 38; Machiavellianism 117; narcissists 76, 87, 88; organizational culture 130, 131; teams 124
complaints 150–151, 153, 167, 169
conflict 32, 124, 133–134; destructive leadership 10; forced conflict resolution 46; organizational culture 130; passive-aggressive leadership 12; psychopaths 104; unethical leadership 66; work and family 135
conformity 67
confrontation 147–149
conscience 66, 96, 97, 100
consistency 79
constructive narcissists 77, 80, 88, 93

control 11, 12, 145; bullies 22, 40; lack of personal control 136–137; Machiavellianism 113, 118, 119; narcissists 78, 82, 84, 88, 89, 93; psychopaths 96; tyrants 45; unethical behavior 64
Cooper, C. 8, 31
coping mechanisms 144–154, 165; negative 144–147; organizational coping 153–154; organizational mechanisms for individual coping 150–153; positive 147–150, 169
corporate psychopaths *see* psychopaths
corruption 8, 9, 64, 65, 66, 114, 116
creativity 57, 77, 127, 129, 166
credit, taking: bullying 29; narcissists 78, 81, 82, 83–84, 92; tyrants 46, 47, 57; unethical leadership 66
crime 95, 98, 104, 156
criticism: abusive leadership 11; bullying 22, 25–26, 33, 35, 39; legal rulings 158; narcissists 76, 80, 84; tyrants 45, 47, 57
cruelty 5, 46, 113, 114
cynicism 73, 74, 115, 117

Dahling, J. 118
Dark Side of Leadership 11–12
Dark Triad 7, 8, 17, 73–74, 120; *see also* Machiavellianism; narcissists; psychopaths
deadlines 35, 59–60
Deborah, Y. 134
deception 149; Machiavellianism 73, 74, 111, 115, 119, 120; narcissists 78, 80; psychopaths 73, 96, 97, 99, 102–103, 109; unethical leadership 66; *see also* lying
decision-making 12, 129; accountability 63; destructive leadership 10; ethical leadership 62, 63; hoarder bullies 28; narcissists 76, 81, 93; psychopaths 100, 107; tyrants 45, 57
defensiveness 14
delegation 12, 84, 89
Delves, R. 63
denial 101, 145
depression 23, 37, 39, 42, 135
derailment 4, 34–35
destructive leadership 4, 8, 10, 65
deviance 11, 74
Diamond, Jared 111
Dimon, Jamie 60
disability 34, 162, 164
disaster hunters 5
discrimination 59, 139; laws against 155, 160; legal advice 152; organizational policies 153; zero tolerance 165

dishonesty 73, 119
dissent 69
distress 11, 36–37, 134, 135–138, 155; *see also* stress
distrust 45, 46, 61, 130, 136; Machiavellianism 117, 118, 119; narcissists 75, 78, 79, 85–86, 93; tyrants 57
documentation 42, 149, 150, 151, 152
Dollard, M. 20–21
dominance 73, 75, 76
Drach-Zahavy, A. 13
drama 100–101
drug use 13, 137, 146
Duffy, M. 6, 8, 128, 134
Dunlap, Albert J. 59
dysfunctional leadership 3, 4–16; addressing 142–170; costs of 13; definitions of 5–6; different terms used for 7–13; history of 4–5; impact on followers 134–139, 140; impact on the organization 123–134, 140; role of power 13–15; *see also* bullying; Dark Triad; tyranny; unethical leadership

eating disorders 13, 137, 146
Ebert, R. 134
Edmondson, Amy 166
EduCap, Inc. 68
education and training 168–169
Einarsen, S. 8, 10, 20, 31
Ellis, Havelock 75
Ellison, Larry 60
embarrassment 13, 136, 138
emotional abuse 8
emotional detachment 73, 74, 104, 117
emotional distress 9, 36, 134, 135–138, 155
emotional empathy 81
emotional intelligence 7, 76, 80, 81, 168
emotional outbursts 45, 57, 98
emotions: addressing the situation 147; bullying 37, 39, 41, 42; checking 147–148; emotional impact of dysfunctional leadership 135–138, 139; narcissists 84–85, 93; psychopaths 98, 100, 102, 103, 107; sociopaths 98
empathy, lack of 73, 76, 79–80, 81, 86, 89, 93, 101
Employee Assistance Programs (EAPs) 151–152
employees: behavioral observations 169; coping mechanisms 144–153; ethical leadership 62–63; impact of dysfunctional leadership on 124–126, 134–139, 140; injustices 129–130; narcissists 88–89; organizational commitment 129;

organizational culture 126–128; psychological safety 166–167; tyrants 58; unethical behavior 66; unvalued 132; Zynga 59–60; *see also* job satisfaction; teamwork; turnover
Enron 4, 65, 67
Ensley, M. 128
entitlement 73, 75, 79, 82, 86, 104
envy 78–79
Equal Employment Opportunity Commission (EEOC) 155
Erickson, K. 7
Erturk, A. 31
ethics: ethical leadership 62–63, 65; ethical principles 63; Machiavellianism 116–117, 119; *see also* unethical leadership
evil 4, 113, 114, 115
exclusion 32; *see also* isolation
excuses 12
executive pay 67
exit interviews 167, 168
exit strategies 92–93, 151
expectations 11, 25; lack of 73; narcissists 84; psychological safety 166–167; tyrants 47; unethical leadership 66, 67; zero-tolerance 165
expert power 14
exploitation 73, 80
extroversion 105

failure, fear of 11
fairness 62–63, 129
falsification of numbers 61, 67, 68, 145
family conflicts 135
Fastow, Andrew 67
favoritism 10, 11
fear 14, 15, 135, 138, 142; bullying 20, 37; of failure 11; financial results 124; Machiavellianism 114, 117; psychopaths 97, 107; of retaliation 69, 89, 100, 107, 139, 142–143, 151, 154, 167; toxic leadership 9; tyrants 55, 56, 60; unethical leadership 69
feedback: asking for 41; bullying 33; narcissists 81, 91–92; passive-aggressive leaders 12; psychological safety 166; psychopaths 96; resistance to 14; 360-degree 91, 167; tyrants 47
Ferris, G. 8
Fields, T. 20
financial crisis 67
financial irresponsibility 104
financial issues 138–139
financial results 124
Fiorina, Carly 90–91

174 Index

followership 69, 88–89, 133, 134; *see also* employees
Forni, P. 75
France 157
fraud 65, 66, 67, 100
Frenkel-Brunswick, E. 46
Freud, Sigmund 5, 7, 75, 76

Gandhi, Mahatma 15, 16
Ganster, D. 8
Geis, F. 115–116
gender: bullying 31–32, 34; harassment laws 162, 164; narcissists 87
Genghis Khan 5, 60
Germany 160
Glad, B. 46, 85
goals 14, 128; abusive leadership 11; ethical leadership 62; job satisfaction 134; Machiavellianism 116, 118; narcissists 76, 79, 82, 84; psychopaths 96, 107; tyrants 46, 47; unethical behavior 64, 66, 67
Goldman, A. 130
Goodwin, Fred 88
gossip 124, 125, 149, 168; bullying 26, 27, 31, 33, 34, 35; humiliation 136; relational aggression 103
grandiosity 73, 75, 79, 86, 107
Grandy, G. 11
gratitude 85, 93
Great Britain 158–159
greed: culture of 100; psychopaths 95, 97, 102; tyrants 60, 65
Griffin, R. 134
guilt 13, 37, 137, 138, 139

Hafkamp, M. 127
harassment 128, 139, 143; bullying 20, 21; laws against 155, 156–164; legal advice 152; narcissists 89; organizational policies and processes 153, 154; zero tolerance 165
Hare, C. 14
Harris, P. 63
Harvey, M. 8
healing 154–155
health 13, 37, 134, 138, 147
healthy conflict 124
Helmsley, Leona 57–59
helplessness 13, 28, 42, 46, 139
Henle, C. 134
Higgs, M. 80
hiring process 106–107, 168

Hitler, Adolf 6, 16, 45, 46, 47, 49, 50
Hoel, H. 8, 31
Hogan, R. 8, 133
Holloway E. 8, 131–132
honesty 63
Hoobler, J. 128
hopelessness 39, 135
Hornstein, H. 46
hostile work environments 33, 155
hostility 75
Howell, J. 15
Human Resources (HR) 150–151
human rights 9, 52, 55
humiliation 33, 128, 136, 154; addressing the situation 147; bullying 20, 21, 22, 35; harassment 161; post-traumatic stress disorder 137; psychopaths 107; relational aggression 103
Hunter, S. 15
Hutchinson, M. 21

illegal practices 11, 145; *see also* crime
impulsive behavior 11, 73, 74, 101, 104
incivility 36
incompetence 8, 9, 22, 25, 33, 136
individualism 66
inflexibility 46, 57
influence 13, 106, 107, 118
information: gossip 34; misuse of 89; withholding 28–29, 32, 35, 42, 117, 119, 124, 128
injustice 11, 129–130, 137
innovation 57, 124, 127, 129, 166
insecurities: bullies 21–22, 25, 40, 42; narcissists 78, 79; targets of bullying 40
insensitivity 11, 12
insider trading 67, 69
insults 22, 38–39, 47, 154; *see also* name calling; verbal abuse
integrity 6, 63, 64
intelligence: Machiavellianism 119; psychopaths 96, 98, 104, 106, 109; toxic leaders 9
interviews 106, 107
Ireland 159
isolation: avoidance 145–146; bullying 20, 21, 24, 28, 32–33, 35–36, 37, 39, 42; emotional impact of dysfunctional leadership 135, 136; harassment 161; narcissists 75, 79; psychological safety 166; psychopaths 107; suffering in silence 143
Italy 160
Ivan the Terrible 5

Jackson, D. 21
Jacques, E. 14
job demands 33
job satisfaction 3, 129, 134; behavioral
    observations 169; bullying 37, 38; Dark Side
    of Leadership 11
job security 22, 33
job switching 99
Jones, Jim 16
JP Morgan 60

Kahn, W. 166
Kaiser, R. 8, 133
Kaufman, Ron 123
KBW 68–69
Keashly, L. 8, 20
Kellerman, B. 6, 8, 59, 65, 132, 134
Kennedy, John F. 15, 16
Kets de Vries, M. 5, 6, 8, 75, 77
Kim Il-sung 45
Kim Jong-un 56
King, G. 75
King, Martin Luther 15, 16
Kohut, H. 77
Kozlowki, Dennis 68
Kusy, M. 8, 131–132

Lambert, L. 134
laws 143, 152–153, 155, 156–164
Lay, Kenneth 88
leadership 3–4; ethical principles 63; Machiavelli
    on 113–115; role of narcissism 86–87; see
    also dysfunctional leadership; senior leaders;
    unethical leadership
Lease, D. 126
legal advice 152–153
legal rights 155; see also laws
legitimate power 14, 15
Lencioni, P. 130
Levinson, D. 46
Levy, P. 118
Lewis, S. 19
Leymann, Heinz 20, 30, 137
Lind, A. 129
Lipman-Blumen, J. 8, 9
listening 154, 167
Liu, K. 127
loose systems 38, 106, 109, 128, 130, 168
Lovelace, J. 15
loyalty 9, 132, 144; Machiavellianism 114;
    narcissists 78, 83, 88, 89

lying 11, 149; destructive leadership 10;
    Machiavellianism 111, 117–118; psychopaths
    95, 96, 97, 102–103, 109; unethical leadership
    64, 65, 66, 68; see also deception
Lynch, J. 123

Maccoby, M. 88
MACH-IV scale 115
Machiavelli, Niccolo 111–115
Machiavellianism 4, 7, 73–74, 111–120;
    characteristics and traits 118–119; definitions
    of 115; ethics 116–117; modern times 119;
    positive lens 118; principles of 117–118;
    research on 115–116; unethical leadership 64
Madoff, Bernie 88, 96
Malcolm X 16
Mandela, Nelson 15, 16, 51
manipulation: financial results 124;
    Machiavellianism 73, 74, 111, 115–116, 117,
    118–119, 120; narcissists 80, 82; psychopaths
    74, 95, 96, 98, 99–100, 103, 106–107, 109
Manitoba 164
McDermmott, James Jr. 68–69
media 55, 90
men: bullying 31–32; narcissists 87
merges and acquisitions 60, 99
Merrill Lynch and Company 68
Meyer, J. 129
micro-management 10, 35; Machiavellianism
    119; narcissists 84, 89; tyrants 45, 47, 57, 60
Millar, C. M. 63
Miller, D. 5, 77
Miller, R. 116
mistakes 22, 23, 92
Mitchell, M. 64
mobbing 20, 30–31, 35, 42, 157, 160
money: Machiavellianism 119; narcissists 87;
    psychopaths 95, 97, 104
Moore, M. 123
morale 13, 123, 125, 134, 151
morality 116, 119; see also ethics
Morin, R. 75
Mother Theresa 15
motivation 11, 60, 116, 118, 123
Mowday, R. 129
Mugabe, Robert 50–51
Murdoch, Rupert 60
Mussolini, Benito 45

name calling 11, 34; see also insults
Namie, G. & T. 8, 20

Index

narcissists 4, 5, 7–8, 73–74, 75–94; addressing 91–92; characteristics and traits 80–86; Dark Side of Leadership 11; dealing with 92–93; definitions of 75–76; gender 87; impact of 87–89; Machiavellianism 119; psychopathy compared with 101–102; reasons for following narcissists 89–91; role in leadership 86–87; two faces of 77–80
Near, D. 116
Negative Acts Questionnaire-Revised (NAQ-R) 35
negative charisma 15–16
Neuman, J. 8, 10
non-verbal cues 40; *see also* body language
norms: ethical leadership 62; narcissists 87; organizational 11, 126, 127–128, 130, 140, 145; psychological safety 166–167; psychopaths 97; tyrants 47; unethical leadership 66

Obama, Barack 111
obedience 69
objectivity 63
Olweus, D. 20
Ontario 163
openness 63
Oracle 60
organizational change *see* change
organizational culture 11, 123, 126–128, 130–131, 140, 155; building a strong 165, 169–170; bullying 37–38; ethical leadership 62; narcissists 88, 93; psychological safety 166, 169; tyrants 47
organizational interventions 165–169
organizational skills 103
organizational structure 131–132
organizations 87–88, 123–134, 140, 150–154
Ostroff, C. 134

Padilla, A. 8, 133
Pagon, M. 8
paranoia 5, 50, 61, 85, 100
parasitic behavior 101, 105
passive-aggressive leadership 12–13
passive coping 144, 147
Paulhus, D. 8, 73
Pearson, C. 36
Pellitier, K. 46
perfectionism 11, 58
performance 13; impact of bullying on 37; job satisfaction related to 134; Machiavellianism 118; results 124, 132; tyrants 46; *see also* productivity
performance management systems 167

personal security 33
personal space 33
persuasion 100, 107
petty tyranny 4, 8, 46
physical abuse 10, 11, 34; *see also* violence
physical distress 36–37, 138
Pincus, Mark 59–60
Pittinsky, T. 75, 81, 86
policies 153, 154, 163; inconsistent application of 33; loose systems 128; zero-tolerance 38, 165, 168–169
political astuteness 106, 116, 117, 118, 153–154
politics 16, 65; Trump 90–91; tyrants 47–57
Pope John Paul II 15, 16
Popper, N. 64
Porter, L. 129
positioning 83, 93
positive leadership 4, 6, 169–170
post-traumatic stress disorder (PTSD) 37, 137, 139
power 13–15; abuse of 4, 11, 14, 57, 58, 116; bullying 19, 21, 22, 28, 40; Machiavellianism 111, 113, 114, 116, 119; narcissists 76, 78, 79–80, 82, 87, 88, 93; organizational culture 130; psychopaths 95, 96, 97; tyrants 45, 46, 57; unethical behavior 64, 65
power wielders 6–7
powerlessness 37, 65
pragmatism 73
pressure 67, 97, 100, 104, 109
prestige 14, 76, 95, 119
proactive narcissists 77, 80, 93
problem solving 147, 148
productive narcissists 77, 80, 93
productivity 3, 8, 165; behavioral observations 169; bullying 37; health problems 13; impact of dysfunctional leadership on 123, 124, 125, 151; job satisfaction related to 134; Machiavellianism 118; *see also* performance
professional help 41, 143, 154, 155
psychological abuse 21, 30–31, 35
psychological problems 138, 146
psychological safety 166–167, 169
psychopaths 7, 64, 73–74, 95–110; addressing 108–109; characteristics and traits 102–106; definition of 96–97; evolution of corporate psychopaths 98–100; followers 107–108; hiring a corporate psychopath leader 106–107; Machiavellianism 119; narcissism compared with 101–102; recognizing 109; sociopaths compared with 97–98
public criticism 11, 35, 45, 57; *see also* criticism

punishment 11, 14, 15, 46, 54, 56
Putin, Vladimir 52, 54–55

Quebec 161–162

race 34, 59, 155, 162, 164
Raknes, B. 20
Rayner, C. 8, 31
recklessness 6
references 149, 168
referent power 14
Reino, A. 127
relationships: emotional impact of dysfunctional
    leadership 135; Machiavellianism 116, 117;
    narcissists 78, 79, 81–82, 93; organizational
    commitment 129; psychological safety 166;
    psychopaths 98
remorselessness: narcissists 85, 88; psychopaths 73,
    96, 97, 100, 102
reporting dysfunctional behavior 133, 150–152,
    154, 161
reputation 6, 28, 37, 63, 130
resentment 12
resources, hoarding 28–29
responsibility: bullies 20, 33; narcissists
    93; psychopaths 103; tyrants 47; *see also*
    accountability
restructuring 131–132
results 124, 132, 165
retaliation, fear of 69, 89, 100, 107, 139,
    142–143, 151, 154, 167
revenge 117–118, 134
reward power 14, 15
rewards 14, 15, 100, 133; Machiavellianism 118;
    narcissists 89; organizational commitment 129;
    organizational norms 127–128; psychopaths 106
rights 37, 97; human 9, 52, 55; legal 155
risk-taking behavior 88, 90, 93, 100, 166
Rosenthal, S. 75, 81, 86
Roter, A. 151
rules 11; ethical 63; inconsistent application of
    33; lack of 128; Machiavellianism 116, 119;
    narcissists 87; obedience to 69; psychopaths 97;
    tyrants 47, 61; unethical leadership 64
rumors 124, 125, 149; bullying 24, 26, 31, 32–33,
    34, 35; harassment 161; relational aggression 103
ruthlessness 60, 78, 105, 113

sabotage 24, 64, 134; bullying 20; derailment
    34–35; injustices 130; unethical leadership 66
Saddam Hussein 16, 45, 46, 52–54

safety 165, 166–167, 169
Sanford, R. 46
sarcasm 35
Saskatchewan 162
scandals 60, 62, 64, 65, 66, 67–69
scapegoating 9, 33, 149
Schanke, M. 8
Schein, Edgar 126
self-absorption 73, 75, 76, 86
self-awareness 80
self-confidence 16, 154–155; bullying 37, 40, 42;
    narcissists 77, 79, 89, 90; psychopaths 100, 107
self-destruction 7, 78, 93, 130
self-doubt 23
self-efficacy 76
self-enhancement 66, 69, 74
self-esteem 11, 13, 154; body language 40; bullies
    19, 21–22, 42; narcissists 75–76, 79, 82, 88, 90,
    91, 92; rebuilding 155; tyrants 46; unethical
    leadership 66
self-harm 13, 137, 146
self-importance 78, 80, 81, 119
self-interest 11; Machiavellianism 73, 119;
    narcissists 75, 76; psychopaths 97; unethical
    leadership 64, 65, 66
self-medication 146
self-promotion 73
selfishness 73
selflessness 63
senior leaders: addressing dysfunctional
    leadership 149, 150, 152; focus on results 132;
    followership 133; HR role 151; opportunistic
    bullies 29, 30; organizational values 127
sexual harassment 89, 143, 153, 158, 161, 163;
    see also harassment
sexuality 34, 59, 87, 162, 164
shame 13, 37, 91, 137, 138
shareholder value 59
Shkreil, Martin 68
sick days 138–139, 151
silence, suffering in 143, 144, 146
silent treatment 28, 89
Skilling, Jeff 67, 88
Skogstad, A. 8, 10, 31
social justice 129–130
social skills 12, 19, 22
social support 147, 150
sociopaths 97–98, 103
soft power 14
Somech, A. 13
speaking up 144

178 Index

stages of understanding 139
Stalin, Joseph 46, 47
Stamper, R. 127
Starratt, A. 11
statements, framing 41
status 11; bullies 19, 28, 42; Machiavellianism 118, 119; narcissists 76, 77, 78, 87; power and 13, 14, 15; tyrants 50, 61; unethical leadership 65
Steers, R. 129
stereotypes 14
strengths, reaffirming your 150
stress 7; bullying 37; emotional symptoms 135; HSE guidelines 159; legal rulings 158; Machiavellianism 117; organizational 131; physical symptoms 135, 138; positive coping mechanisms 147; psychopaths 97, 100, 101, 104–105; tyrants 46; unethical leadership 67; work environments 165; *see also* distress
success 95, 97, 119
suffering in silence 143, 144, 146
suicide 13, 135, 140, 146, 156
Sun, L. 134
superiority 73, 75, 78
supervision 8
support 4, 41, 147, 150, 154
suspicion 45, 78, 117, 136
Sweden 158
sycophants 78, 92

tax evasion 58, 61, 65, 68
teamwork: impact of dysfunctional leadership on 123; injustices 130; lack of team synergy 124; narcissists 83–84, 93; psychological safety 166
teasing 35
temptation 65
Tepper, B. 6, 128, 134
termination of employment 47, 58, 60, 82, 125–126, 137
terrorism 52, 53, 90
Thain, John 68
Thau, S. 131
threats 11, 20, 33, 34, 128
thrill seeking 73, 97, 98, 100, 104, 107
time, lost 125
time off 138–139
timing a conversation 148–149
tone of voice 25, 40, 148
toxic leadership 4, 8–9
training 36, 143, 164, 168–169
trauma 79

Trevino, L. 62
Trotsky, Leon 48
Trump, Donald 90–91
trust: ethical leadership 63; impact of dysfunctional leadership on 130; narcissists 78; organizational culture 169; psychological safety 166; psychopaths 95, 98; unethical leadership 66; *see also* distrust
Tuckey, M. 20–21
Turning Pharmaceuticals 68
turnover 3, 168; bullying impact 37; costs of 9; impact of dysfunctional leadership on 124, 125–126, 151; job satisfaction 134; organizational commitment 129
Tyco 4, 68
Tyler, T. 129
tyranny 5, 7, 16–17, 45–61; defining 45–46; downfall of tyrants 61; organizational tyrants 57–60; petty 4, 8, 46; political tyrants 47–57; unethical leadership 64, 65

uncertainty 15, 38, 90, 104, 111; *see also* chaos
unemployment 139
unethical leadership 10, 17, 62–70; complaints procedures 153; crossover with destructive or tyrant leadership 65; defining 63–64; faceless victims 66; followers 69; Machiavellianism 116, 120; temptation and greed 65; tipping points 66–67; traits of an unethical leader 65; tyrants 47, 61
unfair criticism 33
unfair dismissal 158–159
unions 157

Vadi, M. 127
values: dysfunctional 131; ethical leadership 62, 63; narcissists 79; organizational 126, 127, 129, 140, 145; unethical leadership 64
vanity 73
verbal abuse 8, 10–11; bullying 19, 20, 21, 34, 35; psychopaths 107; *see also* insults
Vickers, M. 21
victimization 158
violence: laws against 160; organizational conflict 134; psychological 31; psychopaths 97; tyrants 45; *see also* aggression; physical abuse
vision 4, 76, 77, 78, 81, 88

weakness 22, 40, 46, 96, 136, 147
Weber, Max 13

weight 34, 162, 164
Whitaker, B. 118
Wilkes, L. 21
Williams, K. 8, 73
Wilson, D. 116
women: bullying 31–32; narcissists 87
work environments 165; conducive 169; hostile 33, 155
workload 33
Workplace Bullying Institute 20, 31

WorldCom 4, 65
Wyatt, J. 14

Yamada, D. 20
Yeltsin, Boris 54

Zapf, D. 31
zero-tolerance policies 38, 165, 168–169
Zinko, R. 8
Zynga 59–60

Taylor & Francis eBooks

Helping you to choose the right eBooks for your Library

Add Routledge titles to your library's digital collection today. Taylor and Francis ebooks contains over 50,000 titles in the Humanities, Social Sciences, Behavioural Sciences, Built Environment and Law.

Choose from a range of subject packages or create your own!

Benefits for you
- Free MARC records
- COUNTER-compliant usage statistics
- Flexible purchase and pricing options
- All titles DRM-free.

Benefits for your user
- Off-site, anytime access via Athens or referring URL
- Print or copy pages or chapters
- Full content search
- Bookmark, highlight and annotate text
- Access to thousands of pages of quality research at the click of a button.

REQUEST YOUR FREE INSTITUTIONAL TRIAL TODAY

Free Trials Available
We offer free trials to qualifying academic, corporate and government customers.

eCollections – Choose from over 30 subject eCollections, including:

Archaeology	Language Learning
Architecture	Law
Asian Studies	Literature
Business & Management	Media & Communication
Classical Studies	Middle East Studies
Construction	Music
Creative & Media Arts	Philosophy
Criminology & Criminal Justice	Planning
Economics	Politics
Education	Psychology & Mental Health
Energy	Religion
Engineering	Security
English Language & Linguistics	Social Work
Environment & Sustainability	Sociology
Geography	Sport
Health Studies	Theatre & Performance
History	Tourism, Hospitality & Events

For more information, pricing enquiries or to order a free trial, please contact your local sales team: **www.tandfebooks.com/page/sales**

The home of Routledge books

www.tandfebooks.com